THE SOUL OF WIT

University of Nebraska Press : Lincoln & London

THE SOUL OF *Witz*

Joke Theory from Grimm to Freud

BY CARL HILL

Manufactured in the United States of America
The paper in this book meets the minimum requirements of American National Standard for Information Sciences – Permanence of Paper for Printed Library Materials, ANSI Z39.48-1984.
Library of Congress Cataloging in Publication Data
Hill, Carl (Carl Dale), 1961–
The soul of wit: joke theory from Grimm to Freud / Carl Hill. p. cm. – (Modern German culture and literature). Includes bibliographical references.
ISBN 0-8032-2369-2
1. Wit and humor – Psychological aspects.
2. Subconsciousness. I. Title.
II. Series.
PN6149.P5H55 1993 801′.957—dc20 93-447 CIP

Contents

ACKNOWLEDGMENTS

Books, like jokes, often appear to be nothing more than products of the wit of a single person. But closer inspection will always reveal roots that lead beyond any one individual. Let me take this opportunity then to subvert my own authorial position and give due credit to at least some of the many people who made this work possible. I would like first to thank my mother, whose unsparing critique of one of my third grade essays—'a little dull' and 'needs to be punched up'—led to an ongoing obsession with humor in writing. These tendencies were fostered by Dian Fitzgerald, whose excellent pedagogy always put creative expression ahead of doing things by the book. Russell Berman has provided me with a model for critically engaged intellectual work and his advice and encouragement were crucial to the completion of this project. Katharina Mommsen went out of her way in giving me help and advice during my time at Stanford. I would also like to thank Sabine Wilke, not only for her useful comments and suggestions during the writing of this work, but also for directing a very lively independent study on turn-of-the-century Vienna. My fellow graduate students Marcia Klotz and Glenn Kurtz gave me marvelously detailed remarks on the chapters they read—they will both make fine professors someday. I must also thank the Fulbright Commission and the Whiting Foundation for grants which provided the material basis for the completion of this work. And finally let me express my undying gratitude to my wife, Sabine, who knows both how to take and make jokes, and always with perfect timing.

THE SOUL OF WIT

VORSPIEL

In the beginning there was God, and God was witty:

> Iu (*den göttlichen personen*) ist ein macht, ein wicz, ein muet, ir drei ein got, ein natur ir drei.
>
> He (the divine being) is one power, one wit, one spirit, these three one god, one nature these three.
> HEINRICH VON BURGUS (Grimm 866)[1]

And to demonstrate His power, God created the world. And He saw that it was good, for it had no other choice:

> Hetten die steine
> witze und sinne . . .
> kunden sie sich verstan,
> si mochten wol geklaget han.
>
> Had the stones
> Wit and sense . . .
> Could they understand themselves,
> They might well have complained.
> HERBORT VON FRITZLAR (Grimm 862)

And then God created man in His own quick-witted image:

> Und blies uns sînen geist in
> und gab uns wizze und sin
> und machet uns redebêre.
>
> And breathed his spirit into us

1. Translations in this book are my own, except for most passages from Freud, where I have relied mainly on the Standard Edition.

And gave us wit and sense
And made us capable of speech.
HARTMANN VON AUE (Grimm 862)

And man in his godlike loquacity attempted to speak to his fellow creatures, but they heeded him not:

> Ich, als die einfalt selbst, ich rede hier mit thieren, an denen die vernunft und witz sind nicht zu spüren.
>
> I, as simplicity itself, I speak here with animals who show no sign of reason or wit.
> MARTIN OPITZ (1638; Grimm 862)

And so God saw that He must give man a companion and thus created woman. But this was no big help:

> Das weiblich geschlecht ist . . . unfürsichtig, weils nicht alles was es sihet und höret, mit witz und vernunfft betrachtet.
>
> The female sex is . . . improvident, because it does not observe all that it sees and hears with wit and reason.
> GEORG NIGRINUS (1592; Grimm 862)

Hardly better than an animal, this female creature. But still man cared for his companion and used his divine *Witz* to protect her from her own lack of foresight:

> Darumb das ein mann sich soll hütten und fürsehen, hat im gott kunst oder witz verlihen, das er dieselbige brauch nach seines nechsten nutz und gottes ehr und nicht zu schanden.
>
> That a man should protect and look out for himself, God granted him art or wit, that he use them for the good of his near ones and bring no disgrace to God's honor.
> VALENTIN SCHUMANN (1559; Grimm 862)

And thus *Witz* is the divine gift with which a man looks after his family and honors his god. At least, so it was in the beginning. But the foundation upon which this Eden of domesticity was built proved to be an unstable one, for *Witz,* showing its predilection for double entendre, carries with it the seeds of its own destruction. Cracks begin to appear in the vault of heaven:

> [Lucifer] wollte aus eigner witze über gott herrschen.
>
> [Lucifer] wanted to use his wit to rule over God.
> JACOB BÖHME (Grimm 867)

Witz, the principle of divine order, takes a diabolical turn, and this quickly infects the world of man. The *Witz* that united and harmonized the heavenly and the secular is no more:

> Diu zwai sint unterschaiden, weishait und witz, wan weishait ist aigenleich ain spiegelschawen götleicher unde übernâtürleicher ding und haizet ze latein sapientia. Aber witz ist ain umbsihtichait in menschleichen werken, daz ze halden ist und daz ze lâzen, und daz haizt ze latein prudentia.
>
> They are two different things, wisdom and wit, for wisdom is actually a mirror of divine and supernatural things and in Latin is called *sapientia*. But wit is circumspection in human deeds, that which is to be kept and to be let go, and in Latin is called *prudentia*.
> KONRAD VON MEGENBERG (Grimm 868)

Of course, 'Witz und Weisheit' had not always been seen as so distinct. Grimm assures us that 'among the words most often paired appear, favored by alliteration, wit and wisdom' (868). At one time the two were assumed to be almost synonymous. So was this postulated unity of the divine and the secular intellects simply a mistake brought about by a fortuitous conjunction of consonants, and so nothing more than a witty *Wortspiel* (word game)? Whatever the case, the spell of alliteration is soon broken and the two concepts are suddenly seen to stand in fundamental opposition to one another. *Witz* finds itself cast from heaven like a shooting star:

> Weiszheit kompt von gott, witz ausz listigem kopf . . . weiszheit hat ihr absehen auf nutz und erbarkeit, die witz allein auf nutzbarkeit.

> Wisdom comes from God, wit from the cunning brain . . . Wisdom looks to usefulness and honor, wit to utility alone.
> CHRISTOPH LEHMAN (1662; Grimm 870)

Man appropriates *Witz* as something purely his own, though admittedly tainted with the diabolical aura of *List* (cunning). Once this split has been effected and *Witz* is no longer concerned with considerations of 'ehrbarkeit,' to say nothing of 'gottes ehr,' then it is free from all moral constraints and no longer bound by the requirement 'nicht zu schanden', to do nothing dishonorable. *Witz* can become a utilitarian, opportunistic principle that threatens to undermine the established orders of religion and society as a whole:

> Solh abtrünig lerer sein verschiener zeit in Teutschland aufgestanden . . . , si vertrauen iren witzen mer dann gemain lerern.

> Apostates have appeared at different times in Germany. . . , they trust their wits more than common teachings.
> BERTHOLD VON CHIEMSEE (Grimm 866)

The relationship between *Witz* and the common knowledge that holds a community together is a problematic one and even Grimm is unable to give us a clear description of it:

> The earliest examples already describe *Witz* as a faculty of the intellect, but perhaps the Old High German *uuizza* as well as the relation with the Old Indian *vidya* 'wissen' (to know) indicates that *Witz* originally also encompassed knowledge itself, and thus the meaning 'ratio, prudentia' would be a derivative one. (Grimm 861)

So did *Witz* fall from grace, or was it never really there to begin with? Did *Witz* grow out of *Weisheit,* or does this critical faculty have an independent existence apart from the body of knowledge embraced by God's omniscience? The debate surrounding the primacy of faith over reason has been played out many times in the past, and I shall not linger over it. Important for our investigations is simply the fact that whatever its initial character, *Witz* has come to be identified with the side of human reason. The split between accepted knowledge and the faculty which does the knowing, along with the increasing identification of *Witz* with the latter, marks *Witz* as the avant-garde of the intellect. It is in the paradoxical position of being both the builder and destroyer of knowledge, tradition, and culture.

Yet if *Witz* is no longer a divine exhalation, but instead a product of the human mind, then must it not be a mortal, transient thing? Keeping one's *Witz* becomes more and more of a challenge, for it can be forgotten: 'sîner wizze vergezzen' (*Rolandslied;* Grimm 864); stolen: 'der witze beraubt' (Peter Suchenwirt; Grimm 864); or, most commonly, lost: 'Ich meine, das heisse vernunft, sinn und witze verloren [I believe that would mean the loss of reason, sense and wit]' (Luther; Grimm 864).

And how many ways there are to lose it. The very pursuit of knowledge itself can cause *Witz* to self-destruct if pushed with too much vigor:

> Durch weniges schlaffen und vieles lesen ertrucknete er ihm selbs das gehirn solcher massen, dasz er allen verstand und witz verlohr.
>
> Through little sleep and much reading (Don Quixote) so desiccated his brain that he lost all reason and wit.
> BASTEL VON DER SOHLE (1648; Grimm 864)

The quixotic quest of these knights of the intellect to recover the state of innocent omniscience that was lost after the fall can only result in failure:

> Darüber er . . . in solchen grim und melancholischen eiffer geriethe, dasz er auch von witz und sinnen kam.
>
> He fell into such wrath and melancholy over this, that he also lost his wit and sense.
> M. C. SCHÜTZ (1592; Grimm 864)

Witz can both lead to and be overwhelmed by melancholy. The criticisms made by its religious opponents—'Je mehr witz, je mehr irrgangen, dann des menschen verstandt gibts nit [The more wit, the more error, for there is no such thing as human understanding]' (Paracelsus [1616; Grimm 865]) — may be internalized, leading to rage and despair against its own powerlessness. But an even more sinister threat lurks on the horizon:

Beraubt . . . aller witz (*durch Circes kunst*).

Robbed of all wit (by Circe's art).
GEORG ROLLENHAGEN (1595; Grimm 864)

Women, we must recall, were excluded from the male world of *Witz,* which forms the basis of both the divine and the secular patriarchal orders. Indeed, *Witz* is the basis of patriarchal succession. Grimm informs us that '*ze den wizzen kommen* [to come to wit] means to mature, become older':

Swenner kumet ze den wizzen
daz er daz erbe sol besizzen.

Swenner came to wit,
that he should possess the inheritance.

Man barg in vor ritterschaft
ê er kœme an sîner witze kraft.

He was denied knighthood
until his wit fully developed.
WOLFRAM VON ESCHENBACH (Grimm 863)

The male heir (and the pronouns are gender specific) cannot move into his adult role until his *Witz* is fully matured. And therefore the robbery of one's *Witz* by a Circe figure is a threat to one's very identity as a man. *Witz* that is used by men to capture women — 'Hatte nun der könig mit Tigranes diese nacht allen seinen wiz angewendet, wie das frl. möchte wieder erhaschet werden [The king with Tigranes applied all his wit this night to how the maiden might be caught again]' (Andreas Heinrich Buchholtz *Herkuliskus* [1665; Grimm 867]) — can also be appropriated by women for their own use in the battle of the sexes:

Diu wîse küniginne
diu kêrte alle ir sinne

und alle ir witze dar an,
wie sî generte einen man.

The wise queen
turned all her sense
and all her wit to,
how she could catch a man.
GOTTFRIED VON STRASSBURG (1210; Grimm 867)

Men are willing to concede this faculty to them, but only at the price of its complete devaluation:

Was ist ein jungferding? Ein thier durchaus gefüttert mit falschheit, wahn und witz, mit stoltzheit gantz begütert.

What is a maiden? An animal fed on falsity, delusion and wit, rich in pride.
JOACHIM RACHEL (1664; Grimm 869)

Women are to be kept on the animal level, and such *Witz* as they might have must be of a similar nature. But just as *Witz* turned against God, so it turns against man in the hands of its new mistress:

Das üch ein wib mit irer witz
hat bracht umb üwer regiment.

That a woman with her wit
has destroyed your regiment.
THOMAS MURNER (Grimm 870)

Patriarchy, the regimented male order, is felled by its own principle of organization. Indeed, the whole social order is threatened here:

Da (*in der welt*) ist immer einer dem andern an witz und vermögen überlegen.

For (in this world) some are always superior to others in wit and wealth.
ULRICH BRÄKER (1789; Grimm 868)

We have previously encountered the connection between *Witz* and inheritance, and so its coupling with *Vermögen* and the idea of an inescapably hierarchical society should come as no surprise. But the upper classes' claim to a monopoly on *Witz* does not go unchallenged:

Wer witz und adel dahin stelt
allein, wo reichtumb ist und gelt
der treugt ander und wird betrogen.

He who places wit and nobility
only among the wealthy,
he deceives others and is deceived.
HANS WILHELM KIRCHHOF (1563; Grimm 868)

Witz as *prudentia,* as selfish and utilitarian calculation, can be seen as the driving force behind the amassment of riches and power and thus as the erector of class boundaries. But arrogance breeds ignorance:

So wenig fried und krieg einander wohnung gönnen
so wenig mögen wiz und stolz beisammen sein—
nur wo die thorheit wohnt, da kehrt die hoffart ein.

Just as little as peace and war can live together,
so it is with wit and pride—
only where foolishness dwells, there does haughtiness enter.
JOHANNES VON GROB (Grimm 868)

As the upper classes become prideful and foolish, the *Witz* that made them what they are leaves them—but not in peace:

Da sinkt die grosze weltherrschaft von Rom vor eines wilden witz zusammen.

There sinks the great world dominion of Rome before a wild wit.
HEINRICH VON KLEIST (Grimm 868)

Rome, the symbol of secular and divine authority, falls before the onslaught of *Witz*.

* * *

Scholarly investigations into the nature of the joke have traditionally been plagued by a bad conscience and invariably begin with an apology to the reader for presuming to waste their time with such a frivolous subject. In breaking with this tradition I have sought to place the principle of *Witz* almost at the heart of the universe, tracing it from Genesis to the dawn of the modern age. And even if the reader is still reluctant to grant *Witz* this metaphysical and world-historical status, it must at least be admitted that it cannot be dismissed as just a joke. To be sure, the evidence presented so far for the importance of *Witz* has been rather sketchy, but what more can one expect from an introduction than a sketch of things to come? This rummaging through the *Urgeschichte* of *Witz* was simply designed to make the reader aware of certain themes which, like bad pennies and bad jokes, have a way of cropping up again and again.

Instead of opening with a definition in the traditional sense, I sought to open up a definition. By refusing to permit the examples the Grimms choose to disappear into their philological glosses of them, I let the voice of *Witz* speak for itself. A similar method will be used on Freud's text, *Jokes and Their Relation to the Unconscious.* Let us listen to the jokes themselves and see what they can tell us about Freud's world and his theories. The themes we will discover there are paralleled quite closely by those we have already seen in Grimm. *Witz* can be both builder and destroyer of tradition. It is both defender of the faith and heretic, elitist snob and roguish buffoon, male chauvinist and radical feminist. *Witz* demonstrates its tendentious nature in setting up cultural, class, and gender boundaries just to smash them once again. These aggressive energies can even turn back on themselves and a moment of melancholic gallows humor is its frequent, if not inescapable, companion. I will argue that there is something about *Witz* that makes it quintessential to the project of modernity and will show how this plays out through a wide range of cultural and social registers.

The reader has undoubtedly noticed by now that I often speak of *Witz* as if it had a life of its own. This will, I hope, not be taken as a sign that I am indulging in a peculiar form of neo-Hegelianism with *Witz* taking the place of *Weltgeist,* nor that I have succumbed to the delusional psychosis common to scholars where their subject of investigation becomes the world to them. My substantiation of *Witz* serves rather both as a convenient narrative device and says something important as to how the discourse which builds up around *Witz* does acquire its own momentum. *Witz* can, I think, be profitably viewed as a historical subject developing over time and transcending the discrete lifespans of the authors who have written about it. Indeed, the historical dynamics of this discourse—the cunning of *Witz,* if you will—often subvert the particular aims and intentions of those who seek to capture it in theoretical form.

Freud himself may have thought that he was simply describing the workings of ahistorical psychological processes, but the material he works with betrays him, forcing him to deal with a culturally and historically conditioned social psyche. The cultural data contained in the jokes Freud chooses as examples is not precipitated out in his theoretical reprocessing of them, but remains to shape, mold, twist, deepen, resonate with and/or mock the theories he constructs about them. And though Freud speaks rather disparagingly of it, there is also a long history of *Witztheorie* from which his own sprang. *Witz* does not come to Freud as a neutral term that lends itself easily to purely scientific purposes. It has a long history through which its meaning shifts innumerable times, a fact that may serve as an indicator for *Witz*'s importance in German cultural history, for this word was fought over.[2] To determine Freud's position on this battlefield and to appreciate the brilliance of the campaign he waged upon it, we must return to the first glimmerings of the Enlightenment. From here we can trace the development of *Witz* as a theme for intellectual investigation and examine the diverse cultural and social issues that were at stake.

2. In view of its cultural specificity, I have chosen to leave *Witz* untranslated, especially since later I will be discussing it with regard to the related but still distinct English *wit.* It should also be remarked that the German *Witz* encompasses both 'wit' and 'witticism,' both the mental faculty and the jokes it produces. Since the blurring of the line between jokes and the theories concerning the creative force behind them is a central theme of this work, this gives the ambiguity of *Witz* an added significance for me. I shall also make use of other German words and phrases where I think it necessary.

Witz and the Enlightenment

Witz first became an issue for German intellectuals after 1671, when Dominique Bouhours in his *Entretiens d'Ariste et d'Eugene* informed them that they didn't have any. Of course, the phrase he used was *bel esprit* [beautiful spirit] and not *Witz,* but we shall see how the one later evolved into the other. This was the offending passage: 'C'est une chose singulier qu'un bel esprit allemand ou moscovite [There is nothing more unusual than finding a *bel esprit* among the Germans or Muscovites]' (180). Both Ariste and Eugene are at pains to point out that it is not really the Germans' fault if they're a little dim—it is just that they live in a cold climate and tend to be fat, factors which naturally slow one's intellectual development. But all attempts at conciliation go for nought, as Max Waldberg tells us: 'There has never been a lack of outrageous insults and ridicule directed at the German people. Gluttony, alcoholism, intellectual inferiority, social clumsiness, pedantry. . . . But no attack, neither earlier nor later, created such indignation and revolt as this one of the Jesuit father's' (91).

Waldberg goes on to describe how Bouhours's remarks, which after all take up about a paragraph in a two-hundred-page book, led to a 'Literaturfehde' [literary feud] that lasted for almost a century. Even making allowances for a certain amount of hyperbole on Waldberg's part, the effect would appear to stand in ludicrous disproportion to the cause. Why should this one disparaging remark be any different from any of the other insults the Germans had received? What we must realize is that *bel esprit* involved much more than the ability to produce amusing small talk. Bouhours was in fact describing a mode of social interaction that had far-reaching implications for European culture. Therefore to be excluded from it was to be denied access to the modern world. But the Germans had no intention of being frozen out of the progress of civilization like the barbarous Muscovites. Their eyes were fixed on France — as a rival and as a model.

The transition, however, from *bel esprit* to *Witz* was a gradual one. Bouhours's *Entretiens* appeared in 1671. In 1687 Christian Thomasius finally took up Bouhours's challenge in a work entitled *Von Nachahmung der Franzosen* [On the imitation of the French]. At the beginning of the essay Thomasius remarks on the present mania for all things French, but refuses to go along with some of his compatriots in condemning this falling away from good old-fashioned Teutonic values. Change and progress are fine with Thomasius, and he acknowleges the French to be the most culturally advanced people in Europe. This makes them deserving of imitation. The trick, however, is not to imitate superficial details of style, but to strike to the heart of French superiority — which leads him to the notion of *bel esprit* as a driving force behind cultural modernism.

On a linguistic level, Thomasius's appropriation of this concept remains uncertain. At times he translates it with 'schöner Verstand' [beautiful intellect], at others he uses 'schöner Geist' [beautiful spirit], and sometimes he just sticks with the original French. In other polemics against Bouhours, translations such as 'geschickte Köpffe' [clever heads] and 'subtil(er) und galant(er) Geist' [subtle and galant spirit] appear (Grimm 871). It is only in 1697 that Christian Wernicke in his satiric poem 'Auf den witzigen Burrhus' forges a definite philological link between *Witz* and *esprit*. Grimm suggests that because Wernicke's mother was English, he may have been influenced by the English concept of wit, opening up another channel of foreign influence that will be explored later.

The original affinity between *Witz* and *esprit* seems to reside in their markedly intellectual character. This aspect of *Witz*, whether viewed as *sapientia* or *prudentia*, comes out clearly enough in the examples from Grimm cited above. Bouhours defines *bel esprit* as 'le bon sens qui brille [good sense which sparkles]' (151). This sparkling quality is by no means incidental to its intellectual character. 'It is gay, lively, full of fire.' Truly a 'fröhliche Wissenschaft' for the seventeenth century, seeking to combine the intellectual and vital faculties in a union that will avoid both scholarly pedantry and enthusiastic obscurantism. But for all its fire, the watchword remains *lucidity.* 'This balanced temperament of vivacity and good sense means that *esprit* is subtle, but not frivolous; that it sparkles, but not too much; that it is quick in comprehension and that its judgments are sound. When one has such *esprit,* one thinks things well, and expresses things just as well as one thinks them. One puts much sense into few words, says all that needs to be said, and says precisely that which needs to be said' (Bouhours 152).

Bel esprit represents intellectual efficiency, wasting neither words nor time. The English concept of wit has similar features, as we see from John Locke's description of it: 'Wit lies most in the assemblage of ideas and [puts] those together with quickness and variety, wherein can be found any resemblance or congruity, thereby to make up pleasant pictures and agreeable visions in the fancy' (chap.11, §2).

Christian Wolff, who was influenced here by Locke, attributes speed and agility to his own concept of *Witz:* 'Ease in perceiving similarities [*Aehnlichkeiten*] is actually that which we call *Witz*' (*Metaphysik* §366). But now this is no longer a question of mere fancy. *Witz* and its ability to identify similarities is an essential part of the 'art of invention' (§861), which involves the combination of old truths to invent new ones. This hearkens back to the scholastic idea of combinatoric thinking, which was further developed in Leibniz's *Dissertatio de arte combinatoria* and was carried on by Wolff. *Witz* is again placed at the avant-garde of the intellect, using the old to discover the new.

But a purely philosophical description of *Witz* would certainly fail to do it justice. Its creative potential was also exploited in the realm of aesthetics. Paul Böckmann recounts the rise of *Witz* as an aesthetic principle in opposition to that which had guided the baroque. Where baroque writing is heavy and ponderous, that of the early Enlightenment is marked by simplicity and brevity. There is also a change in general mood, with the Baroque's gloomy fascination with mortality being replaced by a cheerful affirmation of this world (Böckmann 474–75). We have already seen in Bouhours that *bel esprit* tends toward economy of expression and thus would oppose baroque bombasticism. 'A true *bel esprit* is more concerned with things than with words; he does not however despise the ornaments of language; but he does not search after them either' (Bouhours 152).

More detailed theoretical descriptions of the aesthetic role of *Witz* only appear at midcentury. Johann Cristoph Gottsched declares that a true poet must be possessed of 'einen grossen Witz':

> To be sure, the wit of a poet mainly shows itself in the happy invention of figures of speech. For [*Witz*] is a power of the soul to easily perceive similarity: thus one sees that every word not used literally contains an analogy [*Gleichnis*]. . . . This amuses the reader . . . and with his mind busied in such a pleasant fashion with so many concepts all at once, he takes pleasure not only in the perfection of the poet whose work he is reading, but is also entertained by his own acumen. (324–25)

Wolffian art of invention now manifests itself in the invention of art. The mode of operation remains the same, with the movement from the familiar to the novel over the bridge of similarity which partakes of both. The reader is to be presented with a surfeit of thought, which engulfs one 'all at once,' thus maintaining the surprise and sparkle of Bouhours's 'bon sens qui brille.' And far from becoming passive spectators, readers must engage their own intellectual faculties if they wish to gain full enjoyment from the work. *Witz* thus provides a means of interaction between author and reader that seeks to place them on equal footing. Theoretically at least, the distinction between aesthetic producer and consumer breaks down in this world of rational agents. Here *Witz* embodies an agenda of universal intellectual autonomy that makes it an important part of Enlightenment aesthetics. It should also be noted however that the 'pleasure' of the reader here remains on a purely intellectual level. But the notion of pleasure introduces a non-rational element that in conjunction with *Witz* will prove most disturbing to the as-yet-harmonious vision of the Enlightenment.

Already in Bouhours we can identify an interesting interplay between *bel esprit*'s rational and aesthetic facets. *Bel esprit* should be learned, but is never pedantic. Indeed, too much learning can be counterproductive. It is all too easy for the scholar to become isolated in his intellectual niche, a *Fachidiot* incapable of communicating with even the most educated of laypeople. This state of learned dumbness stands in contrast to the sparkling eloquence of *bel esprit,* which thrives in 'dealings with respectable people' (170). For Bouhours, the three areas in which *bel esprit* expresses itself are 'conversation,' 'lettres,' and 'affaires.' While admitting that specialized disciplines must to some extent remain opaque to the layperson, *bel esprit* still should be able to provide a common ground for scholar, artist, and statesman to communicate among themselves and with an educated public. We have seen that *bel esprit* eschews any sort of jargon, preferring a clear and direct articulation of its insights, which may be expected to appeal to everyone possessed of the requisite *bon sens* (as well, of course, as the social status necessary for admittance to the salons where these 'respectable people' are to be found). *Bel esprit* offers itself as the basis for a public sphere that promises to be able to hold at least the educated classes together.

Bouhours is not shy about making the class dynamics of his notion of *bel esprit* explicit. He laments that 'people have usurped this title in our century with just as much liberty and injustice as that of gentleman or marquis' (149). *Bel esprit* can only remain a patent of intellectual nobility if it remains rare. True *bel esprit* 'lets one know things as they are in themselves, and not come up short, like the people, who remain on a superficial level' (150). *Bel esprit* here loses the egalitarian aura of good sense and becomes the mark of distinction that raises one above the level of the common run of mankind.

But Bouhours's metaphors are not solely borrowed from the world of the nobility. 'A true *bel esprit* is like those rich and wise people who are magnificent in everything and who nonetheless never make foolish expenditures' (156). The 'dealings' in which *bel esprit* engages now take on an explicitly economic character. 'A *bel esprit* is rich with his own money. . . . Above all he would never appropriate the thoughts of others' (158). *Bel esprit* expresses the power of creative individuality, of those entrepreneurs who make their own way in the world. What unites *bel esprit* across all its various manifestations (in polite conversation, scholarship, business/government) is that 'it . . . has something in itself which succeeds in all that it desires to undertake' (174–75). There is a direct correlation between the level of *esprit* and worldly success, and so it comes as no surprise to hear that the highest manifestation of *bel esprit* is in the service of the prince. 'This is the most sublime and the most glorious employment in which the *esprit* can engage itself: nothing is more flattering to one's self-esteem, nothing fulfills ambition better than the resounding titles of ambassador, plenipotentiary and minister of state. Those who are raised to these lofty stations have a character of grandeur and authority which distinguishes them from the rest of men' (176).

Here we find the true province of *bel esprit* — the society of the rich and the powerful. Bouhours's elitist program comes through clearly as he incessantly invokes *bel esprit*'s ability to raise the individual above the level of the masses. To do this, it places itself at the service of the political hierarchies that make up the absolutist state. But it must be noted here that the proffered service is not aimed at increasing the glory of the monarch, but instead that of the servant. Even as a lackey to the powers that be, *bel esprit* remains dedicated to the development of the individual as a creative, self-reliant being, and this will make it, as well as its later appearance as *Witz,* into a most untrustworthy ally of absolutism.

Like Bouhours, Wernicke is well aware of the class dynamics of *Witz,* but takes a completely opposite view of the matter:

EDELMANN UND BAUER
Es dient dem Fürsten gleich, doch nicht um gleichen Preis
Der Edelleute Witz, der Ackersleute Schweiß:
Der Edelmann verzehrt, der Bauer zinset Geld,
Der erste ziert den Hof, den dieser unterhält. (233)

NOBLEMAN AND PEASANT
They both serve the prince, but not for the same price
The nobleman's *Witz,* the farmer's sweat:
The nobleman consumes, the peasant pays money,
The former adorns the court, that the latter supports.

Both Bouhours and Wernicke place *Witz* in service to the prince, but how good a servant it is remains at issue. Instead of being a productive force as we saw in Bouhours, *Witz* is portrayed here as a social parasite, filling at best a decorative function. *Witz* is identified with the idle, amusement-hungry courtier and so comes under attack in a wave of anti-courtly sentiment that swept through eighteenth-century

Germany. That this movement also had anti-French overtones, since French was the language of the court, must not be overlooked. The debate over *Witz* started by Bouhours clearly then had nationalistic and political implications.

Yet it would be a mistake to conclude that Wernicke completely condemns *Witz*. On the contrary, he identifies it as the underlying principle of his writing:

BESCHAFFENHEIT DER ÜBERSCHRIFTEN
Dann lässt die Überschrift kein Leser aus der Acht,
Wenn in der Kürz ihr Leib, die Seel' in Witz besteht,
Wenn sie nicht allzutief mit ihrem Stachel geht,
Und einen Abriss nun von einer Wunde macht. (3)

THE NATURE OF THE ÜBERSCHRIFTEN[1]
No reader will neglect the *Überschrift*
When its body consists of brevity, its soul of wit
When it does not go too deep with its sting
And only leaves an outline of a wound.

Wernicke cloaks his edifying and critical insights in a witty garb to both lessen their sting and make it easier for the reader to accept his message. *Witz* need not be kept within the walls of the court. It can also be used by the popular writer to help in his crusade for the moral and intellectual reformation of society. No longer merely a tool for social climbing, *Witz* becomes a medium for social interaction. Communication is no longer instrumentalized to serve the ends of personal aggrandizement, but becomes an end in itself. Wernicke takes a backhanded swipe at the Frenchman Bouhours's ruggedly individualistic notion of *bel esprit* when he notes that Molière was in the habit of reading his newly penned works to his maid and that he was more than willing to modify his choice of expression if the reaction of the theater audience was less than enthusiastic (260). No longer the product of the single individual, *Witz* is now portrayed as a collective social enterprise. Wernicke applies this principle to himself, explicitly abandoning any claim to absolute originality and declaring himself satisfied

1. *Überschriften* are short, satiric poems.

Wenn ich mit eigner Kürz' entlehnten Witz vermähle,
Und das, was andere wohl erfunden, wohl erzähle. (269)

When I marry my own brevity with borrowed wit,
And that, which others have invented, well retell.

The foundation for this collectivist concept of *Witz* had already been laid in Thomasius's reception of *bel esprit*: 'Thus we Germans should let the objection made by Bouhours that there are no *beaux esprits* among us not only spur us on to trying to prove the contrary, but everyone, both upper as well as lower class, both nobility as well as commoner, both women as well as men must take on the task of striving for a beautiful spirit [einen schönen Geist]' (31).

The French affront to the national honor is responded to with a call for national mobilization, on the intellectual level at least. As Böckmann points out (485), Thomasius takes *bel esprit* out of the court and puts it into the sphere of the educated middle class. *Witz*'s populist potential turns it into an important channel for the Enlightenment. 'This witty, that is to say entertaining and clever, manner of presentation is above all the norm for popular scientific literature. Following Fontenelle's example, a discourse is striven for "whose sole purpose appears to be to please, but whose purpose is actually to educate"' (Johann August Unzer, *Der Arzt,* 1759, Preface) (*Reallexikon,* 921).

Thomasius himself puts his popularizing theories into practice in his *Monatsgespräche,* which Habermas declares to be 'the model for a whole genre of periodical' (39). There is a clear connection between *Witz* and Habermas's notion of the bourgeois public sphere. Habermas claims that the intellectuals of the Enlightenment were trying to create a social space for all people to exchange freely their ideas without fear of reprisals or coercion. The bourgeois public sphere was to be the practical realization of the universalist claims of Enlightenment reason. *Witz* as a stylistic principle provides a framework for the clear expression of thought that appeals to the good sense of everyone. Factors such as the social rank and prestige of the speaker should, theoretically at least, not be taken into account; a battle of wit will be won on individual merit alone. *Witz,* the enemy of all scholarly pedantry, stoutly refuses to collapse into an esoteric discourse designed only for the ears of the initiated, but instead seeks a wider public. 'The critic, as cultural strategist rather than literary expert, must resist specialization' (Eagleton 18). By combining education and entertainment, *Witz* was a perfect tool for the 'cultural strategist' pursuing an enlightenment agenda. *Witz* did indeed have an egalitarian dimension that transgressed class and cultural boundaries as Thomasius indicated.

Yet there is a darker side to Habermas's bourgeois public sphere, for not everyone is permitted entry. 'Education [*Bildung*] is the one criteria for entry—wealth [*Besitz*] the other' (108). Obviously enough, one cannot enter the literary 'Reich des Witzes' without being able to read, a skill possessed by only a very small percentage of the population. And of course one must also have the requisite surplus cash to be able to afford such luxuries as books and periodicals. However populist the rhetoric, this form of *Witz* remained restricted to the upper reaches of society, betraying its elitist origins. As Habermas remarks, 'the bourgeois avant-garde of the educated middle classes learned the art of public rationality by communicating with the 'elegant society' of the courtly nobility' (44). It remains to be seen if and how aristocratic eloquence can be transformed into a mode of communication suitable for a democratic public sphere.

Eighteenth-century England undoubtedly provides the best example of this transition. Habermas points to the importance of satire in the construction of the English public sphere (79–80). Eagleton describes this realm as 'animated by moral correction and satiric ridicule of a licentious, socially regressive aristocracy,' though he goes on to point out that the middle classes never pushed satire so far as to endanger their 'historic alliance with their social superiors' (10). A key theoretical exposition of these trends is given in Shaftesbury's *Sensus Communis: An Essay on the Freedom of Wit and Humor* (1709). Once again we can trace the passage of wit from the court into the public sphere: 'It has passed from the men of pleasure to the men of business. Politicians have been infected with it; and grave affairs of state have been treated with an air of irony and banter. The ablest negotiators have been known the notablest buffoons; the most celebrated authors, the greatest masters of burlesque' (44–45).

Wit is linked to *sensus communis,* with overtones of common sense that tie it to Bouhours's *bon sens,* but also implying a sense held in common by all, as well as a sense for the common good of all. This egalitarian tendency of wit places it outside of the aristocratic world, and Shaftesbury even goes so far as to deny the possibility of wit existing at the court of an 'absolute prince' and his 'slave subjects' (71). In such a repressive environment, people only look out for their private interests with no sense for the good of humanity as a whole that true wit demands.

Wit becomes the most bitter foe of absolutism, and the more the authorities try to crush it, the more it gains in strength. 'The greater the weight is, the bitterer will be the satire. The higher the slavery, the more exquisite the buffoonery. That this is really so, may appear by looking on those countries where the spiritual tyranny is highest. For the greatest buffoons are the Italians. . . . 'Tis the only manner in which the poor cramped wretches can discharge a free thought. We must yield to them superiority in this sort of wit' (51).

Note that the more wit becomes identified with political opposition, the more pronounced its humorous side becomes, while at the same time the good and clear sense that is the essence of wit is distorted in an atmosphere of political repression:

> If men are forbid to speak their minds seriously on certain subjects, they will do it ironically. If they are forbid to speak at all upon such subjects, or if they find it really dangerous to do so, they will then redouble their disguise, involve themselves in mysteriousness, and talk so as hardly to be understood, or at least not plainly interpreted, by those who are disposed to do them mischief. And thus raillery is brought more in fashion, and runs into an extreme. 'Tis the persecuting spirit has raised the bantering one; and want of liberty may account for want of a true politeness, and for the corruption or wrong use of pleasantry and humor. (50–51)

In order to maintain its oppositional character wit must pay a heavy price. The clarity with which it used to be able to express itself fades as it lapses into a defensive unintelligibility. Its politeness and gentility, which had made it the basis for social harmony with its promise of the rational resolution of all conflicts, drops by the wayside as political tempers flare. If reason is outlawed, then violence, discursive or otherwise, will take its place.

But political repression is not the only target of wit. Shaftesbury also directs it against religious dogmatists who would keep people in moral and intellectual subjugation. Wit becomes the bearer of the light of reason that will reveal the falsity of 'certain idol-notions' (43) that one may have received and was too lazy to examine. Raillery and mockery serve an Enlightenment agenda in clearing away the dead wood of traditional superstition. Humor is described as a faculty 'which nature has given us as a more lenitive remedy against vice, and a kind of specific against superstition and melancholy delusion' (85). Though wit may appear to be hostile to traditional notions of morality, it can never be turned against true virtue. 'A man must be soundly ridiculous who, with all the wit imaginable, would go about to ridicule wisdom, or laugh at honesty, or good manners' (86). Wit still wants to remain on the side of common sense, embodied in the healthy moral intuitions of the people, and so is the enemy of moral sophistry. Shaftesbury argues that a 'mannerly wit' can fill an important function in a community's ethical life. For all the progressive talk about clearing away old and outdated ideas, wit still performs the essentially conservative task of maintaining society's moral fabric. 'Nothing is ridiculous except what is deformed' (85). Ridicule can be used to attack the outlandish and unusual, the different, the person who does not quite live up to accepted norms and practices. Wit here acts as the instrument of social discipline, in contrast to its earlier critical role. Whether this duality in its nature constitutes a harmonious balance or an irreconcilable contradiction remains to be determined.

Shaftesbury acknowledges the mischief unbridled raillery can do. Despite its essentially rational and moral character, wit can be made, for a limited time at least, to serve the purposes of vice and obscurantism. Nonetheless, Shaftesbury insists that 'wit is its own remedy. Liberty and commerce bring it to its true standard. The only danger is, the laying an embargo. The same thing happens here, as in the case of trade. Impositions and restrictions reduce it to a low ebb. Nothing is so advantageous to it as a free port' (45–46). The free trade metaphor is apt indeed. Wit serves not only the intellectual and political agenda of the rising bourgeoisie, but is also made to speak for their economic goals. Though appealing to a common sense of the general good, this good is achieved by individuals at liberty to pursue their own ends—both in conversation and in commerce. Wit takes the role of the invisible hand that harmonizes individual and social needs.

Yet for all its universalistic pathos, de facto restrictions still abound. The threat that wit poses to all forms of hierarchy, the danger that 'all professions must fall to the ground, all establishments come to ruin' (52) if wit is taken too far, is dealt with by Shaftesbury as follows: he claims that he is writing only 'in defence only of the liberty of *the club,* and of that sort of freedom which is taken amongst gentlemen and friends who know one another perfectly well' (53). Wit can only safely be exercised among a homogenous group, and of a very exclusive sort. The club of wit is only open to the gentleman—the refined, well-educated male. All others need not apply.

Shaftesbury distances himself from an overtly elitist position by claiming that the restriction of wit to this limited group is done in the interest of the public at large. 'The public is not, on any account, to be laughed at to its face. . . . It belongs to men of slavish principles to affect a superiority over the vulgar, and to despise the multitude. The lovers of mankind respect and honour conventions and societies of men' (53). He later praises the moral common sense of the people, a paradisaical state from which the fine ratiocinations of wit have led members of the upper classes. In order to regain this lost harmony, wit must be turned against itself to cure itself. In this ongoing battle, true virtue will in the end win out and the common people will be vindicated. Wit thus represents the voice of popular moral sentiment in these elite circles even as it excludes the people. The troubling split we discovered between its critical and conformist functions is accounted for by this ideological duplicity, as the allegedly universal appeal of wit is balanced by the need to exclude the masses from the deliberations of the ruling elite. Politics, now described as being infected with the spirit of raillery, is far too dangerous an undertaking for those lacking the proper rhetorical armament. Elitism based on an appeal to aristocratic privilege is replaced by the pretext of solicitous concern for the delicate sensibilities of the public and assurances that they remain the ultimate arbiters of truth.

The tensions in Shaftesbury's idea of wit parallel those found in Habermas's reconstruction of the eighteenth-century bourgeois public sphere. In order to govern effectively, at one point rational debate must cease and legislative power must simply be exercised. The necessary mandate to govern is gained by the idea that the laws express that mysterious entity, the will of the people. The legitimacy of the laws of the state is to some extent dependent on a public sentiment that does not necessarily operate in a rational fashion. Its workings were described in Locke's 'Law of Opinion.' Habermas defines it as 'the informal network of folkways, whose indirect social control is more effective than formal censure.' This is a force which shuns the light of publicity that reason enjoys, instead prefering to operate 'by a secret and tacit consent' (114), striving to maintain the moral fabric of society which unbridled reason would tear asunder. Reason, as embodied in the discourse of the ruling elites (such as Shaftesbury), sees this threat, and so draws for itself a line over which it refuses to cross. Wit appears precisely at this line. It represents the rule of reason and the forces of progress and innovation, but is ready to turn to the irrational intimidation of ridicule should reason overstep its bounds and threaten social anarchy. In this way wit mediates between the ruling elite and the general populace, keeping the elite in check even as it gives it a mandate to govern.

Though not translated into German until the late 1770s, Shaftesbury's work was known in Germany even earlier (Haberland 40–41). But the natures of the two cultures were far too disparate for the English concept of wit to be appropriated directly by the Germans. We find the social agenda of wit buried, distorted, or completely absent in *Witz*. Absolutism in Germany was too strong to permit an unbridled and highly politicized raillery. The free market of wit was probably viewed with suspicion by the German middle classes, which were still not completely receptive to the laissez-faire ethic of their English counterparts. Truth was certainly not something that was to be determined in the rough and tumble world of the intellectual marketplace, but was to be established by those qualified to do so. Leibniz led the rejection of Shaftesbury and his reliance on these market mechanisms, and K. F. Flögel gives us an account of the controversy in his *History of Comic Literature* (1784). Flögel here summarizes the problem: 'Truth is harmony and agreement with itself; how could it contain a contrast or the seed of the ridiculous?' (102).

Truth can never be laughable in itself, but it can be made to appear so; this worries Flögel. For Bouhours, wit was a way to express truth in a clear and interesting manner; a transparent medium. But as the sparkling, humorous side of wit becomes more and more accentuated, menacing ambiguities begin to appear. Recall Shaftesbury's discussion of the use of irony to disguise one's true thoughts against political repression; wit becomes a means of saying one thing and meaning another, splitting truth off from its representation. Wit moves to subvert the 'natural sign' of homogenous and totalitarian truth at whose court it formerly served. In the intellectual free market that it opens up, no point of view gets any special privileges. But the resultant threat of anarchy must also be dealt with, and so we find Flögel praising Shaftesbury for drawing a distinction between the wit of 'a man of education and intelligence' and that of the 'rabble' (105). The fear still remains however that wit may be misused by 'simple or malicious people' (105). The comic side of wit offers a mode of discourse not dependent upon *Besitz* and *Bildung* but open to all, giving the lower orders access at least to the intellectual marketplace. Rather than permit the masses to slip into the public sphere through this back door, Flögel sides with Leibniz in preferring to seal off altogether the realm of truth from that of *Witz*.

An alternative strategy would be to try to appropriate the comic side of *Witz* solely for the educated classes. Such an effort is made by G. F. Meier. Like Thomasius, Meier, in the preface to his *Gedancken von Schertzen* [Thoughts on jesting] (1744), declares the improvement of taste to be a patriotic enterprise. But whereas Thomasius sought to mobilize the entire populace for this cultural reformation, Meier chooses to preach to the converted, appealing strictly to an already cultured elite. The enemy is no longer external, but instead the indigenous population, as Meier seeks to rescue jokes from the prevailing 'corrupt and vulgar taste.' Meier makes it clear that he entertains no hopes of improving the taste of the masses. His task rather is to present a theory of jokes and the *Witz* that creates them that will make both *salonfähig* (presentable).

Witz here manifests all the virtues one needed to be an upstanding member of the German bourgeoisie of the time—above all an abject servility towards the ruling classes. Following Wolff, Meier defines the faculty of *Witz* as that which identifies similarities and draws comparisons between apparently disparate objects (*Anfangsgründe* §400). But some combinations are more acceptable than others. While it is very witty indeed to compare the sovereign to a lion or a father, the great must never be compared with the small. Which is not to say that the small can never be compared (unfavorably, of course) with the great. Meier thinks that this is the basis of the most hilarious of jokes, for he finds nothing more laughable than the futile attempts of the lowly to attain to the level of their betters. Comparisons between great and small may thus be drawn for the purposes of ridicule to keep the lower orders in their places, but may never be directed against the dignity of the nobility.

Other bourgeois attributes also crop up in this theory of *Witz*. For example, the jokes one tells must reflect a strong and independent sense of individuality. 'Fashionable jokes' are therefore condemned as pleasing only to the 'rabble' (*Gedancken* §35). True individuality must be able to express itself as something absolutely unique. Meier extols the beauty of novelty in and of itself (§33) and gives dire warnings against repeating even successful jokes (§38). In its dedication to the new, *Witz* manages to maintain some sort of progressive character, even though Meier constantly subordinates it to the interests of the *ancien regime*. *Witz* also betrays its middle-class affinities in the ethos it represents. One must be honest and not steal the jokes of another, for even a sucessful thief will still be plagued 'with a thousand fears' at the thought of discovery and so will get no pleasure from his ill-gotten gains (§37). One must also be frugal and not try to tell too many jokes. 'A witty man must not be profligate, but rather a frugal housekeeper, who worries about the future' (§40). And we discover that a moderate and regular lifestyle is most conducive to the development of one's *Witz* (*Anfangsgründe* §416).

Indeed, what raises the bourgeois above the level of the masses is precisely this self-restraint. The 'rabble' are prone to laugh at just about anything and so the gentleman of truly refined taste must prove himself to be such by becoming 'unfeeling' against this low humor (*Gedancken* §4). One is not even allowed to take too much pleasure in one's own jokes. 'A person who would be good at telling jokes and wishes to be applauded must appear to be indifferent to his own flash of wit' (§94). In the bourgeois world success only comes with self-restraint, if not outright self-denial. This is as true in the world of business as in that of the salon and it is important to keep this economic subtext of *Witz* in mind. The ideal of self-denial is directed against the perceived decadence of both the upper and lower classes. *Witz*'s appeal to the universal human ability to laugh is here subordinated to a performance principle of production, in this case the production of high-quality jokes that will distinguish one as a member of the educated classes.

The question still remains, however, as to what exactly characterizes the humor of the 'rabble.' For Meier, one sign of this unacceptable wit is an overreliance on gesture. 'The joker hereby turns himself into a fool and harlequin' (§86). Harlequin or *Hanswurst* is the archetypal representative of lower-class comedy. Both Gottsched and Joseph von Sonnenfels explicitly acknowledge Harlequin's lowly origins as they banish him from the stage (Haberland, 57–58). Meier welcomed Harlequin's exile and agreed with Gottsched that a joke must be judged on its intellectual merit and not its physical accompaniment. *Witz* is here made to represent the superiority of mind over body. Remember Bouhours's remark that the German's lacked *esprit* because of their 'corps massifs.' The body is an impediment to wit and so its unwieldy presence must be minimized wherever possible.

The trouble is, despite the best efforts of the aestheticians, members of both the lower and upper classes enjoy Harlequin's antics (55). Flögel recounts the story of two English gentlemen who went to see a popular comedy in Italy. Though expecting to witness a deplorable spectacle and fearing for the safety of their delicate sensibilities, the pair wound up laughing the loudest of all at Harlequin's 'extraordinary gestures' (239–42). It may prove then that the connection between *Witz* and the body runs deeper than at first imagined.

Harlequin's political inclinations are discussed in Justus Möser's essay written in his defense. On the one hand we see in Harlequin the dangerous subversive as he insists on the traditional prerogative of fools to be free to mock the foolishness of the king and his court (26–27). This mockery takes the shape of physical caricature, with the canvas for his fantastic and absurd portraits being that of his own body—'in that I inflate the outer form and diminish as much as possible the inner soul or strength of this form.' Here *Witz* is not solely the product of *Geist,* but arises from the interplay of body and spirit—and in contradistinction to Meier it is directed against 'size without strength' (25). Harlequin's comedy teaches one to see behind fearsome and imposing appearances. *Witz* no longer aims to discourage the lowly, but to reveal the hidden weaknesses of the high and mighty.

This rather provocative gesture does not prevent Harlequin from letting himself be co-opted by the ruling elite. No matter how irreverent the court jester, he still remains the loyal servant of the king. Harlequin in fact brags about the important role he plays in maintaining social order. He takes credit for keeping the people in good spirits and able to continue working happily at their jobs, not the least important of which is procreation (17). Here we see the connection between Harlequin, and lower-class wit in general, with sexuality. Civilization makes great demands on our instinctual lives—'education dampens all passions' (32)—and Harlequin takes it as his mission to recharge our emotional batteries (lest the species die out). Moreover, he provides a safe outlet for those passions which might otherwise destroy society.

Nevertheless, the explicit sexuality of lower-class *Witz* disturbed Meier, who declares himself to be the enemy of any such *Zote* (dirty joke, smut). Since *Witz* here represents a rather puritanical bourgeois ethic, one must not permit oneself such indulgences even in jest. To do so is to lose admission to polite society and possibly find oneself consigned to 'a drunken band of manure haulers' (*Gedancken* §103). Drunkenness and defecation symbolize the loss of both mental and physical self-control so important for middle-class identity. But not only class distinctions are involved here; one's gender identity is also at stake. 'A mature man is thoughtful enough to realize that some witty thoughts are not proper in certain circumstances; consequently we supress them' (*Anfangsgründe* §419). The passage to manhood is marked by the repression of the illicit side of *Witz*.

The relationship between *Witz* and women has been an ambiguous one from the very beginning. Bouhours devotes the last few pages of his essay to the question of whether a woman can be said to have *bel esprit*. Eugene denies this, maintaining that women's physical weakness implies a similarly frail spirit. Though occasionally capable of flashes of brilliance in idle conversation, she will never have the strength to pursue a lengthy and difficult intellectual investigation. Ariste generally agrees with these sentiments, remarking 'there is some sort of opposition between the beauty of spirit and that of the body as that possessed by women' (191). Be it physical beauty or constitutional infirmity, the problem remains analogous to that of the Germans — the body hinders the development of *esprit*. Conceptualizations of the body, whether in its desirability, frailty, or sheer massiveness, are used as instruments of repression and domination as the rhetoric of mind over matter can be directed to create 'inferior' races or genders. The resensualization of *Witz* would therefore have definite emancipatory potential.

On the other hand, Ariste points out that there have been many exceptional women throughout history, citing several examples of those accomplished in the arts and in politics. Though the highest use of *bel esprit* is said to be in the service of the prince, the essay closes with the figure of the princess. The last paragraph reads: 'The reflections in which they both engaged on the admirable conduct of these princesses took them so far into history and politics that they were almost unable to finish their conversation' (193).

Bel esprit, which Bouhours places at the heart of any good conversation, is stretched to the breaking point with the introduction of this feminine element. The masculine discourse of Ariste and Eugene is almost denied the satisfaction of closure, and despite the assurance that this indeed was achieved, an open-ended feeling remains inescapable. Assertion is a poor substitute for the actual deed. Whether the concept of *bel esprit* is modified in their reflections on the princess, or whether she has simply been absorbed by this masculine mode of discourse, is left undetermined. Bouhours leaves us hanging.

Thomasius, as we have seen, accepts women into the world of *Geist* as equal partners. He declares unequivocally that women are as rational as men and sees no reason why they should not be given a chance to study and develop their minds. The essay opens with Thomasius imagining what the Teutons of old would say if they could see their descendants now. 'I think they would spit on us as illegitimate children and bastards, and rather take us, with our French beards, for cowardly and effeminate poltroons, than for respectable, worthy men' (3). But Thomasius refuses to back down in the face of this antiquated patriarchal standpoint, remaining committed to a project of cultural modernization and its attendant development of *bel esprit/Witz*. If this also implies the emancipation of women (and the feminization of men), then so be it.

Sadly, his immediate successors were, on the whole, less enlightened. Wernicke seems mostly concerned with combatting French decadence, but the sexual politics shine through this question of national honor. 'You have just enough wit to be seduced thereby' (2:14). *Witz* is the faculty that makes one prey to the immoral tendencies of French *esprit* (6:10) and to feminine wiles. What is needed is the reassertion of the 'masculine intellect' (6:50; 7:37) to keep *Witz* in check. Bodmer and Breitinger see women as men's equals in *Witz,* but they subordinate this 'feminine faculty of the soul' to its masculine counterpart, *der Verstand* (intellect). Meier seeks to purify *Witz* itself, claiming that its highest form is based on a 'masculine strength' (*Anfangsgründe* §403) that allows it to penetrate to the essence of things. This is in contrast to the characteristically female 'esprit des bagatelles' (§389), again connecting the French with the feminine, which condemns women to irredeemable superficiality.

Meier was a pioneer in exploring the uses of *Witz* as a tool of patriarchal domination. For him, the primary function of women was to produce children (*Anfangsgründe* §389). This initial step out of the way, the question as to their upbringing then arises. Children use their nascent faculty of *Witz* to imitate what they see going on around them. 'Consequently the guidance and proper direction of wit is an important part of child-rearing' (§419). The obvious role models are of course the parents, but the contribution the mother can make to this process remains dubious. We have already seen that her *Witz* is inferior to that of the man. Meier also accuses her of being susceptible to unruly passions (§389), anathema to all intellectual development. It is up to the father then to guide his progeny (especially sons) to maturity, when *Witz* will be properly developed and controlled. Childish imitation must give way to 'masculine imitation' (*männliche Nachahmung*), which follows the rules laid down for all acceptable forms of *Witz* (§415). All this is an important part of a 'masculine spirit,' which 'accords everything its proper value' and no longer shares a woman's delight in 'trivialities' (§407). A well-trained wit focuses on the great, not the small, and accepts the tables of values given it by the high and mighty. Meier's examples of the use and abuse of *Witz* are most illuminating. To draw a comparison between a king and a father is the height of *Witz,* but to write something like 'behold the maiden lying naked there, covered only by the sky' (§406) is outrageous. This is because true *Witz* is supposed to reveal the essences of things, and while a king is very much like a father, the sky could never function as a blanket (which one might suppose to be the point). The essences and proper values that *Witz* deals in are ideologically charged. As long as *Witz* limits itself to singing the praises of patriarchal absolutism, all is well. But as soon as it begins to envision women as naked and free, then it must be supressed. The disciplining of sensuality operates on both the physical and cognitive levels, as is reflected in the words *sense, sens,* and *Sinn.* Because *Witz* partakes of both levels, it becomes the logical point of attack. The political overtones to Meier's plea that ends the second volume of his work are also clear enough. 'All of sensuality must stand under the dominion of reason, otherwise the result is anarchy in the soul, which must necessarily destroy the whole person' (§540).

Ironically enough though, the more severe the repression, the stronger the subversive power of *Witz* seems to become, as Shaftesbury has already remarked. But political repression can have a sexual dimension as well. Flögel claims that under despotism *Witz* 'turns into effeminate delicacy' (146). If the despot forbids free speech, then *Witz* will invent more subtle, indirect forms of communication. For example, the Sicilians developed a secret sign language (a return to the body), which, as Flögel mentions, was also used by wives to deceive their husbands. The patriarch/despot is undermined by the very faculty that was to have celebrated his rule. *Witz,* at first dedicated to the ideals of free and open communication and good sense, is willing to resort to secret signs and threats of anarchy should the freedom of the public sphere in which it thrives be fundamentally threatened. If *Witz* is not permitted the unrestricted use of reason, then it will cultivate irrationality.

This may help to explain the growing predominance throughout the eighteenth century of *Witz*'s humorous side. Meier's *Gedancken von Schertzen* was the first exhaustive theoretical exploration of this tendency. His goal is to explicate the 'rules of joking' (§10). By turning jokes into a science, he hopes to bring them under rational control and minimize their potential for doing mischief. Jokes are constructed on the basis of *Witz*'s ability to apprehend similarities betwen apparently disparate objects. As in Gottsched, the more manifold and various the connections made, the greater the beauty of the joke and the more pleasure it gives. 'It must be similar to an abyss, in which one discovers more and more the longer one looks into it' (§49). Meier tries to disguise the menace that this abyss poses by insisting that these witty connections must be 'true points of comparison' [*wahre Vergleichungsstücke*]. *Witz* should merely reflect the complexity of the real world.

But that *Witz* does not always care to remain the docile handmaid of reality is seen in his discussion of word games. Here *Witz* no longer concerns itself with the essences of things, but simply takes delight in playing with their names. Meier's fury at the practice should make us aware that these games are far from innocent 'childish amusements' (§55). He tries to win sympathy by recounting the tragic story of a noblewoman who was forced to change her name because it lent itself to so many unpleasant puns (all centering on the French word *trou* [hole] thereby opening up both the body and the abyss). Filled with righteous indignation, Meier demands, 'Is it worthwhile to confuse the genealogies just for the sake of a fool?' Play with names threatens the smooth flow of genealogy, the mechanism by which aristocratic hierarchy reproduces itself from generation to generation. We have already noticed the close connection between truth and power, and *Witz*'s increasing separation from the former has implications for its relations with the latter. Patriarchal rationality, which thrives on an essentialist system of values that would collapse signifier and signified, leaving only reified and ideologically charged 'natural signs,' is subverted by the play of *Witz*. Word games provide refuge for all the victims of this totalitarian rationality—the lower classes, women, and children. *Witz* shows that it can go beyond representing the demands of the performance principle and pursue a provocative form of sexual politics. The word game seems senseless to Meier not only because of its subversive tendencies, but also because it is dedicated to the pure pleasure of play, with no other justification being necessary. This opens utopian possibilities which a true 'masculine spirit' must forever flee.

* * *

In summary then we can see that *Witz* is intimately and importantly bound up with the German Enlightenment. This is attested to both by the litany of intellectuals who concerned themselves with the problem of *Witz* and the nature of this concept itself. The project of the Enlightenment was a rational one, and *Witz*'s essentially intellectual character kept it deeply involved in, if not at the very heart of, this broad cultural movement. *Witz* encompasses three forms of rationality—the communicative, the instrumental, and the critical—whose interplay, at times harmonious, at times tense, gives it a dynamic and multifaceted character.

The communicative rationality of *Witz* manifested itself in the public sphere that was both the cradle and the goal of the Enlightenment. Beginning as a mode of social intercourse at the courts of the nobility, *Witz* later provided a form of discourse accessible to a wider audience, translating the fruits of specialist disciplines into intellectual commodities available to all educated people. It became the medium for shaping both national cultural identity and for the interaction with other cultures in a cosmopolitan 'Reich des Witzes.' It erected guidelines of decorum and reasonability that allow a fruitful interchange of various points of view. *Witz*, far from being a purely private intellectual attribute, plugged the individual into a social collective that permits individuality of expression while making it intelligible to others. Here one may influence and be influenced by society. The public sphere created by *Witz* is the ground upon which 'cultural strategists' may pursue their agendas through the rational persuasion of their fellows. That this persuasion often took the form of ideological manipulation must also be acknowleged.

This brings us to the instrumental side of *Witz*. As *prudentia* it gives people a tool to control their world and each other. Following Bouhours, we can say that *Witz* sparkles most brightly in success; a success not necessarily measured in monetary or political terms, but linguistically as well. One expresses oneself with ease and confidence, saying what needs to be said with grace and style. A wealth of thought is packed into a smooth and polished form that threatens to close off further discussion. The *bon mot* can be a rhetorical dagger thrust that finishes off one's conversational adversary, securing victory for one's own ideas with an attendant advance in social prestige and status. The public sphere becomes an arena for the gladiators of *esprit*. *Witz* may also be used to promote not just personal interests, but those of a whole group as well. When *Witz* is made to serve an established hierarchy of values, it can become a formidable tool of social repression.

Witz, however, also subverts its own facade of closure, as the critical intellect refuses to be bound by traditional lines of thought. The wealth of meaning that makes the utterances of *Witz* so imposing opens up a combinatoric abyss that stretches to infinity. Its identification of similarities does not stop at those laid out as proper and acceptable. *Witz*'s drive to link everything with everything else, to play the role of universal mediator, impels it to give voice to those denied access to speech: women, children, the lower classes, the body. Nothing can be left out. The all-encompassing, universalistic strivings of the Enlightenment here show themselves free from the taint of totalitarianism. *Witz* does not impose a preestablished, logocentric harmony, but encourages these oppressed groups to speak in their own metaphors. *Witz* is the faculty which permits people to understand the new as new, and to delight in its novelty. Its self-consciously metaphorical character preserves difference even as it rescues it from the isolation of incomprehensibility. Yet if these new patterns of speech still seem absurd and senseless to the ruling orders, then that is the form that *Witz* will adopt—the joke. The joke is not the primordial form of *Witz*, but arises out of the refusal to hear its message and the ensuing repression of an as-yet-alien rationality.

The connection of *Witz* with repression is of course critical to Freud's theory. But the individualistic psychology of Freud takes on a new meaning in the light of this historical data. The repression of aggression and sexual desire as it manifests itself in jokes is now revealed to be part of a larger system of ideological manipulation, class conflict, and patriarchal domination. The preceding analysis has attempted to demonstrate that *Witz* functions not merely on an intellectual or aesthetic level, but on a social one as well. For reasons of space, a detailed and nuanced account of the class and gender tensions found in *Witz* and in eighteenth-century German society as a whole has not been possible. Yet because these tensions manifest themselves so explicitly in the *Witztheorie* of the time, no great interpretive effort has been required to identify these basic issues as relevant to our investigation and this is all that is necessary for now. A political hermeneutic does not force an alien agenda onto the history of the development of *Witz*. On the contrary, it is the only way to deal fully with the story that *Witz* tells us about itself. I shall argue that this story continues all the way through Freud, who finds himself caught up in projects and problems of the Enlightenment of which he may have been only dimly aware.

REVOLUTIONARY WITZ

Witz and *Genie*

The tensions I have identified in *Witztheorie* through the first half of the eighteenth century would lead to its gradual demise as a dominant aesthetic principle. 'Around 1760 *Witz* loses its function as a central principle of poetics to the concept of *Genie*' (Renner 922). This should not be taken to mean that *Witz* is completely absent from the world of *Genie* (genius). Despite the often hostile rhetoric employed by the theoreticians of *Genie* against *Witz,* this new aesthetic principle can in fact be viewed in part as an outgrowth of the former and indeed as another phase in the course of its development. Heinrich von Gerstenberg, a key early proponent of *Genie,* declared that, along with other highly developed intellectual faculties, the *Genie* also possesses 'the fastest *Witz*' (218). Yet this does not put him on the side of a representative of the older aesthetic order like Gottsched, who sought to reduce *Genie* to purely intellectual faculties, with *Witz* being chief among them. *Witz,* though important, was rejected as inadequate precisely for what was perceived as its purely intellectual nature. '*Witz* was criticized for being too superficial and, because associated with the cold intellect, for being unable to grasp the warm feelings of the heart' (Renner 922). This was to be the dominant theme in the critique of *Witz,* that its lack of passion consigned it to superficiality. 'Thus we find a first case for which the style of *Witz* is inadequate; as soon as the expression of passion is demanded, it fails' (Böckmann 531–32).

After witnessing all the forms through which *Witz* has passed, it must strike us as highly suspect to speak of '*the* style of *Witz*.' The truth is that *Witz*'s inability to deal with passion has nothing to do with anything inherent in its nature. If *Witz* appears coldly rational now, it is because the theoreticians of the early eighteenth century made it that way, doing their level best to beat all the passion out of it. Confining *Witz* to a purely intellectual level made it safe for the upper class males who controlled the institutions of education and therefore admission to the 'Reich des Witzes.' Attempts to integrate *Witz* with the emotions, sexual feelings in particular, were fiercely resisted as signaling a return of the repressed: the body, the female, and the lower classes. The breakdown of *Witz* on the literary level and its loss of status as a dynamic aesthetic principle are therefore to be ascribed to a failure to resolve these social problems. *Witz* became so firmly absorbed into the ideology of the ruling elite that it lost all utility for the increasingly autonomous artists of the Sturm und Drang.

Genie turns its back on the sophisticated complexity of *Witz,* favoring a more natural simplicity. Just as *Genie* itself cannot be learned or taught, so too are its products not as dependent on *Bildung* for their appeal as those of *Witz.* By relying more on passion than intellect, the artist could hope to reach a much wider audience (an important consideration for the *freie Schriftsteller,* authors who tried to support themselves by their writing and so were dependent on the volume of sales for their livelihoods). Johann Lavater poses the question, 'Who is the poet? . . . A spirit, who feels that he can create, and does create—and whose creation not only *innerly* pleases him as his *own work,* but about which *all tongues* proclaim—"Truth! Truth! Nature! Nature! We see what we have never seen and hear what we have never heard—and yet what we see and hear is flesh of our flesh and bone of our bone"' (334).

The true poet evokes the immediate, the natural, and the body. As *Genie* he becomes the 'speaker of unspeakable things' (347). What was denied access to the learned eloquence of *Witz* now regains its voice, as *Witz*'s elitist exclusivity is swept away by the mass response to the *Genie.* All tongues celebrate the recovery of the flesh, for the body has regained its tongue. Indeed, was not Lavater's whole project of physiognomy designed to give the body speech by making it legible to us?

With *Genie* an effort is made to open those lines of communication that had been closed off in *Witz. Witz* relied on a highly metaphorical language whose dense aphorisms could only be unlocked by the cultivated intellect. Its resolutely nonliteral discourse and delight in a multiplicity of interpretations here gives way to an immediacy of intuition that seeks to collapse the difference between signifier and signified. The poet's feeling overwhelms both himself and his audience in the passionate revelation of the truth. Gerstenberg makes a similar move, describing *Genie* as 'the power to form an image of nature in the soul as if it were really there' (222). This is done through 'vivid words, expressions of the deity or muse, which creates things around itself through words' (223). With *Genie* the word recovers its power of divine fiat.

Both Gerstenberg and Lavater surround *Genie* with religious imagery. For Gerstenberg its power rests on its ability to create 'the illusion of God's presence' (222) and Lavater refers to them as 'human gods' (347). The rational skepticism that marked the reign of *Witz* gives way before a 'torrent of enthusiasm' that would seem to sweep in an era of religious revival. This move is foreshadowed in Lessing's play *Der Freigeist* [*The Freethinker*], where it is said of the title character that his *Herz* is better than his *Witz,* and that in the end he will return to the faith he now mocks. *Genie,* like the English wit before it, seeks to moderate the effects of *Witz*'s critical edge and ground itself in the moral intuitions still held by the public at large. But instead of maintaining that these intuitions are ultimately capable of rational justification, *Genie* glories in an aura of mystification. Moral community is resurrected not on the rational, but on the aesthetic plane, taking the form of mass hallucination. Gerstenberg explicitly acknowledges the irreal effect of the *Genie,* refering to it not just as 'illusion,' but also as 'deception.' We are too far into the Enlightenment now for a return to religion to be accompanied by anything but a bad conscience; it cannot escape overtones of sheer manipulation and fraud. But the ones being deceived were not the common people, who of course had no inkling of these writings and no need to recover a faith they had never lost, but these bourgeois intellectuals themselves. Excluded from political power, and with no viable public sphere which might give them access to it, they abandoned the social and communicative ethic of *Witz* for the individualistic and prophetic visions of *Genie.* But the redemptive *Kraft* (power) of the *Genie* never breaks out of the realm of the imaginary and so remains a harmless *Machtfantasie* (dream of power).

Even in these heady dreams of virtual omnipotence one can detect an undercurrent of melancholic despair that has in fact resigned itself to the very order from which it fled (Lepenies 88). Lavater refers to the 'Genieen' as 'kings of the world' (347) and Gert Mattenklott remarks on 'the aristocratic traits of the cult of the *Genie*' (44). Indeed, one could say that Lavater's physiognomy, in showing us how to discern levels of *Genie* on the basis of a person's physical appearance, is nothing more than a form of heraldry for the new intellectual aristocracy. He discusses at great length, for example, the meaning of various shapes of the eye as evidencing greater or lesser signs of *Genie.* One mark of true *Genie* is the 'Blitzblick' (350). Earlier he had written of Hamann: 'the gaze of the prophet, which annihilates with the lightning of wit (Blitze des Witzes)' (331). *Witz* appears as reunited with the body, but previous lower-class buffoonery has given way to the terrible glance of the *Übermensch.* The body is permitted to speak, but only in the language of hierarchy. The *Genie,* whose divine powers were supposed to create a new world, winds up simply affirming the reified logic of the status quo. 'He only describes after all the configurations of possibilities already statically predetermined in the sacred language. The blind *principium determinationis* is the divine plan of salvation' (Mattenklott 44). *Genie*'s commitment to immediacy of representation leads it to close up the space that *Witz* had carved out for itself for the purposes of speculation, critique, and subversion. Despite its blustering radicality, *Genie,* because it is incapable of changing a repressive reality, winds up reproducing it.

This is not to say that *Witz* gained nothing from its *Geniezeit. Genie* freed *Witz* from the stifling clutches of traditional aesthetics and helped it to recapture an oppositional spirit. *Genie*'s gesture of radical individualism would also be absorbed by *Witz,* which now loses its previous function of smoothly integrating the individual into society. In romanticism it will become the foundation of critical subjectivity, helping creative individuals maintain their distance from the dominant social order while providing a framework for communication that keeps them from falling into isolation and silence. As such, *Witz* will help form the beginnings for a counterpublic sphere.

Witz and Romanticism

Friedrich Schlegel stands as the last great theoretician of *Witz* in the eighteenth century, whose speculative audacity would lend *Witz* an unprecedented degree of importance. Yet for all his originality, the influence of his predecessors can also be detected. As before, *Witz* is the faculty which brings together apparently disparate ideas. Schlegel often speaks of 'kombinatorischer Witz,' a phrase that hearkens back to the Leibnizian tradition. 'Many witty ideas are like the unexpected reunion of two friendly thoughts after a long separation' (*Kritische* 2:37). The element of surprise is here balanced by the idea that *Witz* in fact creates nothing new, but only unites things that belonged together in the first place. In this manipulation of thoughts *Witz* retains its markedly intellectual character, with its creations being called 'logically beautiful' (Notebooks 763). The connection between *Witz* and *Bildung* is also maintained. 'Witty ideas are the proverbs of cultured people' (*Kritische* 2: 29). Schlegel resists the increasingly popular opinion that would confine *Witz* to the province of the joke. 'There is a type of *Witz* which is not at all funny' (Notebooks 1143). Not only does it manifest itself in all the literary genres, but also in politics, philosophy, and even science. 'The most important scientific discoveries are *bon mots* of this sort' (*Kritische* 2:220). *Witz* is the activity of the creative intellect, and as such penetrates into all spheres of human endeavor without being confined to any one in particular. In the end, 'everything is *Witz,* and *Witz* is everywhere' (Notebooks 782).

Which is not to say that we cannot identify differences within *Witz* itself. Helmut Schanze points out that Schlegel turned away from the so-called negative *Witz* of Voltaire in order to emphasize its 'combinatoric-creative function' (73). Steven Alford draws a distinction in Schlegel between simple *Witz,* which discovers an already present unity, and a combinatory *Witz* that lives up to its name in that it actually unites antithetical forces, proving to be an early form of dialectical thinking (52ff.). *Witz* was always capable of uniting opposites on a purely linguistic level, but Schlegel wants more than that. Not just the appearance of unity, but actual harmony must be created between antitheses if *Witz* is to escape the fate of becoming just a joke. Like *Genie* before it, *Witz* is endowed with power, which Schlegel often expresses through the metaphor of chemistry. 'The understanding is mechanical, *Witz* is chemical and *Genie* is organic spirit' (*Kritische* 2:366). There is indeed a line of progression being drawn here, which runs not only through the realm of the spirit, but also affects the physical world. 'It is natural that the French should somewhat dominate this age. They are a chemical nation, the chemical sense is most widespread among them, and they always conduct their experiments even in moral chemistry on a grand scale. The age is also a chemical age. Revolutions are universal chemical, but not organic movements' (*Kritische* 2:426). The chemical force of *Witz* acts as a solvent to break apart the world of the understanding and its ossified structures. Turmoil and confusion therefore mark its age, but this too shall pass. 'According to the analogy of this thought, an organic age would follow the chemical' (*Kritische* 2:426). The prophetic character of *Witz,* which Schlegel often remarks on, is demonstrated as it prepares the way of the *Genie.* The world of *Geist* is no longer restricted to the arts and sciences, and so the stage for *Witz*'s dialectic becomes the whole of human history. Yet its forward-looking, progressive character is made ambiguous by the projected return to a state of original organic wholeness. '*Poesie* is the original as well as the final condition of humanity. . . . Only through *Poesie* can a person enlarge his existence to the existence of humanity. Only in her are all the means for each. — *Witz is the return to Poesie*' (Notebooks 1786).

Poesie is here certainly not confined to literature, but represents a whole utopian ideal. Of course, literature remains a favorite haunt of *Poesie* and *Witz,* as Schlegel's revolutionary novel *Lucinde* will attest. In the 'Allegorie von der Frechheit' Julius, Lucinde's lover, declares himself to be 'wit's favorite son' (*Kritische* 5:23). The religious/prophetic chord is again struck, but unlike its similar use in *Genie,* the divine insights of *Witz* do not lend themselves to immediate apprehension. ' "You must not seek to transmit the eternal flame pure and raw," spoke the familiar voice of my friendly companion [*Witz*]. "Shape, create, change and preserve the world and its eternal forms in a constant flux of new separations and unions. Cloak and bind the spirit in letters [*Buchstaben*]. The true letter is all-powerful and a genuine magic wand" ' (5:20).

The metaphoricity of language is recaptured by foregrounding its inescapably representative function as expressed in its basic unit, the letter, an ultimately arbitrary sign that seems to have the magical property of transmitting meaning. But its very arbitrariness gives it a flexibility that permits the free play of the intellect. *Witz* thrives on novelty, transgression, and chaos. It has shed its coldly rational character and recovered pleasure as one of its attributes — and a pleasure which is by no means purely intellectual. The intoxicating 'romantic confusion' inspired by *Witz* is used in this work to plead for a more open and accepting attitude toward sexuality. One of the boundaries transgressed by *Witz* is the one erected against sensual pleasure. And with the revaluation of sex and the body comes an attendant rise in the status of women. Women, so long despised and repressed, now become the bearers of redemption. 'Just as women's clothing has an advantage over men's, so does women's spirit in that one can, through a single bold *combination* transcend the prejudices of culture and bourgeois convention and find oneself in a state of innocence and in the lap of nature' (5:20; emphasis added). Women take the lead in *Witz*'s transgressive and messianic functions. But this privileging of the feminine lasts only a short time, as the whole distinction between the genders is called into question. Julius writes to Lucinde that 'one thing above all is the most witty and beautiful: when we exchange roles and with childish delight compete to see who can best imitate the other, whether you are more successful at the considerate ardour of the man, or I at the attractive devotion of the woman . . . I see here a wonderful and meaningful allegory of the perfecting of the masculine and feminine in the complete totality of humanity' (5:12–13).

These allegories of *Witz* presage a future *Aufhebung* (sublimation) that will unite the sexes in overcoming the distinction between them that had been used as a tool of repression. Unfortunately this provocative vision of an androgyny that might open up possibilities for a true multiplicity of sexual expression gives way in the course of the novel to the reestablishment of more traditional gender roles. 'When Schlegel has to present the subsequent development of the relationship between Julius and Lucinde, he seems to be at a loss and adopts the conventional idealized treatment. The 'Zwei Briefe' episode is spoilt by mawkish sentimentality and trite images. Julius reacts to fatherhood by feeling 'Zuversicht und Mut, als Mann unter Männern zu wirken, ein heldenmäßiges Leben zu beginnen' and Lucinde turns into a priestess of joy ministering over the family hearth' (Flavell 559).

Schlegel's critique of the *Witz* of others could equally be applied to himself, as his own utopian allegories provide only the appearance of unity, with real contradictions being left unresolved. Though plotting a sweeping cultural revolution, *Witz* still lacked the necessary muscle to effect fundamental changes in actual social institutions, its appeal to the 'magic wand' of the letter notwithstanding. Indeed, this appeal only serves to remind us that Schlegel's *Witz* remains the possession of an intellectual elite. Its link with *Bildung* gives it an exclusivity that belies its universalist project. 'The perfect republic would have to be not only democratic, but at the same time aristocratic and monarchical; within the legislation of freedom and equality, the educated [*Gebildete*] would have to outweigh and guide the uneducated, and organize everything into an absolute whole' (*Kritische* 2:214).

The old triangle of *Witz*, *Besitz*, and *Bildung* reappears. For all its subversive threat and emancipatory vision, Schlegel's *Witz* leaves its class origins uncriticized and so lapses back into the old hierarchical ways of thinking. Enlightenment is still coming from the top down, implying that *Witz* has failed to create a world in which there is no top. Schlegel must however be given credit for making explicit a revolutionary agenda that has been implicit in *Witz* since its inception. Unfortunately its conservative elements also remain, and so it comes as no surprise to find Schlegel retreating in his later years to the comfortable world of an elitist mysticism.[1]

With Jean Paul (Richter) we find ourselves just entering a new century. His theory of *Witz* stands as both a summation of the old and a ringing in of the new. *Witz* had always contained a highly subjective element, which, despite the attempts of various earlier critics to stamp it out in the name of an objective reason, grew steadily in prominence. Jean Paul's is a very complex and nuanced interpretation of the relationship between *Witz* and the individual. An initial reading of his

1. See, for example, his essay 'Bruchstück eines dritten Gesprächs über Freimauerei' (*Kritische* vol.3).

chapter on *Witz* in the *Vorschule der Ästhetik* could easily give one the impression that it had severed all its ties to Enlightenment rationality and completely gone off the deep end. The product of *Witz* is not deducible by the rules of ordinary logic, but instead is described as 'the miraculous offspring of our creative ego,' which he goes on to connect with Schlegel's 'fragmentarische Genialität' (171). *Witz,* we are told, 'denies the existence of spirits and gods . . . it respects and despises nothing.' Having regained the lost innocence of an amoral paradise, *Witz* 'wants nothing more than itself and plays just for the sake of playing—each minute it is complete . . . it is atomistic, without real connections' (201). Volker Müller seizes upon these playful and dissolute traits of *Witz* in his interpretation of Jean Paul, distancing *Witz* from any hope of practicality or praxis. *Witz* may provide the individual with a vision of freedom, but its anarchistic sympathies allegedly make it more concerned with freedom from the state than with realizing freedom within it.

Though this strain of cheerful anarchy is undeniably present in Jean Paul's theory, it can be overemphasized. His invocation of a radically amoral and nonrational individualism in rebellion against a repressive society is balanced by his awareness of the problems such a rugged individualism poses. The Germans, he points out, already have a very highly developed sense of privacy, but this has in fact undermined the development of true individuality. 'Because nothing is public with us, but everything private, everyone blushes at the mere sight of his name in the newspaper' (118). Jean Paul is keenly aware of the lack of a public sphere in Germany in which individuals would be free to express themselves as such. This has led to the 'grammatical suicide of the ego,' where the good German will go to great lengths to avoid all reference to himself in speaking or writing. 'A German is happy to be anything except himself' (135). Jean Paul goes on to link this grammatical self-deprecation with a servile attitude towards the powers that be. These antiegoistic trends in German society are part of a whole power structure that one could not expect to overcome simply through the fantasies, however witty, of the discrete individual. Jean Paul's theory of *Witz* therefore not only prizes creative individuality, but also envisions the construction of a public sphere in which this individuality may be expressed, giving *Witz* a most practical thrust indeed. The subject cannot constitute itself through its own fiat, but instead must find its place in an intersubjective world—it must communicate or die. To be the true expression of the creative individual, *Witz* cannot just be an atomizing force, but must also be one of the 'social forces . . . for what would a witty hermit have to gain thereby?' (169).

That *Witz* does not lapse into a completely subjective irrationalism is clear enough from Jean Paul's discussion of the 'need for learned *Witz*.' This form of *Witz* recaptures its role as bringer of enlightenment and popularizer of knowledge. Jean Paul points out that '*Witz* is useful in everything as the abbreviator and epitomizer of the intellect' (472). Remarking on the growing importance of encyclopedic and journalistic writings, Jean Paul finds he can recapture the universalist project of the Enlightenment. 'The man of the world, the student, the businessman, all have different circles of knowledge. *Witz*, if it does not wished to be banished from one circle to another, must form the middle point for them all; and for better reasons than its own advantage. Namely, the earth must eventually become *one* country, humanity *one* people' (205).

Learned *Witz* establishes a global village through the exchange of information, bringing the customs and traditions of exotic lands to one's own doorstep. And this exchange of information not only promotes harmony and understanding on a worldwide scale, but also proves to be subversive of repressive domestic orders. Jean Paul disingenuously relates how descriptions of distant Oriental despotisms have gradually become familiar in Germany and are now 'useful for all witty heads' (207). The cloaking of dissent by displacing it to faraway countries is of course an old trick, and the utility of *Witz* in encoding and deciphering these dangerous messages should be readily apparent.

The link therefore that Jean Paul makes between freedom and *Witz* is both substantial and practical, with the progress of one conditioning that of the other. 'Freedom gives *Witz* (thus equality too), and *Witz* gives freedom' (201). *Witz* is not simply a foretaste of an ever elusive utopia, but is an active soldier in the army of the revolution, and Jean Paul explicitly holds up the French as his model for freedom. *Witz*, 'the equalizer [*Gleichmacher*] of all things,' puts its irreverence at the service of egalitarian ends. Yet even as it serves the cause of the revolution, *Witz* seeks to counterbalance its totalitarian tendencies. 'A person can easily take equalizing so far that he forgets the dissimilar, as the revolution proves.' Jean Paul's theory of *Witz* does indeed draw on the Enlightenment, whose theorists viewed *Witz* as the faculty for identifying similarities between apparently disparate things. But he also makes clear that similarity must also imply dissimilarity, or else it would collapse into tautologous equality. *Witz* plays both sides of this line, establishing parallels and connections while at the same time preserving distance and difference.

True individual emancipation, however, takes place on more than just the political level. The German repression of individuality extends to its most visible manifestation, the body, in particular the lower half (135). Because *Witz* can work across distances without first collapsing them to a common term, it can mediate between 'incommensurable magnitudes' (172), enabling it to bridge the gap between mind and body. *Witz* is not only an intellectual principle but also a vital one, with its two most inexhaustible sources of material being life itself and 'the relationship through which life as well as the dirty joke is created' (204). The community of communication has its erotic side as well, where 'the community of ideas is ordered like the women in Plato's *Republic,* and all copulate with each other' (202). The emancipation of sensuality would continue to fascinate progressive German thinkers from Jean Paul through *Junges Deutschland* right up to Freud and beyond. *Witz* will be there as well, maintaining the link between intellectual, sensual, and political liberation.

This is not to say that it has so quickly and cleanly broken its ties with its repressive past. Though Jean Paul may now acknowledge the importance of sensuality for *Witz,* the method of appropriation of the former by the latter may leave something to be desired. It still seems mostly a matter of sublimation, of letting off steam, of dealing with a necessary evil. The potentially explosive character of sensuality must be defused. 'There is just as little *seductive* indecency in the genuinely comic as in the art of dissection (and is not the former an example of the latter, just more spiritual and sharper?); and so just as the spark passes along an iron rod through gun powder without igniting it, so the flame passes in comedy as *Witz* through inflammable sensuality' (138). This remark is preceded by an interesting description of Swift: 'Swift, known for his cleanliness, which was so great that he once put nothing into the hand of a female beggar because it had not been washed, and even better known for his more than Platonic abstemiousness . . . which with him and with Newton had been in the end transformed into the inability to sin' (137). In the figure of the dirty female beggar we can see those who still remain excluded from the bourgeois public sphere — women and the lower classes — and even at the price of impotence. *Witz* retains its intellectual character, permitting it to draw on the scientific / ascetic ethic represented by Newton in its dissections of sexuality and other 'indecencies.'

This repressive function is carried on by the intellectual character of the 'learned Witz.' 'How differently, more mild and easily do women read in this regard! If they should run into learned *Witz,* they do not scream unduly or complain about the disturbance, but keep on quietly reading and do not want to know — that they may more easily forgive and forget — what was actually being said' (206). Women are to remain blissfully ignorant in their exclusion from the male public sphere opened up by 'learned Witz.' The subtle reinsinuation of hierarchy is again to be observed in the relation between mind and body, where Jean Paul continues to maintain the privileged position of the spirit. This has political implications, for the progressive praxis of *Witz* is thereby limited to the sphere of *Bildung,* with little appreciation for life's grimier realities. 'Uncouth or shabby people . . . usually draw their analogies from eating or even more from war' (203). It seems only natural that food and war would be of interest to the lower classes, since they do most of the fighting and starving. That this remains beneath the dignity of proper *Witz* simply shows that, as we begin the nineteenth century, it remains, for all its revolutionary pathos, firmly in the hands of the educated classes.

Witz and Junges Deutschland

With *Junges Deutschland* we reach a high water mark in *Witz*'s development as a tool of cultural criticism. The Young German writers would seek to fully realize *Witz*'s emancipatory potential, which had been theoretically articulated over the past century but never really put into practice. This would entail working with and against the literary tradition that had both nurtured and supressed *Witz* since its appearance as an important aesthetic and philosophical concept. I shall take Ludwig Börne as the key transitional figure here, for he was the one who prepared *Witz* for its appropriation by the Young Germans. We shall focus on his reception of Jean Paul, who may be seen both as summing up the subversive potential of Enlightenment *Witztheorie* and showing its limitations. The Young Germans, with Heinrich Heine chief among them, would actively pursue the emancipatory vision of *Witz* that Börne had sketched out for them. First and foremost, they sought to make good on *Witz*'s populist potential in providing the basis for a truly democratic public sphere. The boundaries of the literary realm had been greatly expanded since the beginning of the eighteenth century, offering the writer a much better chance of reaching a mass audience. But the simultaneous capitalization of the literary marketplace to serve this larger public confronted *Witz* with an entirely new set of economic conditions to which it had to adapt itself. Fierce competition among authors for a share of this market would result in pitched polemical battles that would put a premium on a highly aggressive and tendentious species of *Witz*. Its long-repressed erotic side would also be permitted greater freedom, as utopian vision, rhetorical weapon, and saleable commodity. Thus this section will prove to be a chronicle of confrontations: Börne versus Jean Paul, Börne versus Weimar classicism, Young Germans versus Wolfgang Menzel, Heine versus August Platen. Throughout these skirmishes we will be concerned with tracing the roles of tradition, economics, sexuality, and aggression. These four factors will continue to condition the development of *Witz* all the way into Freud.

While Jean Paul would exercise a tremendous influence on *Junges Deutschland,* his reception by these writers was not completely uncritical. In his 'Eulogy to Jean Paul,' Börne comes both to bury and to praise him, or better, to bury him with praise. Jean Paul is described as a star fallen from the heavens and as a king who has lost his crown. The demigod has proven to be mortal after all, leaving his successor with a most problematic legacy, for one can neither be certain that one is worthy of bearing the mantle of the illustrious dead nor that the immortal one will even have the decency to stay put in his grave. The specter of the return of Jean Paul in one form or another will haunt Börne throughout his eulogy. Though Börne is to preside over these last rites, he is continually confronted by the image of Jean Paul as the priest. He first appears as 'the high priest who prayed for us in the temple of nature—he is gone and our prayers no longer have an interpreter' (1:790). Clearly one does not need a priest as mediator unless one has first fallen from the state of grace/nature. To make up for the lost paradise, people turn to both priests and poets. The poet 'gives to us that which nature denies: a golden age, which does not rust, a springtime which does not wilt, cloudless happiness and eternal youth. The poet is the comfort of humanity' (791). In this role Jean Paul will only appear to us again 'at the gates of the twentieth century' when his literary utopia will be realized. In the meantime, however, his death signals the end of the ersatz utopian function of literature, at least so far as Börne is concerned, who sees his own role as a writer not in comforting people but in arousing them.

As a priest Jean Paul not only put us in touch with nature but also with each other. 'He is the priest at every golden wedding' (792). This is reminiscent of Jean Paul's famous description of *Witz* as 'the disguised priest, who joins every pair' (*der jedes Paar kopuliert*) (173). We have already seen how Jean Paul's concept of *Witz* involves both intellectual and sensual emancipation, and Börne goes on to praise him for championing these causes. But these goals can only be attained through the strengthening of the egos of individual Germans. Börne laments that the Germans are never permitted to give public expression to their private feelings and credits Jean Paul's writings with providing a safe haven for emotional development. This cultivation of a strong sense of individuality will lead to the eventual emancipation of Germany. 'He was the first to speak the word *ich*, dreadful to the ears of every German, and if freedom does not consist in people living without laws, but that each becomes his own law-giver, then it was Jean Paul who sowed the seeds of German freedom for our grandchildren' (793). We have witnessed the increasingly important role played by the subject in the revolutionary period of *Witztheorie* from Sturm und Drang through romanticism. The Young Germans will continue to develop the importance of the subject and attempt to turn it into the basis for a liberal social order.

This brings us to Jean Paul's third ecclesiastic manifestation, the 'priest of justice' (794), in which the subversive erotics of his works now passes over into political agitation. Here he appears as the 'judge of mankind . . . hounding the nobility and Germany with his *Witz*' (794–95). Despite the apocalyptic imagery, however, Börne must admit that Jean Paul was only a prophet and not the Messiah himself. The humorist, for all his critical power, remains a 'court jester,' whose saturnalian festivals in the end serve only to comfort people for their lack of real freedom. Once again we see Jean Paul's work filling an ersatz function that could become dangerous if pressed too far. Börne displaces this criticism onto 'those false prophets' (796) who, in trying to imitate Jean Paul, betray him. 'They think themselves free, because they can rattle their chains.'[2] Börne sets himself up as the true heir to Jean Paul's priesthood and its promise of paradise—a promise that can only be kept by the angry priest of justice. The worshipers of nature and love must, for the moment at least, retire and await better times. Börne's eulogy buries not only Jean Paul, but the whole aesthetics of the *Kunstepoche*.

The utopian promise of art remains, however, reflected in the imagery of wealth with which Börne describes Jean Paul's work, a metaphor which raises questions as to the status of the latter's legacy. At the end of his eulogy, Börne describes Jean Paul as being fantastically wealthy, and so already living in a state of utopian overabundance. He goes on to claim that Jean Paul was a great friend to the poor, a nonsensical assertion if taken at face value, for the lower classes certainly neither comprised Jean Paul's readership nor profited from his literary gems. It is only ten years later that we discover that Börne had himself in mind in his defense against Gustav Kühne's charge that he had been illicitly plundering the riches of Jean Paul's humor (2:1023ff.). Börne describes himself as a poor man who has accepted his lot in life. He

2. 'Sie dünken sich frei, weil sie mit ihren Ketten rasseln.' A modification of a line of Lessing's, which Freud will cite later. See chapter 5.

knows he lives in a lean and hungry time, and is grateful for scraps from the rich man's table. Not as an heir but as a beggar does Börne approach Jean Paul, always aware of the gulf between them. Which is not to say that Börne gained nothing from Jean Paul. Unlike Swift's poor female beggar, Börne is able to enter the cultured and witty milieu of the educated classes. Not only did Jean Paul help to inspire his own humoristic style, but both share as well a faith in the larger emancipatory project of *Witz*. '*Witz* is the democratic principle in the realm of the spirit; the people's tribune, who, despite the will of a king, can say: *I will not have it!*' (2:811). The ego again reasserts itself, but unlike the case of Jean Paul, where in practice it remained isolated in its purely private reception of the literary work, Börne envisions a much more public 'realm of the spirit.' For Börne, 'the critical act is a dialogue with the public. Börne's style, too, is designed to accord with this goal: it is terse, sparing, but effective in the use of rhetorical figures; it avoids abstract formulations wherever an example can make a point more concretely. This style—for which even the skeptical Heine cannot refuse respect—probably affects the younger generation more than any other aspect of Börne's work. His writings are a signal: with this mode of writing, one would be able to conquer the public sphere' (Hohendahl, *Criticism* 224–25).

'Terse, sparing, but effective'—Börne pushes the economic rationality of *Witz* to its limits. Whereas we have seen *Witz* in the past as capable of producing a wealth of imagery, it has also been associated with the principle of intellectual economy and efficiency. Börne turns to this latter facet of *Witz* in the face of the growing capitalization of the literary marketplace. No longer responsible solely to the promptings of the poetic muse, the creative writer now falls under the discipline of productivity and marketability.[3] The popularizing journalism that Jean Paul himself envisioned as the natural outgrowth of *Witz* demands a style that is antithetical to his own. Börne's engaged journalism has no room for the intricate sentence structures or delicate and

3. Not that conditions in the *Kunstepoche* were ever really all that idyllic, save for a very few privileged writers. See for example Köster 51ff. Still, the nature of social pressure on writers had changed from dependence on the aristocracy (however tasteful and enlightened) to dependence on the marketplace.

myriad allusions that were Jean Paul's stock-in-trade. Humor was certainly marketable, but in order to achieve the popularity necessary for both literary and political success, it had to be of a simpler, more accessible nature. Börne is unwilling to live off Jean Paul's wealth, which would reduce him to the status of a parasitic epigone doomed to extinction. He accepts his relative poverty, but does not resign himself to it; rather he tries to turn the tension between rich and poor, ideal and real, to good aesthetic and political account. Even while adapting himself to present austere conditions, he still holds out hope that we can recover Jean Paul's luxurious standards by the beginning of the twentieth century, thereby supplementing *Witz*'s critical power with a utopian dimension.

The second literary tradition with which Börne had to deal was that of Weimar classicism. Here Börne makes a much cleaner break with the past. Unlike with Jean Paul, there is no question of turning Schiller and Goethe into some sort of internalized literary ego ideal. Börne sees no politically redeeming features in their art and so feels free to lambast them with a wide array of reproaches, among them being a lack of *Witz:* 'I was always astounded that our two greatest poets were so completely lacking in *Witz;* but I thought, they have nobility of spirit and are reluctant in their public appearances to show any familiarity with *Witz,* which is of plebeian descent. At home when no one is around they are probably very witty. But when I read their correspondence, I found that in their nightgowns they have no more *Witz* than they would a dagger at their side' (2:810–11).

The public sphere here becomes a place where plebeian *Witz* drives its aristocratic counterpart from the field. In contrast to Shaftesbury, the public sphere now is depicted as unsafe for the nobles, unarmed as they are. Börne has seen the great ones in their dressing gowns and discovered them to be daggerless. Any Oedipal conflict with these literary forefathers is avoided by a simple reversal of the castration threat. Börne appropriates *Witz,* which as we have seen has traditionally been associated with the passage to manhood as well as admittance to the public sphere, for himself, taking it away from the effete/elite writers lounging about in their pajamas, exchanging their carping letters. This subliminal sexual attack with *Witz* playing the role of the dagger of castration will return in a much more explicit form in Heine's attack on Menzel.

As if to make amends for the aggressively erotic character of the *Witz* he directs against Schiller and Goethe, Börne hastens to give it a more positive function. He declares that, while providing a channel for criticism, *Witz* also serves to soften its impact, assuring that civilized discourse can be maintained. Though having moved beyond the salons of the aristocrats, it still maintains its *délicatesse.* This by way of helping to assuage fears about the brutal anarchy that might be unleashed should the plebes, however witty, come to power. Indeed, *Witz* is to be a force that draws society together. During the French Revolution it provided the bridge upon which the bourgeoisie could make contact with progressive elements at court in common cause against the repressive monarchy (2:199). Now it must overcome the gap between rich and poor. 'It is the arm with which the beggar draws the rich man to his breast, with which the small vanquishes the great' (2:811).

But Börne may be on shaky ground here, and not just in his views on Schiller and Goethe. Peter Hohendahl points out the naiveté of 'the attempt to reach the masses with the stylistic means of *Witz* and irony, which developed out of the culture of the literary salon' (*Literaturkritik* 112). Despite their populist intentions, *Besitz* and *Bildung* remained the criteria for entrance to the literary and even journalistic world for which the Young Germans were writing. This not only resulted from their style of writing, however, nor only from the subjects with which they dealt, but was also aggravated by government censorship regulations. The *Karlsbader Beschlüsse* mandated precensorship for any book less than 320 pages. This forced progressive writers to produce works whose very size made them unaffordable to the general public. Still, the fact that these conditions presented obstacles for *Witz* to make the transition from salon to mass culture and gain the practical impact its proponents desired should not lead us to dismiss its emancipatory potential, especially in the light of its development in popular journalism up to 1848 and beyond. Whatever the actual political status of Börne's appeal to the masses, his imagery does succeed in drawing our attention to the increasingly aggressive and erotic character of *Witz*. The poor will vanquish the rich, but it will be done with a loving embrace. The Oedipal ambivalence Börne directed at his literary forefathers has been moved to the political sphere of class conflict.

Ludolf Wienbarg also gives voice to this more combative tone in his pugnaciously entitled work, *Ästhetische Feldzüge* (Aesthetic campaigns), which was probably the closest the Young Germans came to producing a literary manifesto. 'Recent prose has on the one hand become more vulgar, betraying its origins, its community with life. But on the other it has become bolder, sharper, more innovative, betraying its warlike character, its struggle with reality' (189). Again, an aggressive form of *Witz* is associated with its traditional source, the vulgarity of the lower classes, though now in a much more positive manner. He goes on to hold up Heine as the model for this new style of prose and declares that 'it is *Witz* that gives Heine's writings their wide distribution and effect, but which at the same time mobilizes the strait-laced gentlemen, the aristocratic gentlemen, the religious gentlemen against them.' Wienbarg concludes his work by citing a passage from Heine's review of Menzel's *Die deutsche Literatur*: 'The polemic form of *Witz* known as satire has its uses in these bad, useless times. No religion is still capable of restraining the desires of the world's rulers. They taunt you without being punished and their horses trample your fields. Your daughters hunger and sell their blossoms to dirty parvenus; all the roses of this world fall prey to a puffed-up race of stockbrokers and privileged lackeys, and nothing can protect you from the arrogance of wealth and power except death and satire' (194).

Note that *Witz* preserves here its traditional function as an instrument of social control, being called on to fill the moral vacuum left after the collapse of religion (to which the witty jabs of the Enlightenment contributed). Whereas before the desires of the lower classes were the ones to be controlled, the focus is now on both the old and the new aristocrats—the parvenu and the stockbroker. *Witz*'s erotic and tendentious qualities are developed by the Young Germans in the face of this moral and political crisis. *Witz* stands against this violence of the upper classes (which is described here in a highly sexualized imagery), by trying to fight fire with fire, by channeling these energies back against themselves in taunting the taunters. But this jujitsu of *Witz* is a perilous maneuver, fraught with the danger of co-option by the very power structure which it resists and with which it has so much in common. And death, the end of all struggle and desire, is not merely the alternative to satire, but will prove to be its constant companion.

Even looking solely at issues of class, the progressive nature of *Witz* is far from unambiguous. Though claiming to speak for the poor, the ones actually doing the talking are always bourgeois intellectuals who have their own scores to settle with the aristocracy—and each other. Comparing the situations of Heine and Lord Byron, Wienbarg remarks that the former lacks the advantages of wealth and nobility enjoyed by the latter and so must fall back on 'just one weapon, *Witz*' (180). This new breed of autonomous writers who live by their *Witz* and not the largesse of aristocrats are now free to criticize their former patrons. Yet this lack of a guaranteed income also brings them into increasing competion with one another, as Ingrid and Günter Oesterle point out. Confronted by increasing competition in the literary marketplace, these writers themselves prove they can be as violent and aggressive as any stockbroker. *Witz* as an instrument of polemic has not just political and moral thrusts but also an economic one, often blurring rather than drawing the line between parvenu and poet. As the Oesterles demonstrate, Menzel's attack on the Young German writers and the resulting suppression of their works can be seen as an attempt to squeeze out his economic competitors (160).[4]

We should keep in mind that before their falling out, *Witz* was a unifying bond between these future antagonists. Heine, no mean judge in these matters, refers to Menzel as 'one of Germany's wittiest writers' (7:247). Though Heine admits that Menzel's *Witz* often serves 'to fill the gaps in his knowledge,' he finds this understandable in an age, not unlike our own, that suffers from a surfeit of information. 'It is to be doubted that a young scholar could be so deeply knowledgeable of all possible disciplines that we could expect a thorough critique of the present state of affairs from him. Herr Menzel knew how to help himself along with divination and construction. He is often very fortu-

4. See also Werner's discussion of Heine, who viewed censorship as an assault on his property rights (146–47).

nate in his divinations, and his constructions are always ingenious. If his assumptions are on occasion arbitrary and wrong, he is unsurpassable in juxtaposing similarities and contradictions. His procedure both combines and conciliates' (248–49).

The position of the critical intellect is almost overwhelmed by the sheer immensity of its object—the modern age and its various 'disciplines.' Mastery of the requisite knowledge for a broad critique seems beyond the hope of the individual subject. But rather than remain boxed up in the narrow confines of a specific discipline, critical subjectivity recovers itself in the intuitive combinatorics of *Witz.* Börne as well draws on the classical tradition of *Witztheorie,* defining it as a 'rapid judgment' that dispenses with the plodding steps of deductive proof in favor of inductive leaps. 'A newcomer to the natural sciences wants to familiarize himself with a certain species of tree; he digs up the roots, he peels off the bark, he splits the wood, he puts the fruit in his mouth. Then along comes a botanist, who is familiar with the reproductive system; he takes a look at the blossoms and a single filament leads him through the labyrinth. This latter is *Witz,* the former judgment' (1:471). Interesting that the reproductive system should prove so important to the judgments of *Witz.* As we shall see, this insight did not have to wait for Freud in order to be developed.

At first, Menzel, Heine, and Börne shared a similar analysis of the political situation, with a lack of precision in their witty barbs helping to gloss over their differences. Heine approvingly quotes Menzel's description of the contemporary struggle between the progressive liberalism of the 'educated middle classes' and the outdated feudalism of the aristocracy and the 'uncouth masses' (7:250). But the bourgeoisie itself is by no means a homogeneous group; the *Freiheit/Einheit* split that would become so important around 1848 is already in evidence. What shall be the main goal of the rising bourgeoisie, political emancipation or national unification? *Witz,* which in the past has seen plenty of ideological battles, will also play host to this one as Menzel and the Young Germans begin to go their separate ways. In this first round it seems that the forces of political progress win a complete victory (at least on the battlefield of *belles lettres*). Here is how Hohendahl calls the action: 'The attack is led in such a manner that Menzel is annihilated by means of wit. . . . Neither Börne nor Heine, in his *Über den Denunzianten,* allows Menzel's arguments to be taken seriously. Their ironic style sacrifices the opponent to his own ridiculousness' (Criticism 232).

Yet it would be a mistake to reduce *Witz* purely to the level of a stylistic technique, no matter how effective. At stake here as well is the ideological character that *Witz* has developed since the beginnings of the Enlightenment, with the victory of the progressives, however witty they themselves may be, being by no means assured. Old motifs again come to the fore. *Witz*'s traditional association with the French becomes a burning issue as Menzel 'der Franzosenfresser' leads the nationalistic assault against it. Yet now the French connection is no longer with the absolutist court of Louis XIV, but with the popular uprisings against Louis XVI and Charles X. As in the time of Thomasius, the French are looked to by progressives as a model for the future. The Teutonic ghosts of old are shunted aside, with Börne ridiculing the patriotism of Menzel, whose eyes are still fixed on the glorious deeds of Teutoburger Wald, the battle in which the German tribes vanquished the Roman legions. Börne sees that the nationalism or, as Menzel himself puts it, the 'enthusiasm and *Witz*' (Börne 3:894) aroused in the Wars of Liberation against Napoleon have lost their emancipatory character. *Witz* is now used by the Germans to mock their earlier enthusiasm for freedom, with nationalism being used to maintain their hatred for the French, thereby deflecting it from its appropriate object, the ruling aristocracy. In order to recover its progressive thrust, *Witz* must regain contact with its French roots and break with the repressive nationalistic order which Menzel and others would have it serve. The nationalists, of course, have other ideas. Börne reports the following comment made by a German in Paris: '"Pas mal pour un Allemand" [Not bad for a German.] How do you like that? I was furious. Just wait! When we have Alsace again, Lorraine, Burgundy and turn your king into the Count of Paris — then we will show you that we are wittier than you' (3:704).

Bouhours's slight lives on, and as the aggressive character of *Witz* grows stronger, polemic begins to give way to militarism and plans for war. This has its counterpart in the strictly literary realm, with Heine challenging Menzel to a duel. Menzel's refusal leads Heine to invoke the code of honor of the highly nationalistic German fraternities against him (Oesterle 180–81). 'Herr Menzel is not a Westphalian, is not a German. Herr Menzel is a coward' (Heine 4:314). Both Börne and Heine have compared *Witz* to a dagger, which Heine, having once ascribed it to Menzel, now tries to strip him of, leading him to call into question not only his national, but also his gender identity:

> A certain shame is part of the essence of the German; he would never draw his sword against the weak or defenseless. . . . But Herr Menzel preferred to swing his flashing blade at women, he cut them down by the dozen, the German authoresses, poor creatures, who, in order to buy bread for their children took up their pens, and can only counter this rough public ridicule with hidden tears! He has certainly performed an important service for us men in freeing us from the competition of these female writers, and perhaps he has thereby served literature as well, but I would not want to win my spurs in such a campaign. (4:312)

Menzel prefers to engage in swordplay with women instead of with men and so is discredited as a patriot and as a writer. The discourses of both the literary and nationalistic fraternities establish themselves in part through the exclusion of women, with the 'ridicule' of tendentious *Witz* being used to keep them at home with their undernourished children where they belong. We have seen *Witz* play the male chauvinist before, but now its role in the creation of exclusively male groups begins to assume a homoerotic character. Heine envisions Menzel's punishment at the hands of the literary fraternity: 'German youth has never beaten a poorer sinner with wittier rods' (4:308). The increase in the tendentious and erotic character of *Witz* brings it to the point of sadomasochism.

The connections between homoeroticism and polemic are made even more clearly in the attack on Platen at the end of Heine's *Die Bäder von Lucca*. This feud, however, was not begun over questions of sexual orientation, but was touched off by some *Xenien* (satirical epigrams) directed by the writer Karl Immermann against Platen, which Heine had appended to the end of *Die Nordsee III*. Heine makes light of the contrast between the short and sharply satirical form of the *Xenie* and the massive five-act play that Platen wrote in response. If brevity is the soul of wit, then Platen is no James Brown. Nonetheless, in *Der romantische Oedipus,* Platen, through the allegorical figure of *Verstand* (intellect), claims to be a master of polemical *Witz.*

> Ja, gleichwie Nero, wünscht' ich euch nur *ein* Gehirn,
> Durch einen einzigen Witzeshieb zu spalten es. (Act 5)

> Yes, like Nero I would wish you all one head,
> To split with a single stroke of *Witz.*

Verstand's role in the play is to represent a classicist, formalistic aesthetics against that of the romantics. By subordinating *Witz* to *Verstand,* Platen seeks to return it to the purely intellectual character it had in Enlightenment theory, but at the cost of its political and sexual dimensions which are now beginning to penetrate the bourgeois public sphere in the works of these Young German writers who, following Börne, have broken with the classical tradition. *Verstand* defends itself against charges of harboring aristocratic sympathies by blandly stating that it is merely against *Anarchie,* and earlier Platen makes clear that the poet must shun sensuality and concentrate on art. It is to this purely aesthetic level that Platen largely confines his own polemic, albeit with certain critical exceptions.

Heine will have none of this. Though the nature and ferocity of Heine's attack on Platen in *Die Bäder von Lucca* offended many of his contemporaries, several of whom were, on the whole, sympathetic to him, Heine refused to recant. Jost Hermand documents that the contemporary reception of the work was for the most part highly critical of the down-and-dirty level on which the polemic operated (154–55). Heine seems to go out of his way to provoke this reaction. He saw that a 'fair' fight over mere aesthetics would accept the tacit repression of the issues dearest to him, thus guaranteeing the victory of his opponent in advance. Heine is therefore intent on uncovering the political, economic, and especially sexual subtexts of Platen's poetics, linking him with the forces of aristocratic authoritarianism, sexual repression, and the accountant mentality of Hyazinth, a character in *Die Bäder von Lucca* who likes to have both his books and his poems balanced. Furthermore, by associating Platen's poetry with defecation, Heine mobilizes the scatological traditions of lower-class humor to oppose Platen's refined *Witz*.

This segues nicely into his attack on Platen's alleged homosexuality. To borrow an image from Heine, the ostrich may try to hide its head in the sand, but its ass sticks out for all to see. Heine invokes the lower body to humiliate Platen's elevated pretensions. But Heine's attack on Platen's homosexuality is not without ambivalence. Seizing on Platen's Nero analogy, Heine writes, 'the verse is poor. But the hidden joke [*versteckter Witz*] is this: the count [Platen] actually wishes that we were all Neros and he, on the contrary, would be our one dear friend Pythagoras' (3:367).

Heine turns the would-be Nero into the passive member of the homosexual pair, projecting masochistic desires onto Platen that he will later prove willing to oblige. As in the case of Menzel, Heine envisions Platen's future beating, though this time not at the hands of enraged fraternity brothers but by the Eumenides, representing the wrath of the female world Platen has shunned. To what extent is Heine's own *Witz* complicitous in this homoerotic, sadomasochistic complex he ascribes to Platen? And by identifying with the Eumenides, does not Heine feminize himself? The situation becomes even more convoluted when we recall that Heine justifies his assault on Platen's sexuality by referring to the disparaging remarks Platen made concerning Heine's own Jewish ancestry. Amazingly he censures Platen for having failed to carry out his attack forcefully enough. Mocking his claim to having 'true *Witz*,' Heine suggests a number of much more effective Jewish jokes that could have been used against him. Who is the one asking for punishment now? Heine claims to have discovered the *versteckter Witz* in polemic by showing how it boomerangs back on itself, either in homosexual masochism or Jewish self-hatred.

Still, Heine is not without sympathy for Platen's difficult situation. 'The lack of natural tones in the poems of the count perhaps stems from the fact that he lives in a time in which he cannot speak his true feelings, in which the same mores that oppose his love even forbid him to express his anguish without disguise' (3:357). Society's sexual repression forces Platen to seek refuge in the formalistic, antisensual poetics that Heine attacks. Parallels could easily be drawn between the situation of the homosexual and that of the Jew, forced by society to take up the trade of money lending and so living up to the stereotrypes of greed and venality that Heine himself so bitterly mocks. As Börne remarked in the case of Menzel, the emancipatory polemics of *Witz* can be turned against itself, rechanneling aggression back onto the individual. This is *der versteckte Witz* of *Witz,* which after 1848 will transform it into self-deprecating *Humor.* Instead of providing common ground against a common enemy, we see *Witz* here reducing the world to an interchangeable relationship of beating and being beaten.

Heine continues in his helpful vein, suggesting to Platen how he might have improved his treatment of the Oedipus story. According to Heine, Platen would have been truer to his 'genuine sentiments' if he had had Oedipus kill his mother and marry his father. The homosexual is portrayed as killing off the feminine in the name of a purely homoerotic bond, justifying the wrath of the Eumenides. Yet as we have seen, Heine himself, at least as far as literature is concerned, has no objections to the exclusion of women. But male identity becomes a rather slippery thing once its female counterpart has been removed. Heine declares that Platen, 'is a woman, and moreover a woman who delights in the feminine; he is thus a male lesbian' (3:355). Both Menzel and Platen are accused of having too much to do with women in order to discredit them among the male intellectual fraternity. But Heine here goes beyond the crude sexism he used against Menzel to engage in a truly metaphysical flight of fancy. He claims that there is a 'miraculous conditioning relationship' (3:357) between the sensual and spiritual nature of a poet, rendering the homosexual, who has killed off the fecund principle of the mother, barren in both regards. But the example Heine chooses to illustrate the act of poetic creation is that of Athena springing from the head of Zeus, a form of birth that dispenses with the mediation of the mother, exactly what Heine accused the homosexuals of doing. Because women remain excluded from the world of *Witz,* the gender identities of the men remain unstable. Have too much to do with them, like Menzel, and one is expelled from the literary fraternity. But to have nothing to do with them leads to the mock femininity of Platen or Heine's fantasies of literary immaculate conception.

The dialectic of the excluded other, however, is operative not only for women. Menzel tried to cast aspersions on *Junges Deutschland* by associating it both with the French and with the Jews. With two of their leading lights being Börne and Heine, this was not at all difficult. Wienbarg ascribes a highly developed *Witz* to Heine and to Jews in general, both because they are denied the possibility of speaking their minds directly and because, as foreigners in their own country, they maintain the distance needed for good satire. But elsewhere he gives voice to a literary jingoism worthy of Menzel himself and cannot help but bemoan the fact that Heine had not been born a full-blooded German like Jean Paul. The attitude of the Young Germans toward Jews is just as ambiguous as that toward women, with both Heine and Börne distancing themselves from their Jewish ancestry even as they seek to avoid falling into the camp of the anti-Semites.

What seems to be at the root of all the contradictions we have discussed regarding the Young Germans is the change in the economic status of the writer per se. The project of the popularization of *Bildung* through *Witz* envisioned by Jean Paul and others is not the smooth and inexorable process of rational enlightenment that had been intended. Instead they find themselves engaged in a pitched polemical battle, where emotion tends to overshadow reason and where their very existence as writers is at stake. This is true not only in the crass material sense of making ends meet; the whole question as to what it means to be a writer becomes more and more pointed. Almost all the Young Germans, while promoting a more journalistic prose style, still cling to an ideal of literature that would somehow keep it above the sordid world of politics and economics.[5] What they were beginning to realize, and Heine's works are full of jokes on the subject, was that literature was becoming a commodity much like any other. Their im-

5. Börne would seem to be the exception here. Wienbarg remarked that Heine was a much more careful stylist, presaging a break that Heine would make explicit in his *Denkschrift* on Börne. At the end of this work he insists upon the timeless, aristocratic nature of true literature. Similar ambivalences can be seen in Karl Gutzkow's *Goethe* essay.

mediate reaction seems to have been one of denial in projecting undesirable qualities onto a convenient object of ridicule. We have seen Heine take jabs at the parvenu, the competitive woman, and the grasping Jew. *Witz* was deeply involved in the new economic order of the literary marketplace, reflecting the dialectic of popularization both in its democratic sympathies and its uses in playing on popular prejudices in the service of a repressive political order. Though these progressive writers could identify and work against overt forms of political repression such as censorship, they lacked a thorough critique of the subtly repressive forces of the 'free' market, racism, and sexism, and their effects on their literary praxis — their *Witz,* whose progressive character remains plagued by ambiguity.

It really should come as no surprise then to discover Freud's interest in the works of this period. He was an avid reader of Börne and Heine, both of whom clearly had a tremendous impact on his conception of *Witz.* Norbert Altenhofer's claim that Freud picked up on their association of humor with the recovery of a lost childhood happiness is well taken (27), as is his connection of *Witz* with censorship, both psychic and political. Walter Hömberg (84) and Richard Gray (48–49) point out *Witz*'s importance not only in baffling external political censorship, but in overcoming the internal resistance of the reader through the use of the bribe of pleasure that humor can offer, providing an obvious link to Freud's later theories. Freud explicitly credits Börne with inspiring the technique of free association — a term that would seem to epitomize the psychic process of *Witz.*[6] Freud must surely also have been interested in the Young Germans's linkage (following Jean Paul) of *Witz* to the development of an independent, critical subjectivity (a strong ego, if you will) within the context of the rise of mass culture. And the crises of both the liberal ego and society, which would become so intense by century's end, are already in evidence. The overture for the politics in a new key that will resound in fin-de-siècle Vienna can be heard in the strident polemics of the 1830s. Freud himself would give much discussion to the tendentious side of *Witz.* The association of Jews with *Witz,* though begun in the late

6. See Freud, 'A Note on the Prehistory of the Technique of Analysis,' vol. 18.

eighteenth century, reaches a high point here and takes on added political and erotic dimensions. The eroticization of *Witz* as a whole certainly did not escape Freud, who develops it in both its utopian and apocalyptic aspects. Here we have an early battleground for the forces of Eros and Thanatos.

THE SCIENCE OF *W*ITZ

Freud begins his introduction to the joke book by listing four important theoreticians of *Witz*: Jean Paul, Friedrich Theodor Vischer, Kuno Fischer, and Theodor Lipps. His selection is by no means arbitrary. Jean Paul both summarizes the progressive side of *Witz* as developed through the eighteenth century and provides the basis for its appropriation by the Young Germans (who also appear in Freud's book, mostly by way of examples taken from Heine). Vischer's leftish Hegelianism situates *Witz* and *Humor* within the midst of the revolutionary activity surrounding 1848. Though Fischer's book was not published until 1889, it was based on lectures given in 1871 and will bring *Witz* through the postrevolutionary crisis of liberalism and its 'resolution' in the founding of the German Reich. Lipps's work, *Komik und Humor*, appeared in 1898 as the crowning achievement of attempts to turn *Witz* into an object for a scientific psychology—a project in which Freud himself would be deeply involved. But Freud presents us with this thumbnail sketch of the history of *Witz* only to dismiss it. He laments the fact that *Witz* has failed to receive the attention it deserves and seems to feel that what has been written about it has been of rather low quality. Be that as it may, I will argue that Freud failed to escape the influence of his less than illustrious forebears and that some rather direct connections can here be made. The generally liberal, progressive character of *Witz* is fundamentally called into question through the century by the pretensions to philosophical rigor of the Hegelians, who had little place for *Witz* in their system, by the resignative force of *Humor*, a spin-off of *Witz*, and by the apolitical project of scientific psychology which turned *Witz* into an object to be studied. The supression of *Witz*'s revolutionary potential had a tremendous impact in shaping Freud's thought on this issue, so I shall devote the next chapter to discussing it.

Witz and the Hegelians

Hegel was not fond of *Witz,* having little use for it either stylistically or in the systemic rationality of his philosophy. In his *Ästhetik* he dismisses it as hopelessly subjective and arbitrary (302–3). Lacking the organic qualities necessary to partake of the truth of the *Idee,* the rational order that is the ultimate telos of history, *Witz* is condemned to superficiality and irrelevance. It is just a game that has lost the historical significance others had ascribed to it, for apparently the *Weltgeist* does not play dice. *Witz* simply has no basis in reality for Hegel; it is a wonder that it exists at all. That it does exist, however, is never doubted, and therefore it must be incorporated into the system, it must be explained. Hegel's rather skimpy attempts at this left many of his followers dissatisfied, and they sought to do better. But reconciling the basic tenets of Hegel's philosophy with *Witz* was no easy matter, as *Witz* again proves resistant to easy incorporation by a thought which makes much of its systematic rigor. This, as we shall see, is not to be blamed so much on the supposedly inherent irrationality of *Witz* as on its association with certain cultural forces and values which themselves resisted assimilation to the scientific rationality of the nineteenth century.

A first attempt is made by Christian Weisse, whose *Ästhetik* of 1830 greatly expands the Hegelian view of *Witz.* Weisse restricts it to the province of the comic, declaring any of its other manifestations to be 'a dry game of the intellect' (242). But he goes on to criticize Hegel for having failed to recognize the role the comic plays in aesthetics. For Weisse the comic is 'sublimated [*aufgehobene*] ugliness' leading to the 'restoration of beauty' (210). As the vanquisher of ugliness and bringer of beauty, the comic seems to be a truly dynamic principle in aesthetics. *Witz* is able to play both sides of the line, both destroying and transfiguring the undesirable through laughter. Even its subjective character, which Hegel found so distressing, proves of value, as the individual is raised through the comic to become conscious of itself as the true substance of the ideal. The negation is negated, the universal and the particular are wed, and *Witz* plays a decisive role in bringing about the happy ending.

Still, one may wonder about the truly dialectical quality of this *Aufhebung*. According to Weisse, ugliness is always just on the brink of dissolving into beauty, going even so far as to suggest that 'in truth there is no ugliness.' How real then is the force which negates it, which itself soon collapses into the truth of beauty? The system very much needs a dynamic force to run, but its totalizing character cannot permit any real opposition, only the appearance of such, thus reducing its dynamic to the level of mere appearance as well. Likewise, the system needs individuals to embody it, but cannot tolerate true individuality. The comic was to replace the contemplative passivity of the subject with the 'free play of his intellectual powers' (214). This outburst of spontaneity and creativity must however remain confined to the realm of aesthetics—remaining, by Weisse's own admission, 'purposeless.' The subject is not really active, just playing at it. *Witz* is compartmentalized in the system where it can have no real effect on the whole, included and excluded at one stroke.

In order to elucidate his views on laughter, Weisse abandons theory and decides to tell a story, a myth from the golden age of the Greeks. Parmeniskus loses in the cavern of Trophonius the ability to laugh and Apollo tells him that he will only recover it in the house of his mother. Of course, Apollo means his own mother Leto, and Parmeniskus finally laughs again upon visiting her temple and seeing what is supposed to be a statue of her, but is in fact a 'formless lump' (236). Weisse's gloss of this myth is most interesting. He connects both Trophonius and Leto with the terrors of the underworld. It is only when Parmeniskus sees Leto reduced to a formless lump that laughter overcomes his initial fright.

What is being affirmed here is the power of classicism to vanquish the now-mythological forces of ugliness and impose order on the world. The Greeks were able, through Apollonian art, to overcome their barbarous past, represented by Leto, the mother goddess. And not only the sinister past of matriarchy, but even contemporary political threats can also be dealt with: 'In the comedies of Aristophanes the historical element of the fall of the old Greek customs and religion into immorality and infamy would be, viewed in itself, more tragic than comic;—what is actually comic is the manner in which a material element (the democratic and anarchic masses) behave as if the highest political, historical and religious ideas were their own. What was necessarily ugly and evil in historical reality is transformed in the work of the comic poet into something funny, in that it is depicted as something unreal' (233).

Witz and the comic in general are to be enlisted into the service of an aesthetic conservatism which is also amenable to reactionary politics, though Weisse avoids an explicit politicization of the aesthetic. *Witz* is thereby appropriated by the Biedermeier right to counter the democratizing thrust of the 1830 revolution and the growing challenge of the Young German writers to classicist aesthetics. The true joke, of course, is that the formlessness of Leto stands not in submission but in steadfast opposition to the well-formed world of her son. Weisse's dialectic never reaches the level of synthesis, but only of crass negation, incapable of either reconciliation or opposition. The real gets rationalized with a vengeance here as *Witz,* which was to be the dynamic principle of change, comes to represent the deadening weight of the status quo.

Witz fares little better even with a left-Hegelian like Arnold Ruge. Ruge commends Weisse for his rehabilitation of *Witz* for Hegelian theory, but is very much aware of Weisse's failings:

> The essential failing of Weisse's distinction is that these two, the possibility and the reality of the comic, are kept apart superficially; as in the expression of *Witz,* it is the transformation of the object into something comic, in which the idea of objectivity is not sublimated [*aufgehoben*], the true connection left unarticulated. One should also have added that this creation is an act of self-creation, where one cannot speak of transformation insofar as the object of *Witz,* the confounded spirit, is sublimated in the knowledge of *Witz,* and so is no longer an object; but *Witz* itself has only as knowledge and in knowledge no other objective existence as itself and in itself. (*Vorschule* 147)

Ruge sees that the distinction that Weisse has set up between the potentially laughable (the ugly) and what is in fact laughed at (the comic) is an illusory one; the dialectic lacks any tension here, for the former collapses so quickly and effortlessly into the latter as to make it a distinction without difference. Ruge therefore takes the logical step of attempting to reestablish the dialectic solely within the confines of *Witz* itself. *Witz* becomes *Wissen* coming to know itself. Ruge is trying to make the best of what he sees as *Witz*'s self-absorbed subjectivity by turning it into a pathway for self-knowledge.

Yet we should not imagine that the subject can attain this knowledge solely by means of introspection. Following Hegel, Ruge ties any increase of self-knowledge on the part of the subject with the saga of its emancipation in general. If the freedom of the subject were to depend completely on itself, then the dialectic would again lack any invigorating tension, for nothing would stop the subject from blandly asserting its freedom and getting on with the rest of its life. This is indeed what *Witz* would like to do. 'This expresses the truth that spirit by all means wishes to appear as free, but also the falsehood that it cannot so appear in the recognition of grave misfortune (142). Ruge illustrates this point with the story of Charles I of England who, in captivity, starts to cry when he is offered cold water with which to shave. Tears running down his cheeks, he declares that he has not fallen so low that he shall not have warm water for the purpose. *Witz* is therefore the 'consciousness of contradiction' in that it both recognizes and seeks to deny its actual lack of freedom. Far from being completely self-absorbed, *Witz* is in fact struggling against the limitations of its environment.

This emancipatory framework is definitely a step beyond Weisse, but Ruge winds up falling into a similar trap. For Ruge, *Witz* still remains irredeemably subjective. Though representing the 'outer limit of self-liberation' (*Werke* 10), it achieves this only by refusing to sublate the individual into the universal. Thus, in the Hegelian order of things, the freedom it offers must remain arbitrary and illusory. As with Weisse, *Witz* just isn't real in a rational world. Indeed, as the consciousness of repression, it may be assumed that it would disappear with the removal of repression. But Ruge goes beyond this, moving not only against repression, but also against the repressed. The harmony of dialectical *Aufhebung* gives way to outright exclusion as *Witz* continues to be a rallying point for elements that bourgeois rationality simply cannot process.

A good example of this is to be found in Ruge's discussion of *Doppelsinn,* which is used to tease the listener, to arouse a desire for meaning which the witty *Pointe* must satisfy. The double entendre and its resultant tension is thus resolved in the reassertion of a reason which removes the tantalizing but troublesome ambiguity. Jokes make sense and desire is satisfied. But this satisfaction is only made possible through the suppression of some desires, as Ruge explicitly excludes dirty jokes from his discussion (*Vorschule* 153). Intellectual titillation is all well and good, but its physical counterpart has no place in polite society.

He makes a similar move in his critique of Heine, whom he accuses of ironizing all desires, all 'desire for positivity' (172), thereby denying the reader any restful satisfaction. He compares Heine to a coquette who is always flirting, but never delivers (*Werke* 31). But perhaps Heine's wit is just delivering the wrong things. Ruge accuses him of lechery (37) and has no sympathy for the Young German program toward the 'emancipation of the flesh' (*Vorschule* 172). Heine's remark that he has a passion for 'love, truth, freedom and crab soup' strikes Ruge as simply frivolous, betraying an allegedly innate Jewish realism that has little appreciation for the purity of the ideal (*Werke* 28). Heine is repeatedly associated (indeed associates himself) with *Kot,* the great equalizer:

> Selten habt ihr mich verstanden, selten auch verstand ich euch;
> Nur wenn wir im Kot uns fanden, so verstanden wir uns gleich.

> Rarely did you understand me, and rarely did I understand you;
> Only when we found ourselves in the muck did we understand
> each other at once. (Heine, 1:130)

The comic deflation of high ideals in the name of everyday realities of food and sex and other dirty things has traditionally been linked with lower-class humor. The negativity of *Witz* that makes it unsuitable for *Aufhebung* to the level of theory, the fount of all progress, according to Ruge, really boils down to its ties with Jews, women, and the lower orders. These elements will not only prove difficult for Hegelian theory to assimilate, but also for liberal society as a whole during the course of the century. Even at the moment of its greatest revolutionary ardor, the bourgeoisie cannot bring itself to embrace these undesirables. While appreciating Heine's utility as a critic of the old order, Ruge and his fellows are already working to make sure that the emancipatory stirrings expressed in his *Witz* do not get out of control. 'These demons are in our power for now' (60), he writes on behalf of his fellow liberals. But while the forces embodied in *Witz* — most noticeably the rehabilitation of desires like hunger and sex — represent a recognition of the physical realities of daily life and might have offered some material basis for a revolutionary project, Ruge fails to exploit them to engage a mass audience for such an agenda. Instead he places his hopes in a return to the spirit of religion, a vague religion of the deed. The *Wissen* (knowledge) that was to have replaced *Witz* passes over into mysticism, for it appears to have lost all connection with the realities of the political situation.

Vischer follows Ruge in siting *Witz* within the context of an emancipatory struggle, but criticizes what he takes to be Ruge's overemphasis of *Witz*'s negative facets. While admitting *Witz*'s subjectivistic, atomistic qualities, Vischer takes Ruge's idea of *Witz*'s self-transcendence a step further. *Witz* is not merely to be supplanted by something fundamentally different from it, such as the beautiful or knowledge — Vischer's *Aufhebung* seeks to preserve its comic element. When the subject turns *Witz* back upon itself, sees itself as funny, a negation of the negation has occurred and the subject is reunited in laughter with the world it had previously mocked. This is the level of *Humor* which affirms even as it criticizes. To be sure, Ruge, Weisse, and Jean Paul all discuss *Humor* and often assign to it similar features, but Vischer claims to make the definitive statement.

The ability to laugh at oneself is no guarantee that one has reached a higher level of being. 'When, for example, the sexually dissolute person uses *Witz* to help him deal with the evil consequences that spring from his vice, like Falstaff, this is not the free comic [*freie Komik*], as is the case with the person who knows the weaknesses of the flesh, but does not need *Witz* to exonerate himself, but can rather freely grasp this evil in its universality as the limit and flipside of true love' (463). Vischer is much more tolerant of the smutty double entendre than Ruge, recognizing that it can be useful 'to sublimate spiritual and sensuous love in pure and beautiful harmony' (431) and pointing out that obscenities were enlisted by Luther and Johann Fischart in the cause of virtue. Sensuality in and of itself, however, remains suspect, at best a necessary evil, the presence of which permits an unscrupulous character like Falstaff to pervert *Humor.*

An even more subtle form of what Vischer calls 'gebrochener Humor' (broken humor) is represented in another Shakespearean character, Rosalinde of *As You Like It.* Again, the problem results from a libido gone out of control. Having lost her beloved she seeks comfort in a melancholic wit. 'She smiles at the pain in whose bashful beauty she at the same time delights; she is in love with it, for it is the disguised picture of her beloved' (464). It seems that 'noble feminine natures' are especially prone to this sort of pathological, one might even suggest neurotic, form of *Witz.* The link between melancholy and *Humor* has a long tradition. Jean Paul had remarked on it, tracing it back to the medieval notion of physical humors that affected individual temperament. Vischer must break this link if he is to save *Humor* as a liberating force. But no woman is capable of this. 'Only the masculine spirit can at the same time look into the depths of the misery of the whole world and overcome this consciousness in the form of a joke' (465).

Of course, not all men are able to pull this off either. Not only obvious libertines like Falstaff, but anyone too given to the passions, such as Byron and Heine, will never reach the level of *Humor* untarnished by 'bitterness and despair' (465). This melancholic *Humor,* which Vischer also associates with Jean Paul, leads to an apolitical *Innerlichkeit* that feels for the sufferings of humanity but shuns any activity in the public sphere that might provide any real sort of relief. 'That still and secret *Humor* of effeminate men, amiable, rural, small-town types, appears as frivolity when one looks at the manly struggles of public life, which he cannot bring into his private circle and whose sight disconcerts him. But to watch the fall of a moral world order like the manly spirit of Aristophanes or to see, with Shakespeare's fiery gaze, ingratitude, injustice, impotence of the laws, bribery, and feuds hold sway and still cast one's *Humor* over these ills, that is the highest and most difficult' (469).

Once again we see gender-specific definitions of the comic being used to articulate the possibility of action in the public sphere. The feminine, representing both the disorderliness and the self-absorption of the passions, must be excluded. The trouble is that a male body is no guarantee of a manly spirit. As was the case with the polemics of the Young Germans, when gender distinctions begin to blur, the possibility of androgyny, of 'effeminate men,' must be admitted. Yet even they are not completely beyond all hope of redemption. Vischer admits, for example, that Jean Paul has a strong side that can take on the harsh realities of the public sphere. Indeed, as long as his sympathy for the sufferings of the poor is kept from dissolving into sentimentality by a tough-minded realism, then 'there stands before us a republican, a communist, a democrat. The comic is democratic, not only in the narrow, but in the widest sense.' (470). It appears that the animus-anima conflict, at least for the men, is to be resolved in favor of the masculine through the pursuit of a radical political agenda. Passion is sublimated into political action.

As may be expected, however, the class differences that would lead to the failure of the revolutions of 1848 are also in evidence. *Humor*'s affirmative character makes it all too susceptible to co-option: 'I believed that I would also have to give things up for the comic, since it began with something sublime pushing its way in; my daily mood, my comfort, my needs, my little passions, my appetite, my soup and my roast were all supposed to become contemptible to me. But now it is different; I am at home in the world, I am content, completely content, without sacrifice' (475).

The denial of sacrifice here is not utopian, but represents a somewhat premature reconciliation. Indeed, the critical sacrifice has already been made, as the 'little passions' of the comfortable bourgeois replace the real passion that has been previously repressed. *Humor* can cut both ways, inspiring either heroic sacrifices in the name of freedom or permitting reconciliation with 'necessary evils.' In fact, Vischer is not able to keep these two facets apart, for the distinction between *gebrochener* and *freier Humor* was incorrectly formulated. The bitterness of Heine and Byron was not the result of sensual indulgence but of an uncompromising political stance that refused to be at home in the world of the Restoration. The demand for both sensual and political liberation was an important part of this radicality. Vischer remains entangled in a moralistic worldview that undercuts his revolutionary ideals. The acceptance of personal sexual repression makes it easy for one to treasure the pleasures one is permitted and resign oneself to an apparently ontological *Weltübel* (world misery), especially if other classes are bearing the brunt of it.

Viewing the Hegelian appropriation of *Witz* as a whole, we seem to have learned more from its failures than its successes. Even on a stylistic level there is probably nothing more antithetical to *Witz* than the turgid prose of Hegelian theory. The faith in the almost magical powers of theory as a force for change in the world leads to an abandonment of witty popularization; the philosopher writes for the *Weltgeist,* not the general public.[1] Passionate polemic also seems to have no place here, being replaced by a scientific objectivity that will be easily recouped by the status quo after 1848. The attempt to scientize *Witz* has proven to be just as regressive as eighteenth-century efforts to do the same. Again, it is where these theoreticians have the greatest difficulties that they are most instructive—when they encounter women, Jews, and the lower classes, all problematic groups that Freud, who himself claimed a measure of scientific rigor for his own method, will also have to deal with. The valorization of *Humor* over *Witz* in the context of 1848 should also be noted. Vischer has initiated a discussion of *Humor* that will lead directly to Freud, though by the time it reaches him it will have lost almost all of its progressive pretensions. *Humor* appears at the point at which Hegelian reason, the liberal faith in progress and perfectibility, begins to break down. If *Witz* is the consciousness of contradiction, then *Humor* is the reconciliation to it. But by Freud's time, even this consolation in resignation will have become increasingly untenable.

1. Which is not to say that the general public was dependent on the philosophers for their jokes. *Witz* as a popular and critical tool proved itself in the revolutions of 1848 in spite of the suspicions of the Hegelians. Carl Elbinger, for example, has documented the quite lively *Witzkultur* that arose in revolutionary Vienna. Unfortunately we must pass up a detailed examination of *Witz* as political praxis and continue following the theoretical path that leads most directly to Freud.

Witz and *Humor*

After Vischer, the discussion of *Witz* was for a time eclipsed by that surrounding *Humor,* as is the case in Moritz Lazarus's book *Das Leben der Seele.* This work is important as an early effort to unite aesthetics with scientific psychology, which, as Lazarus himself remarks, is still in its infancy (232). Lazarus sees that the dominant Hegelian paradigm is breaking apart and credits Vischer with helping to bring this about. Nonetheless, both Vischer's and his own work are replete with Hegelian motifs. *Witz* continues to be marked as superficial, especially when compared with *Humor,* which is cast as representing the demands of the ideal.

The break with Hegel comes in the articulation of the relationship between the ideal and the world of history and politics. The project of realizing the ideal within a social whole has been abandoned, at least as far as *Witz* and *Humor* are concerned. No longer part of an emancipatory narrative, *Humor* lapses back into the individualism with which *Witz* was once reproached: '*Humor* . . . belongs only to the individual who stands at the pinnacle of culture' (246). *Humor* would appear to correspond to the mood of an educated elite which feels that history has slipped beyond its control. Though remaining interested in politics, these humorists, apparently exhausted by the efforts of 1848, no longer have the requisite *Energie* (247) to participate in public life. *Humor* loses contact with the political world and concerns itself with private ethical and religious redemption. The often-noted reconciling power of *Humor* takes a resignative turn. *Weltanschauung* replaces *Weltgeist* and the return, on his deathbed, of the prodigal Heine to the flock of the faithful is noted with due approval (257).

Still, Lazarus recognizes that history does go on; it is no longer made by individuals, however, but by larger groups. If radical liberalism has not survived the revolution, nationalism still remains a force to be reckoned with. Though *Humor* is too individualistic to form the basis for a *Nationalgeist,* it can nonetheless aid and abet the ethical upturn consequent upon any nationalistic revival. 'Only then, when a deep and mighty communal spirit shall have seized the whole, so that reader and writer unfailingly know themselves to be of the same disposition, which is both universal and ideal, only then I say will history appear not only in the mirror of poetry, but also in *Humor*' (270). Completely lost here is the liberal model of a rational public sphere. Agreement between author and public is effected through a violent eruption of 'communal spirit' and not a rational discourse that would preserve the integrity of both parties. The critical faculty of *Witz* that might have provided for this has been engulfed by *Humor.*

J. H. Kirchmann, in his *Ästhetik* of 1868, takes a somewhat different tack, hearkening all the way back to the courtly beginnings of *Witz.* Following Hobbes, Kirchmann bases the comic moment on a feeling of superiority, in this case a 'pleasure of knowing better.' 'Just as the prince is neither for himself nor for other princes something sublime, only for his subjects, so the comic is only comic for the person who recognizes its weakness of intellect, its absurdity, and stands above it in his stronger intellect' (45). According to Kirchmann, *Witz* itself seeks to effect 'a genuine elevation above others' (58). But this aristocracy of *Witz* is in fact a purely personal affair, with no class basis. The true struggle in fact takes place between the individual and society as a whole, as *Sittlichkeit* (social mores) comes into conflict with the rough edges of individuality. *Humor* becomes the main defense against this, taken here in the English sense of the cultivation of personal eccentricities and quirks, and so admits its own marginalization. 'In real life such persons never amount to much; one does not know what one should make of them; they are seen as spoiled children, as failed geniuses, and are avoided. They lack perseverance and firmness of action, and they vainly seek to make up for this with ingenious paradoxes and by casting their inaction as something noble' (69).

Thus runs Kirchmann's verdict on 'contradictory *Humor,*' which he views as having been developed in contemporary comic theory in reaction to the conditions of the modern age. The whole project of *Humor,* along with *Witz* as its subsidiary, to raise the embattled individual above the fray through the ability to laugh at the world and oneself is now seen to be dysfunctional. Resistance is no longer collective, but takes place at the level of the individual eccentric. In the face of the imperatives of 'real life,' *Witz*'s only choice seems to be between marginalization and assimilation.

It is Fischer who effects its complete integration into society. To be sure, he sees a 'heightened self-esteem' (109) as the driving force behind *Witz*. The ego's increased confidence is not of its own making, however, but is a decidedly social construct. 'Certain conditions help more than others in raising self-esteem and maintaining it at a constant height' (112). He gives as examples students and 'professions which constantly nourish the feeling of personal superiority and demand that one feel oneself to be and be felt as the master' (113). *Witz* is no longer a sign of eccentricity, but instead of domination, having abandoned its revolutionary aspirations for the standard of the educated, managerial elite. As Hohendahl points out, the project of *Bildung,* to which *Witz*'s fortunes had traditionally been linked, lost its emancipatory ideals and became merely a tool to serve the purposes of the state (*Kultur* 273). The emphasis shifts from a cultivation of critical thought to rote memorization and a blind reverence for the 'classics.' This raises certain problems, however, for a modern state: if it is to govern effectively, it requires servants who not only know a lot but know how to use it. The ability of the state to inspire dedication and loyalty through a sense that one's service to it is valuable is also a must. But the educational system neither developed the students' critical faculties nor gave them a framework of values that could arouse a deep personal commitment. Rather it became just one more branch of a bureaucratic state prone to suffer recurrent moral crises.

Fischer seems very much aware of this threat, for one of his favorite targets is the learned dunce, the idiot savant. The first joke he analyzes is Heine's comparison of certain professors with the pyramids of Egypt, 'only in these academic pyramids, no wisdom dwells' (62–63). This ponderous vacuity is contrasted with the lively *Mutterwitz* of the *Volk* that the scholars lack. 'What is this motherless *Witz* which comes into the world already an orphan and has a father, but no mother? It lacks that which *Mutterwitz* has: the sense for sense!' (152–53). The absence among certain intellectuals of *Witz*'s creative powers of intuition, 'that natural talent and inspiration, which involuntarily hits upon the right thing,' is keenly felt.[2] The result is not just an intellectual

2. One is reminded here of Wolff's *Erfindungsgeist,* the element of nonrational inspiration necessary to keep even the most rational machine running.

crisis but possibly a social one as *Mutterwitz* undermines the foundations of *Meisterschaft*. If the mastery of the educated classes is just puffed-up self-delusion, then the *Mutterwitz* which exposes it and the common folk it represents may become the true masters.[3] But Fischer only lets this threat go so far, having raised it to spur the *reformation* of the higher orders, not their overthrow. Indeed, as soon as the people enter the political arena and make a claim to the power to which their cleverness would appear to entitle them, all *Mutterwitz* abandons them. Fischer recounts the following story from the heady days of 1848. A crowd has gathered in front of the German parliament to demand freedom of the press. But when an official announces the lifting of censorship someone cries, 'When they give something, they take something else away; now we want both freedom of the press and censorship!' (160). This sort of simple-mindedness on the part of the vulgar is just the lowest form of a susceptibility to muddled thinking that permeates all of humanity and for which *Witz* must provide the cure. Fischer sees this omnipresent confusion symbolized in Goethe's witches' arithmetic (thereby counterbalancing *Mutterwitz* with a diabolized feminine figure) and goes on to give a telling illustration of its effects: 'There are now perhaps some people in France who would like to take Alsace-Lorraine from Germany, but do not want a war; just like in the last war there were those who may have counted up the German armed forces on the basis of the witches' arithmetic: "And nine is one and ten is none!"' (161). The marvelous clarity of brute force dispels the witches' wiles and unites the whole German nation in the great joke they have played against the French. The 'literary feud' touched off by Bouhours has become the real thing, as Börne predicted. In a later passage, Fischer cites the arrogant remark of Alexander the Great to one of his subordinates to demonstrate how *Witz* expresses the triumph of strength over weakness. The heightened self-esteem becomes that of the conqueror who sweeps both the 'indecision of the masses' and 'empty learnedness' (175) of the carping liberal intellectuals before him. The male warrior vanquishes the female witch (and

3. Fischer touches upon this situation in the following verse: *Auch war einmal ein Abt, ein gar stattlicher Herr, / Nur schade, sein Schäfer war klüger als er!* [*There was once an abbot, a fine gentleman, / Just too bad that his shepherd was more clever than he!*]

the French have been traditionally connected in the German mind with the feminine) and so solves the crisis of mastery and of values in general. War both rejuvenates the ruling elite's sense of purpose and serves to mobilize the masses around it. *Witz* remains the popularizer of liberalism, but now it's liberalism Bismarck-style.

Yet *Witz*'s oppositional character has not been completely lost. Fischer admits that the Jews and the French, however despicable, are still witty, if in a devious and cunning sort of way. In fact it would seem that social groups who are frequently made the butt of jokes, and Fischer mentions the Jews in particular, develop a high degree of *Witz* out of sheer self-defense. This tendentious sort of *Witz* becomes 'to use the Darwinian phrase, a kind of "struggle for existence"' (116). As we have seen, this struggle is played out not just between individuals, but among classes and nations as well.

Still, if even a victorious *Witz* tends to conjure up its own antithesis as it provokes an oppositional *Witz* among the downtrodden, the position of the conqueror must remain forever unstable. Fischer therefore calls for the supersession of *Witz* by *Humor*, where all antagonisms are smoothed over in an all-encompassing 'aesthetic freedom.' Even the conqueror learns to laugh at himself. And why not? His victory over the French and over the revolutionary ideology of 1848 is thereby secured. Early on in the essay, Fischer cited Jean Paul's equation of *Witz* and freedom (72), but reduced the latter to a purely aesthetic sense. *Witz* as 'playful judgment' allows us to escape from the tension of everyday life (69). Fischer's linking of *Witz* with a reduction in psychic tension is an idea that would continue to be common in later psychological discussions, including Freud's own theories. But we should not be blinded by either an aesthetic or psychological facade to the real tensions that we have seen being reduced here: those of class, national, and gender conflict.

Witz and Psychology

Histories of *Witz* remark on an important change in its meaning from the eighteenth to the nineteenth century as it is increasingly restricted to the province of the comic. *Witz* loses its status as a faculty of the intellect participating in all manner of creative activity and becomes a humble jokesmith. It is important, however, to be aware of the gradual nature of this shift, for *Witz* was slow in giving up its other roles, which, as we have seen, still crop up in theories of *Witz,* if only in vestigial form. Its cultural-critical momentum starts building in the Enlightenment, but only reaches full steam in the nineteenth century, with Jean Paul, Börne, and Heine.

The Hegelians, too, allotted *Witz* a critical role, albeit one that was soon sublated into *Humor.* Hegelian theory, though suspicious of *Witz,* still gave it a broad enough foundation to serve the purposes of what Terry Eagleton has called the 'cultural strategist,' namely, to speak to the needs of culture as a whole. But after the failure of the revolutions of 1830 and 1848 to bring about radical social change, the two bases from which this comprehensive critique was launched—the attempt by the Young Germans to erect a democratic public sphere and the speculative, progressive philosophical framework of the Young Hegelians—were called into question. *Witz* has a vantage point from which it could participate in an all-encompassing critique snatched out from under it, and so its wide-ranging style of free association, dedicated to the violation of all boundaries, succumbs to the old charge of superficiality. The new spirit of realism can be seen precisely as a reaction against the patent failures of this sort of dilettantism (Hohendahl, Criticism 256). The sphere of *belles lettres* ceases to offer a safe haven for the free exchange of ideas, falling more and more under the dominance of an expert literary criticism. Philosophy loses its speculative edge as well and takes a positivist turn. Even Marx's theories of revolution must claim to be scientific in order to gain legitimacy, with little room left for joking around. Any lingering claims to a broader social relevance *Witz* may harbor are easily co-opted by a nationalistic realpolitik, as we saw in Fischer.

The knockout blow, however, comes after 1870 and is delivered by a relatively new breed of expert, the psychologist. Lazarus had declared scientific psychology to be in its infancy, but it had been growing quickly ever since, and with Lipps would prove itself well able to take on *Witz.* Still, this preparation took time, for *Witz* itself had to be transformed into an appropriate object of study. This hinged on its restriction to the comic, for science requires a well-defined material upon which to conduct its investigations. Since positivism uses a physicalist paradigm to understand the world, we may think of positivistic investigation as always requiring a body to dissect, and the restriction of *Witz* to the comic presented it with just that. In the first place, one has a canonical body of jokes, or rather, one may create such a body from the works of acknowledged wits of the past. The writings of previous theoreticians also provide an important, if suspect, corpus upon which to build. But the truly new basis for a revaluation of past theories comes with the introduction of the body itself through the analysis of laughter, the physical expression of the comic and so of *Witz*.

Theoreticians had traditionally concentrated on the psychic causes of laughter, with its inherent physicality remaining somewhat mysterious. Certainly attempts at physical explanations were made (by Vischer, for example), but remained sketchy and of secondary importance. Only in the middle of the nineteenth century do we see this hierarchy of mind over body begin to be reversed. The seminal essay so far as the comic is concerned is Herbert Spencer's 'The Physiology of Laughter' (1860). Drawing upon Darwin, Spencer sees laughter as the discharge of excess nervous energy stemming from a disappointed expectation. Not a new idea, to be sure, but one that would gain increasing prominence in joke theory. What Spencer does is give this qualitative feeling of comic deflation a quantitative basis—excess energy and the need to discharge it in order to restore equilibrium. Though this energy operates on both the psychical and physical levels, it definitely seems to follow the accepted laws of physics, thus bringing the mind as well under this scientific model. Notions of surplus energy, tension, and the need for equilibrium would also form the basis for Freud's own conception of psychic economy. It should also be remarked here that Richard Keller Simon (179ff.) has placed Spencer's essay in the context of his dispute with George Meredith, an author and an important theoretician of laughter. But their standpoints are radically opposed; it is the witty novelist versus the 'great compartmentalizer.' At issue is not just laughter, but the growing specialization of intellectual life and of society as a whole. As Simon points out, the specialists seem to have carried the day.

Ewald Hecker takes somewhat of a different tack in his *Physiologie und Psychologie des Lachens und des Komischen*. Rather than postulate an energy that shuttles back and forth between the mind and the body, he contents himself with establishing a parallelism between the two. The physiology of laughter is to elucidate the psychological process of the comic, though neither one is reducible to the other. Both, it seems, are the result of an oscillation between pleasurable and painful sensations. Laughter's effects on respiration and circulation help the body retain its equilibrium when subjected to the stimulus of being tickled. As far as the mind is concerned, pleasure is measured by the ease with which it can assimilate a new idea or sensation. Similarity (*Ähnlichkeit*, which has long been associated with *Witz*) certainly helps smooth the process of assimilation, with the standard of similarity being our accepted logical, aesthetic, and ethical norms. *Witz* thus has the conservative function of adapting the new to the status quo. Hecker does claim that the man of high ideals will be more resistant to tyranny than his fellows, but this gesture of resistance remains undeveloped and seems more directed at the slavish uneducated masses than at any real despot. In fact, Hecker goes out of his way to supress the political implications of some of the examples he discusses (69). Even more suggestive are his remarks on the hunchback, whose hump offends us but at whom we can still laugh when the pleasant thought of our own superiority occurs to us (34). Or take the case of the obese man, whose revolting corpulence is only outweighed by the thought that it serves him right for being such a glutton (35). The oscillating force of laughter leaves our smug faith in our own values unshaken. Physiology's conservative paradigm, dedicated to following the path of least resistance and maintaining equilibrium at all costs, is easily assimilated by the intellect and the social values it represents, assuring the continued dominance of mind over body. Parallelism becomes hierarchical as the body loses its subversive character in this conservative physiology and is even turned by it into a sign for inferiority and moral degeneracy.

Interesting that Henri Bergson, cited by Freud in *Jokes and Their Relation to the Unconscious* as an opponent to the oscillation theory of laughter (8:188), reaches conclusions similar to Hecker's: 'Laughter is simply the result of a mechanism set up in us by nature or, what is almost the same thing, by our long acquaintance with social life' (188). This blending of nature and nurture, of mind and body, seems at first to be a liberating move. 'The comic character is one with whom, to begin with, our mind, or rather our body, sympathizes' (186). Bergson also connects the comic to dreams and the infantile here, with Freud seizing upon the latter point (8:222–23). But before this alliance of irrational forces can go too far, order is restored. The weight of social discipline has been thrown off only temporarily, with laughter appearing on the scene like 'a stern father' who has played along with these childish pranks for a time but now decides that enough is enough. 'Laughter is, above all, a corrective. Being intended to humiliate, it must make a painful impression on the person against whom it is directed. By laughter, society avenges itself for the liberties taken with it' (187). Laughter's perceived physiological appeal, the sympathy of the body that it arouses, is again used against the body to make it, and so the individual as a whole, vulnerable to the influence of social norms. The naturalization of social mores blurs the distinction between Hecker's physiological and Bergson's more socially oriented theory of laughter. Perhaps this may be traced to a common reliance on Darwin, as both men sought to show the utility of laughter in the evolutionary scheme of things. But the resultant naturalization of values upon which laughter is based does not serve to make them any more natural, only more effective. Frank Sulloway has demonstrated the tremendous impact Darwin had on Freud as well, though it is also important to see how Freud went beyond Darwin. Any chances of success to restore a subversive value to laughter will therefore depend on Freud's ability to modify the conservative economy of Darwinian physiology and denaturalize dominant social values. He must recover laughter for the body and, as indicated by Bergson, for dreams and the infantile. All three are linked through laughter to a given set of social values. But whether this is a purely one-way relationship—that is to say, whether laughter can only follow the agenda set by these social mores without having any counterinfluence on them—remains to be seen. Though the spirit of the age is a conservative one, Freud has a long tradition of physical and infantile humor to draw on — and Heine did dream some very funny and very subversive dreams.

This brings us to a closer examination of how the comic tradition was constructed in the late nineteenth century. *Witztheorie* had been going on long enough for a definite canon of jokes to have been built up and subjected to repeated analysis, which at the very least succeeded in proving that jokes told too often do indeed cease to be funny. A more intriguing question is what happens to them after they have been torn from the time and culture that gave birth to them. Witticisms are plundered from all ages of the Western tradition. Though many are anonymous, most come from famous authors or public figures, themselves part of the canon of the great ones. Aristophanes and Cicero, Cervantes and Shakespeare, Lessing and Lichtenberg, and of course Heine and Börne, all have their places in the pantheon of wit. Or do they? In fact they usually have been reduced to one or two memorable and oft-repeated jokes. The theoretician recounts a couple of these one-liners, makes his point about them, and moves on to the next exhibit, with little attempt being made to place these jokes within the overall literary or public activity of the teller. This type of theory shatters history into a collection of discrete and timeless moments. Its atomizing effect can be seen in the change in the concept of *Witz* itself. *Witz*'s restriction to the comic leads to a devaluation of *Witz* as a general faculty of the intellect and to more attention being paid to *Witz* as signifying a particular joke. *Witz*'s facility for intuitive leaps, which had traditionally made it a difficult subject for theory to get a handle on, is overcome by confining *Witz* to the province of the comic, a designated zone of irrationality, and by further breaking it down into the bite-size pieces of the canonical jokes, a.k.a. 'Stop me if you haven't heard this one before.'

Freud, while clearly indebted to these theoreticians, also has a sense for their limitations: 'It is striking with what a small number of jokes recognized as such the authorities are satisfied for the purposes of their enquiries, and how each of them takes the same ones over from his predecessors. We must not shirk the duty of analysing the same instances that have already served the classical authorities on jokes. But it is our intention to turn besides to fresh material so as to obtain a broader foundation for our conclusions' (15).

Freud's contribution to the canon would take a rather provocative form: the inclusion of Jewish and 'dirty' jokes. The Jewish question was of course a major social issue of the time and its introduction might be expected to lend Freud's work an air of immediacy not enjoyed by other more traditional theories. Though the Jews were stereotypically perceived as being witty, jokes about Jews were rarely recounted in mainstream *Witztheorie,* save for an occasional jab at their venality. Society's attitude towards sexuality was also coming under scrutiny (in part due to the efforts of Freud and other sexologists) and so the admission of the long banished *Zote* to theoretical discourse was certainly not without import. Sexuality might also prove useful as a fulcrum to raise physiological theories of jokes and laughter to a more critical vantage point.

The problem, of course, is not just with the canon, but with the whole structure of these physiological theories. Emil Kraepelin provides us with a good example of this. Kraepelin explicitly acknowledges the sociocritical nature of much of the canon, citing a number of political jokes and discussing Beaumarchais's battle with the censors. But this recognition is really no more than reminiscence, with the polemics of the past having no theoretical grounding in the present. Kraepelin himself declares that his psychology rests on 'the division of our entire experience into an outer and an inner' (128). Similar to the general anatomy of a physiologist, Kraepelin the psychologist concentrates on the workings of an idealized discrete mind. The comic is an individual matter, the ego's overcoming of unpleasurable sensations. Laughter is based on a feeling of superiority and so requires a certain amount of distance from its object, be it other people, one's own body, or even oneself. Social norms do play an important role, but they are taken as something given; though possibly forming the basis of criticism, they themselves are left uncriticized. In the absence of a lively public sphere or even some notion of an unfolding rational world spirit, the basis for collective action has been undercut. The atomizing, ahistorical tendencies of this theoretical paradigm simply leave no place for it. Critical reason has been replaced by scientific rationalization, a problem that bedevils not only Kraepelin but Freud as well.

Yet we must also recognize that the foundations of scientific rationality are none too firm. Almost all these theoreticians of the comic at one time or another lament over how difficult it is to get a clear and distinct picture of this subject. Lipps, a most self-confident theoretician, deals squarely with the theoretical slipperiness of the comic. Indeed, for him it constitutes its essence, for the comic is the nonsensical. Following Karl Groos's appropriation of Kant, he describes our experience of the comic as one of 'Verblüffung und Erleuchtung' (amazement and comprehension); we are at first astonished by the comic utterance (and Lipps does in fact concern himself mostly with verbal and not physical humor), but then come to understand it, we get the joke. Taking as an example Heine's 'famillionär' joke that would later be so important for Freud, Lipps divides the act of understanding into two stages. In the first phase of illumination we sift out the joke's cognitive content, the 'message' of the joke, which in this case is Heine's dig at the familiarity 'of a puffed-up millionaire [*Millionär*]' (95). But the truly comic moment only comes in the second stage upon our realization that the word *famillionär* is itself meaningless. Our astonishment arose through a frustrated expectation of meaning, with the psychic energy involved in this expectation being transformed into laughter once the unsuitability of its object has been demonstrated. The comic is a 'resolution into nothingness' and so meaning is something perfectly incidental to it. It is in itself senseless and thus has been completely marginalized by comic theory.

Perhaps another example from Lipps may serve to make us suspect the purity of his scientific motives for this marginalization of the comic. Imagine, he says, that you are expecting a very important person when in walks a beggar. Anticipation may at first lead you to accord him a status that will soon prove undeserved. 'The beggar abruptly collapses back into his nothingness' (58), thereby sharing the fate of the millionaire. Lipps's dichotomy of sense and senselessness operates on a level seemingly untroubled by social realities. The economic tensions that are manifestly present in these jokes themselves disappear into nothing under the cover of an all-encompassing comic deflation, the universality of which guarantees its emptiness. Freud himself will tell quite a few jokes about beggars and millionaires and we shall see to what extent his own theory of psychic economy draws on and is in turn drawn into economic issues which give it more critical weight than those of his predecessors. The comic regains its traditional role as social critic and thereby recovers its 'meaning' in this newfound sense of purpose.

This is not to say that Lipps emerges unscathed from his battle with the comic. The latter does exact its revenge, though in a most subtle way, through the infiltration into theory itself. In his mockery of Groos's definition of the comic (27), Lipps cites Jean Paul's remark that 'the ridiculous never fit into the definitions of the philosophers, except involuntarily.' He subjects Heyman's ideas to comic deflation (77) and dismisses Hecker's as merely 'witzig' (81). The comic thus turns and consumes theory in the abyss of its own meaninglessness—at least, those theories that Lipps throws to it. But the introduction of this tendentious wit in dealing with one's scientific opponents can get out of control, as Lipps himself suffers the same fate at the hands of Freud. After surveying the works of his predecessors, Freud declares, 'they contribute to our knowledge of jokes no more than would a series of anecdotes to the description of some personality of whom we have the right to ask for a biography' (14). Theory is swallowed by anecdote, the witty story.

This theoretical instability was a threat to Freud's own work. As Samuel Weber has pointed out, a lot is riding on the success of the joke book. Freud's use of free association in his interpretation of dreams could be seen as a fascinating but ultimately meaningless play of wit. Indeed, Freud specifically points to the fundamental connection between the 'logic' of dreams and jokes. To avoid having his own theory become just a joke, Freud must rehabilitate *Witz* by filling the vacuum of meaning left by Lipps and other theoreticians of the late nineteenth century.

His suggestion in the introduction to *Jokes and Their Relation to the Unconscious* as to how this gap might be filled is most instructive. Recall the opposition he set up between a 'series of anecdotes' and a 'biography.' After reviewing the disordered state of contemporary theory, he recommends the expansion of the canon along the lines discussed above. He declares that he will rely not only on traditional examples, but jokes 'by which we ourselves have been most struck in the course of our lives' (15). As was the case in *The Interpretation of Dreams,* Freud's own biography will be interwoven into this text, using the force of his own personality to help provide theoretical coherence. For example, it is known that he began collecting Jewish jokes after the death of his father. This allows for a reading of the joke book in the light of this personal crisis as one more phase of Freud's self-analysis from which he gained so much theoretical insight.

Freud continues to make a biographical argument for the importance of *Witz,* with the last line of the introduction reading, 'even men of eminence [*bedeutende Männer*] who have thought it worthwhile to tell the story of their origins, of the cities and countries they have visited, and of the important people with whom they have associated, are not ashamed in their autobiographies to report their having heard some excellent joke.' *Witztheorie,* and so perhaps psychoanalytic theory as a whole, is saved from triviality by the prestige of the lives of the 'men of eminence.' Freud's conception of *Witz* remains tied up with its traditional bearer, the great man, the bourgeois individual. The hermeneutic circle becomes complete, and probably vicious, when we find psychoanalytic theory returning the favor by giving coherence to the lives of these men themselves in the form of psychobiography, thus saving them from dissolving into a 'series of anecdotes.' This applies to the individual in general. Psychoanalysis gained a great deal of its legitimacy from its apparent ability to explain individuals to themselves. Dreams, jokes and the whole psychopathology of everyday life stand at the beginning of the psychoanalytic enterprise because their analysis can make these theories real to people. But this affirmation of the individual only takes place in the context of its dissolution. The subject appears not as an autonomous rational agent in an ideal speech situation, but as a therapeutic object no longer transparent to itself; it is sick and must be made whole again. Freud calls on *Witz* in his attempt to reconstitute a now-problematic subject, giving it a renewed vigor that it had not seen in many years.

Freud also presents us with a second object of analysis, for the importance of *Witz* is based not only on its importance for the individual, but also on its social role: 'We may also bear in mind the peculiar and even fascinating charm exercised by jokes in our society. A new joke acts almost like an event of universal interest; it is passed from one person to another like the news of the latest victory' (15). Freud will go on to expound upon this inherently social character of *Witz* that makes it impossible to restrict it to the isolated individual. This offers *Witz* the chance of recovering its role as social critic and social unifier. Unlike dreams, jokes can be directly shared by all, transforming psychodynamics into sociodynamics. The problem of the meaning of psychoanalysis is thus raised from the biographical to the political level.

That the relationship between these two levels is not necessarily a harmonious one can be seen from the case of Freud himself. Take for example Carl Schorske's interpretation of the influence of politics on Freud, or William McGrath's updated and expanded analysis of this question. Both offer a great wealth of insight into the effect Freud's political situation had on the development of his theories. But in both cases the biographical in the end overwhelms the political. Freud, to some extent, resolves his personal crises — death of his father, lack of professional advancement — but only at the cost of turning his back on direct efforts to deal with the general social problems of turn-of-the-century Vienna. The political becomes an alien element in Freud's allegedly ahistorical theoretical framework, a residue from the past left in a nebulous state of sublimation. Whatever validity this view may have in regard to Freud the man, and it is true that he was not a political activist, one still must wonder to what extent these traces of political engagement — Freud's revolutionary dreams if you will — can be used to push his theories beyond the limits that Freud the scientist had set for them. But for this we must get beyond a simple biographical perspective (though biographical information, to the exent that it reveals the nexus of the personal and the political, will remain important for me). This is why I have spent so much time tracing the history of *Witztheorie,* for now we can place Freud's own *Witzbuch* in the context of this far-reaching discourse. The structure of this discourse, its rules and imperatives, theories and examples, traditions and aspirations, will shape Freud's own thoughts on the matter as well as help us to determine their significance for the social and cultural institutions of which *Witz* had been and was a part. The book takes on a life of its own and resists any attempt by Freud, himself a *bedeutender Mann,* to impose his own meaning upon it, to turn it into his own biography. The dynamic interpenetration between the social and the personal will be a driving force throughout the book, a book that one might therefore describe as the analysis of a social psyche.

THE ECONOMICS OF WITZ

In the first three chapters we have seen that the history of *Witz* and *Witztheorie* is closely tied up with that of its principal practitioner, the bourgeoisie. The bourgeoisie turns *Witz,* originally appropriated from the aristocratic salon, into a medium through which it comes into contact with the aristocracy on the common ground of *Bildung,* while continuing to exclude the uneducated masses. From romantic *Witz-theorie* at the time of the French Revolution on, we see attempts made to widen and diversify the public sphere of *Witz,* as *Witz*'s potential as a forum for enlightening the masses and effecting progressive social change is explored, especially by the Young German writers. The collapse of this revolutionary project after 1848 left *Witz* in the hands of a scientific elite, where it was at best depoliticized and at worst co-opted to the purposes of a jingoistic nationalism. Freud's book, written in 1905, brings *Witz* up to the turn of the century, a time of great crisis in bourgeois society.

The bourgeoisie as a class had lost much of its cohesiveness by the end of the nineteenth century. As Peter Gay puts it, 'what the nineteenth-century bourgeois had in common was the negative quality of being neither aristocrats nor laborers, and of being uneasy in their middle-class skins' (*Education* 31). This space between aristocrat and laborer was wide indeed, with the difference in income between the upper and lower ends of the scale being simply enormous (24–25). These differences were no longer to be smoothed over in the name of class solidarity in the struggle against the aristocracy, which had wound down to a considerable extent, largely in the favor of the bourgeoisie. Though Austria remained a monarchy, much governmental power was in the hands of a middle-class bureaucracy (Macartney 624) and the truly dominant class was the *Geldaristokratie* of big business, made up of both aristocrats and commoners. The bourgeoisie was no longer interested in revolutionizing the political system, which may have maintained many feudal structures but still worked largely to the grand bourgeoisie's advantage. Its attention was shifted to economic questions, such as the intraclass conflict between big and small business, as capital became concentrated in fewer and fewer hands (Hobsbawm 52, 181). We shall discover that economic issues play an important, if not dominant, role in Freud's *Witztheorie,* the class origins of which remained strongly in evidence.

It must be admitted that the social crisis at the turn of the century was not limited to the bourgeoisie but encompassed a wide range of social and cultural factors. While not arguing a position of economic reductionism, I do want to stress the importance of economic influences in this situation. In Austria the crash of 1873 and resultant revelations of corruption among the ruling elites centering around the Ofenheim railway scandal were instrumental in destroying public confidence in the political institutions of bourgeois liberalism and its entrepreneurial economic ethic, both of which were made responsible for the disaster (McGrath, *Dionysian* 46–47). Indeed, this entrepreneurial spirit, which might have helped hold the bourgeoisie together, becomes the victim of its own success and begins to break down at this time throughout Europe. Hobsbawm tells us that the efficiency of the capitalist system in producing wealth had been such that more and more members of the bourgeoisie abandoned the work of production for the pleasures of consumption (169), leading to a general moral crisis marked by fears of leading a useless, parasitic existence (186). It is quite plausible that this shift in economic relations played into the general cultural atmosphere of decadence, each conditioning the other. Thomas Mann, in his novel *Buddenbrooks,* presents us with a study of how a Schopenhauerian *Weltmüdigkeit* (world-weariness) was sapping the will of the bourgeois entrepreneur to go out and conquer the world. We have previously seen the connection of *Witz* to this entrepreneurial spirit as well as its intimate ties to the world of *Besitz* and *Bildung.* That these two former pillars of bourgeois society are now at odds must surely affect the status of *Witz* as well, for it has always been caught between economic and cultural factors. We shall therefore begin this chapter with a discussion of decadence and *Witz*'s relation to it. Though beginning on a purely cultural level, the economic tie-in will quickly become apparent, thematized in both the material of the jokes and in Freud's theory itself. That *Witz* has been bound up with a cultural-critical discourse from its very inception must lead us to expect from it more than a mere description of the problems at hand. Both an analysis of and potential solutions to these difficulties will also be in evidence. We shall find that Freud draws upon the rich tradition of *Witz* to restore to it a measure of its former role as an instrument of social communication, analysis, and critique. That we have come a long way from Thomasius and the optimistic project of the classical bourgeois public sphere will also be made quite clear.

Keeping this sociocultural background in mind, we do indeed find that Freud's jokes resonate deeply with it. Freud himself characterizes jokes as inherently social phenomena, and so it is no surprise that, by admitting them into his text as examples, his own work becomes infected by this wider social discourse. For example:

> Here I recall a joke which has remained in my memory owing to the special circumstances in which I heard it. One of the great teachers of my young days, whom we thought incapable of appreciating a joke and from whom we had never heard a joke of his own, came into the Institute one day laughing, and, more readily than usual, explained to us what it was that had caused his cheerful mood. 'I have just read an excellent joke,' he said. 'A young man was introduced into a Paris salon, who was a relative of the great Jean-Jacques Rousseau and bore his name. Moreover he was red-haired. But he behaved so awkwardly that the hostess remarked critically to the gentleman who had introduced him: "Vous m'avez fait connaître un jeune homme roux et sot, mais non pas un Rousseau."'[1]

Before we even begin to discuss the joke itself, please note that it has been framed as something able to break the routine of even the

1. 'You have made me acquainted with a young man who is roux (red-haired) and sot (silly), but not a Rousseau.' 'Roux-sot' would be pronounced exactly like 'Rousseau' (8:29–30).

most stolid professor. This remarkable quality is what made it stick in Freud's mind. And though no one would accuse Freud of being as humorless as his former teacher, his own jokes have a similarly disruptive effect on his theoretical expositions. Freud is always wrestling with his jokes, adjusting his theoretical model before the eyes of the reader as new data comes in. Rather than smooth over the conflict between *Witz* and *Theorie* as so many of his predecessors tried to do, Freud plays it to best advantage, using it to spur the reader's interest and understanding. And if this textual dynamic that Freud has set up is more than a rhetorical device, if this truly is a work in progress, then this gives the book's readers an opening to make their own contributions. As with the dream book, jokes are something everyone is familiar with, and this connection to the everyday world brings theory within the reach of the layperson — the home version of psychoanalysis, if you will.

At the same time we must resist the tendency towards what one might call 'pointecentrism,' which would restrict *Witz* to the ability to create one funny moment, the punchline. Freud himself buys into this approach by highlighting the punchlines of his examples with italics or bold type, a textual artifice I have dispensed with in order to encourage the reader to pay attention to the joke as a whole. If we see *Witz* as responsible for the telling of the entire joke, then its horizons, and so those of our analysis as well, broaden considerably. For example, in the joke we have just heard, the setting is a Parisian salon, the cradle of *esprit*. But a long time has passed since the days of Bouhours, Voltaire, and Rousseau, and it is precisely the passing of time and the decay this has entailed to which this joke draws our attention. *Witz* is here reflecting (on) its own situation, acting out its own decline as the invocation of the name of a great *esprit* from the past literally falls apart before our eyes into boorishness and stupidity. The question is raised, does *Witz* still have a home in the bourgeois salon? This theme is touched on in several other places as well, especially in some of Heine's cutting remarks concerning the salon scene of his own time. We seem to hear *Witz* wondering out loud whether it still belongs in high society.

Probably not, since a genuine Rousseau, a fiery prophet of freedom, had little to hope for from the bourgeoisie. As was discussed regarding Kuno Fischer, bourgeois *Bildung* had lost its emancipatory thrust in the repressive environment that followed upon the failure of the revolutions of 1848. Though the works of the old masters would continue to be taught, they had been stripped of their original provocative character, and so their modern appearance could either take the form of a pedantic antiquarianism or absurd self-parody. But then why did Freud's professor, who was usually proof against any sort of joke, find this one so funny? Of course, we have already learned from Fischer that there were many jokes *about* professors, and Freud himself tells a few, but a joke being told by a professor is something new and must be accounted for. Perhaps the answer lies in the explanation Freud later gives of this joke in conjunction with the following one: 'Once when the Antigone [of Sophocles] was produced in Berlin, the critics complained that the production was lacking in the proper character of antiquity. Berlin wit made the criticism its own in the following words: "Antik? Oh, nee."'[2]

Once again we witness the disintegration of a famous name from the past, a past that cannot be brought to life again in the present. Both jokes pose a similar technical problem for Freud. The psychic principle he identifies at the root of each is that of *Ersparnis*.[3] What exactly is being saved in these two jokes? 'We save having to express a criticism or give shape to a judgement; both are already there in the name itself' (43). Remember that we are dealing here with two luminaries in the pantheon of Western culture. These names contain in their own right considerable ethical power to critique a decadent society through the ideals they stand for, but their unadulterated invocation would not save us the trouble of constructing a detailed critique of the times. Quite the reverse, they would demand it. Only in their witty transformation do these names and the ideals they represent become broken ruins, relics of a lost golden age. They are used to criticize anything unpleasantly modern, anything that might disrupt the tranquility of salon or stage, but pose no imperative to change. Nietzsche gives a

2. 'Antique? On, no.' The words, in Berlin dialect, approximate in pronunciation 'Antigone' (31).

3. Translated in the Standard Edition as 'economy,' but specifically in the sense of savings or thrift.

good description of how the monuments of the past were being used at this time as bastions to maintain the status quo by spreading the feeling that all had been done before, and done much better. The hostess, professor, and theater critic ridicule those who, however involuntarily, would make a claim to resurrect bygone glories. These keepers of the bourgeois order are thereby spared any self-criticism, using *Witz* to deafen themselves against the claims of the past with their own laughter. This, I would suggest, is one way to understand the nature of the *Ersparnis* offered by these two jokes.

The general crisis in *Bildung* would naturally have a great impact on the status of *Witz*. We have already seen *Witz* change from a productive intellectual and aesthetic principle to being gradually restricted to the province of the joke. Yet even here it has maintained contact with the world of high culture. As is well known, jokes often rely on allusion and double entendre, on what is simply taken to be *understood* to achieve their comic purposes. This would be impossible without a shared cultural tradition. Freud recounts many highly literate jokes, and, though he does not explicitly acknowledge it, it is precisely this common heritage that allows these jokes to make the economies they do, to leave so much unsaid. Therefore Freud's principle of *Ersparnis* has not only psychological but also social significance as *Witz,* which has ceased to be a creative force, must instead rely on the dwindling cultural capital of the past. *Witz*'s relegation to such a parasitic status is symptomatic for a society that has been plagued with visions of *Epigonenthum* from Immermann to Nietzsche. Bourgeois *Witz* therefore must seek to preserve the past if it wishes to preserve itself, but all its thrift comes to nought, as it leaves each and every shade of the illustrious dead that it summons up debased and worthless. In the jokes we have discussed so far, *Witz* has revealed how empty these ideals have become in the modern world, often doing with one aphorism what it would take a professor a whole semester to accomplish.

But not only the philistines are arrayed against classical *Bildung*. Take for example the following remarks by Heine: 'This lady resembles the Venus of Milo in many respects: she, too, is extraordinarily old, like her she has no teeth, and there are white patches on the yellowish surface of her body' (70). That this archetypal representation of classical beauty is not what it used to be is attested to in yet another passage in Heine, where we find the distraught poet lying at the feet of the statue of this goddess in the Louvre, seeking solace but receiving only a pitying look which seems to say, 'I would like to help you, but as you can see, I have no arms.' Heine's *Witz* stands at the beginning of the break with the classical tradition, both of antiquity and of Weimar. This ideal of beauty gradually gives way before forces that will culminate in the aesthetic exploration of ugliness and nonclassical ideas of beauty found in naturalism and expressionism. *Witz*'s natural tendency to debase the sublime makes it complicitous in this broader aesthetic shift. Thus we need not only see it here as a defender of the status quo's traditional notions of cultural literacy, but also in league with forces of progress and innovation.

Yet the dangers arising from the loss of the firm cultural basis which the classical tradition provided are also indicated by the jokes Freud tells. Far more than questions of taste are at stake, as we see in the following: 'Here is a joke that is said to have been made during an examination in jurisprudence. The candidate had to translate a passage in the Corpus Juris: "'Labeo ait' . . . I fall, says he." "You fail, say I," replied the examiner, and the examination was at an end. Anyone who mistakes the name of the great jurist for a verbal form, and moreover one wrongly recalled, no doubt deserves nothing better.'[4]

The fall that is at the center of this joke is one away from the classical tradition embodied in Latin. The ancients were looked to not only for aesthetic norms, but also for those of jurisprudence, and so as Latin begins to die as a language, there is a danger that the legal ethics and tradition of public virtue it represents will go with it.[5] It seems that these days a good Roman is hard to find, and those few would-be good citizens just don't measure up and soon retire from public life. 'Like Cincinnatus, he has gone back to his place before the plough,' remarks

4. 'In German . . . the same word *fallen* is used for both "to fall" and "to fail an examination." Labeo is in fact the name of a famous Roman jurist, and the Latin words should really have been translated "Labeo says"' (34).

5. For a more literary treatment of this theme, see the third chapter of Joris-Karl Huysmans's novel *A Rebours* where the hero, Des Esseintes, disparages the literature of the Roman republic in its bloom in favor of that of the Roman Empire in its decadence.

the witty Herr N., or as he says of another failed politician, 'he has a great future behind him' (27, 26).

And what exactly led to this politician's failure? Freud merely remarks that 'times changed.' He has already told us that *Witz* can spare us the need to formulate a critical judgment of the situation. Rather than determining the real causes of the political and cultural decay that was engulfing Europe, everything is blamed on the mysterious force of time. The past that cannot be recaptured continues to haunt the present with its lost youth, cast in a joking form as laughter seeks to vanquish the angst these shades of the past arouse. The *Witz* of the age sinks into an almost senile melancholia—or 'anecdotage,' as one joke would have it (21–22). 'Human life falls into two halves. In the first half we wish the second one would come; and in the second we wish that the first one were back' (66). This joke is recounted in connection with two others that give voice to an equally pessimistic view of the passage of time. Kant and Hegel's ideal of history as the chronicle of the progress of man into his self-created future is replaced by the suprahistorical, almost metaphysical, concept of time. We have our future behind us because we have turned our backs to it, gazing longingly towards a forever irrecoverable past. And yet not quite all has been lost, for one relic from the golden age of Greece has survived intact, the sign of its decline, the sophistic joke. For Freud, the basic trick of sophism lies in the process of fragmentation, of focusing on the parts rather than on the whole. Though he discusses this in terms of other examples where the rules of logic themselves become the objects of this fragmentation, we have to a certain extent seen this technique played out for us on a literal level in the dissolution of 'Antigone' and 'Rousseau.' All of this comes together in an ideology of time and its *Zerfallenheit* (decay).

Nietzsche, too, in his essay 'The Use and Abuse of History,' complains about this cultural fragmentation, attributing it to the increasing massification of the age. The fact is that the subject of bourgeois history, the world-historical individual, the great man whose fall Nietzsche laments, is no longer viable. It is this loss that has resulted in history's collapse into time. Let us again turn to Herr N. for a suggestive commentary on the contemporary situation:

> Herr N.'s attention was drawn one day to the figure of a writer who had become well-known from a series of undeniably boring essays which he had contributed to a Vienna daily paper. All of these essays dealt with small episodes in the relations of the first Napoleon with Austria. The author had red hair. As soon as Herr N. heard his name mentioned he asked: 'Is not that the *roter Fadian* that runs through the story of the Napoleonids?'[6]

As with the *roux et sot* fellow we are again confronted with a red-haired usurper to the throne of one of the great men of the past. But not only Napoleon is involved here. Freud informs us that the phrase *der rote Faden* on which the joke *der rote Fadian* depends comes from Goethe's *Wahlverwandtschaften.* And Goethe himself got the idea from the British navy, in whose ropes this red thread was woven which 'cannot be extracted without undoing the whole' (23). But history itself has come unraveled to reveal this red thread in all its inadequacy. The combination of history and literature, the meeting of Goethe and Napoleon, has come apart as the great events of the past are reduced to boring triviality in the contemporary journalism of the feuilleton, which itself has degenerated considerably since the days of Heine and his *Ideen,* where the problematic legacy of Napoleon is handled with far more *esprit.* The joke itself remarks on this dissolution even as it seeks to restore the lost unity, wittily bringing Napoleon and Goethe back together again. The process of *Verdichtung* (condensation), which Freud is trying to illustrate, is much more than just superficial word play—it is a game with *Dichtung* and *Wahrheit.*[7] *Witz* not only mirrors the decadence of its time, it also criticizes it and does its best to put things right, constructing what Freud identifies as the complement to *Verdichtung, Ersatzbildung* (substitution). But *Witz* alone is an inadequate *Ersatz* for genuine *Bildung.* It takes *Witztheorie* to restore this act of reflective judgment that *Witz* itself can both hinder, in its conservative role, and at the same time make possible. Like a neurotic symptom, the joke is maladaptive yet provides the key to the understanding and cure of the illness.

6. *Roter* means 'red.' *Fadian* means 'dull fellow.' *Faden* means 'thread.' So the play is upon 'red-haired dullard' and 'red thread.'

7. *Dichtung und Wahrheit* (poetry and truth) is the title of Goethe's autobiography.

Freud's own theoretical model goes a long way toward opening up jokes and allowing them to speak their full message, though at times it is, at best, merely suggestive. Take for instance his model of psychic economy, especially as it manifests itself in the joke book in the principle of *Ersparnis.* Suppose, in our desire to truly explain the fall of the Great Man and not just leave everything to the mysterious wearing action of time, we feel the need to go beyond the psychological processes of the individual and to investigate the larger social factors at work here. For example, what if we were to give Freud's psychic economy a nudge in a more literal direction? But for that perhaps we need a little outside help.

In *The Eighteenth Brumaire of Louis Bonaparte* Marx also discusses the problems the modern world has in mastering the past. 'Humanity makes its own history, but not freely, not under self-chosen, but under immediately present, given and handed-down conditions. The tradition of all dead generations weighs down on the brains of the living like a nightmare' (8:115). The past has at times been used to successfully revolutionize the present, as suggested by the examples of Luther masquerading as the Apostle Paul or the French Jacobins pretending to be Romans. But in 1851 the masque suddenly turns into farce as Louis Napoleon woefully fails to live up to his famous name. Since he is such a ridiculous figure, 'le roi des drôles' (207), it is only fitting that Marx should mock him with a joke which, happily enough, Freud also discusses. One of Louis Napoleon's first acts was to confiscate the goods of the house of Orleans. A witty countess called this 'le premier vol de l'aigle.' The pun, as Freud explains, is on *vol,* which can mean either 'flight' or 'theft' on the part of the eagle. It is significant that this is the first joke that Freud analyzes after declaring the explicitly economic principle of *Ersparnis* to be at the root of all *Witz* techniques (42–43). The subject of the joke itself would seem to lend this principle more than a tinge of ambiguity, raising the uncomfortable question of when thrift passes into theft. What Freud leaves unexplained is the political context in which the described confiscation took place.

Marx suggests that the joke was telling the truth, that this was indeed only the beginning of a long series of expropriations. 'He wanted to steal the whole of France in order to present it to France, or rather, to buy back France with French money, for as the head of society after December 10th, he has to purchase that which should belong to him' (206). Louis Napoleon is forced to use his ill-gotten gains to buy the respect that really should belong to him in the first place. Unlike his famous ancestor, he cannot rely on his own charisma to inspire personal loyalty and insure his authority. Political power no longer magically flows from the personality of the leader, but instead must be bought, like any other commodity. This is what has turned him into a laughable parody of the past—not the force of time, but the force of money. More than just a play on words, the true joke lies at the point of transition from psychic to political economy. Though Freud's psychologized recounting of it may cause the contemporary reader to smile, this joke itself undoubtedly aroused hearty laughter at the time of its creation among those conversant with and involved in the politics of the day, such as Marx.

So whereas Freud's theory provides us with only a pale reflection of the political situation that gave rise to this joke, Marx uses its political embeddedness to wrest it away from its originator, an aristocrat, and turn the conservative critique of a revolution gone wrong to his own advantage. Though probably not greatly concerned with the fate of the house of Orleans, Marx does see the joke as a sign of trouble, a sign that something funny is going on, and through his analysis takes this joke far beyond what its originator would ever have been capable of grasping. On the one hand, this gives us a glimpse into the possibilities for an engaged appropriation of jokes. Theory greatly expands our understanding of the joke, and the joke helps sharpen the theoretical point. On the other hand it is also clear that theory retains its dominant position, not surprising given Marx's Hegelian background. The joke is at best an illustrative appendage to the theoretical framework. So even though Marx is useful in showing us how to deal with the specific social data contained within a given joke, he neither gives us an account of the 'logic' of the joke in general, be it social or psychic, nor does he permit such a witty way of thinking to infect his own rigorous scientific model of analysis. In this regard Freud seems to have the upper hand.

If the memory of Napoleon has become a bit tarnished, then he might at least take comfort in the fact that the memory of his nemesis, the Duke of Wellington, has fared no better. Take for example the story from the memoirs of Jacob von Falke, whom Freud has already mentioned at the end of his introduction as one who mixes the lives of the great with witty anecdotes. Here we find how revealing this can be. A group of tourists is being led through a wax museum in Ireland. '"This is the Duke of Wellington and his horse," [the guide] explained. Whereupon a young lady asked: "Which is the Duke of Wellington and which is his horse?" "Just as you like, my pretty child," was the reply, "you pays your money and you takes your choice"' (71).

Again we are confronted with the inability of the present to adequately represent the greatness of the past, as expressed in the first joking question of the young woman. It is in the equally witty comeback of the guide that we begin to get an idea of why this is so. The proprietor of the wax museum is literally cashing in on the memory of past heroes. In his gloss of the joke Freud rightly points out how a witty displacement permits the swindler to find refuge behind a protestation of his high business ethics, taking the maxim 'the customer is always right' to its limits. Yet the joke also points to the complicity of the dupes themselves. The guide seems to be saying, 'So, you thought you could buy your way into the presence of the great Wellington? No wonder you can't tell him from his horse!' Marx, in his essay on money in the *Economic and Political Manuscripts of 1844,* describes the apparently limitless power it has to buy anything. Here we find *Witz* showing the limits of the power of *Geld,* making light of a venality that has succeeded in destroying the moral fiber that produced the heroes of the past and now finds that it cannot buy them back into existence again. Furthermore, both *Witz* and *Geld* are related in that they both rely on a mechanism of exchange. But whereas the financial exchange is supposedly one of equality, of exactitude, of all books balancing, *Witz*'s is that of *Ähnlichkeit,* of similarity that presupposes difference, of something left over. *Witz* thus provides a natural parody of the exchanges of *Geld* (money) as *Wechsel* (bill) becomes *Verwechslung* (confusion) and *Tausch* (exchange) *Täuschung* (deception). But *Witz* is not simply a master of deception, for its punchlines also contain a moment of revelation, combining both astonishment and insight. It is the trickster that reveals the tricks of others. In the *vol de l'aigle* joke, the financial dealings of Louis Napoleon are shown to rest on theft. The joke of the tour guide can also be seen as *Witz*'s mockery of money. Not satisfied with an all-too-vague resemblance? Then let the power of money smooth over the distressing difference of a distant *Ähnlichkeit*. You pay your money and you have the choice, don't you?

The peculiar relationship of *Witz* and money is thematized in the first joke that Freud subjects to extensive analysis. 'In the part of his *Reisebilder* entitled "Die Bäder von Lucca" Heine introduces the delightful figure of the lottery-agent and extractor of corns, Hirsch-Hyazinth of Hamburg, who boasts to the poet of his relations with the wealthy Baron Rothschild, and finally says: "And, as true as God shall grant me all good things, Doctor, I sat beside Salomon Rothschild and he treated me quite as his equal—quite famillionairely [*ganz famillionär*]"' (16).

Here we have a fine example of *Verdichtung mit Ersatzbildung* [condensation with substitution] as *familiär* and *Millionär* are combined to form a *Mischwort* in *famillionär*. But more than words are getting mixed up here. On the one hand *Witz* seems to have been assimilated to the rationality of the banker even before Freud identifies *Ersparnis* to be its guiding principle. *Witz*'s traditional association with intellectual efficiency makes this connection a natural one, though one not untainted by the subservient posture that Hirsch-Hyazinth assumes before Rothschild. Yet while the two men are socially far apart, they are united by an entrepreneurial ethic and the creed of good business sense. Their relationship is indeed one of 'famillionairity' as they are both members of the bourgeois family of go-getters, to which *Witz* itself is no distant cousin. Which does not mean that *Witz* is completely at ease with its new relations, the bankers and industrialists who have to some extent displaced the old aristocracy as the leaders of society. *Witz* has accompanied the bourgeoisie in their rise to the top, but as this class starts to lose its former solidity, *Witz* too begins showing signs of internal division. But for *Witz* to distance itself from the bourgeoisie now after their long association would require a leap that would transcend the economic ideology which helped create and nurture it.

To understand how this might be possible we must ask ourselves what exactly is being saved in this joke. Freud suggests, for one thing, words. To express in normal speech the thought contained in the punchline we would have to say something like, 'R. treated me quite as his equal, quite familiarly . . . that is, so far as a millionaire can' (18). Yet in a later passage Freud makes clear what an odd sort of savings this really is. These savings

> may remind us, perhaps, of the way in which some housewives economize when they spend time and money on a journey to a distant market because vegetables are to be had there a few farthings cheaper. What does a joke save by its technique? The putting together of a few new words, which would mostly have emerged without any trouble. Instead of that, it has to take the trouble to search out the one word which covers the two thoughts. Indeed, it must often transform one of the thoughts into an unusual form which will provide the basis for its combination with the second thought. Would it not have been simpler, easier, and, in fact, more economical to have expressed the two thoughts as they happened to come? (44)

So is the relationship of *Witz* to *Ersparnis* really an ironic one, a joke on its own alleged driving force? The critique of economic rationality operates on two levels here. On a more literal level the joke itself functions as a subtle reproach to the money-mad Rothschild and his incapacity for genuine human contact. This point we shall return to, but let us stay for a moment on a purely theoretical level. Freud had hoped to use *Ersparnis* to encapsulate a whole list of diverse joke techniques that he had identified (41–42). But this purely formalistic/linguistic understanding of *Ersparnis* and so of *Witz* itself, which Freud admittedly borrows from previous theoreticians, is clearly inadequate, as he demonstrates in the course of the chapter. Like his predecessors, Freud draws a distinction between thought and word. And since the thought alone is not funny, Freud concludes the joke must lie in its expression. This methodology clearly lends itself to a highly formalistic approach. But, to somewhat oversimplify the matter, the attempt to explain *Witz* on the basis of word counting fails. Consider the following diagram offered by Freud:

F a m i l i ä r
M i l i o n ä r
———————————
f a m i l i o n ä r

This goes along very well with the economic rationality of the *Millionär* part of the joke that is concerned only with the quantifiable, the measurable, the bottom line. But the veneer of mathematical rigor that this diagram evokes is a thin one. The sum lacks the clarity and self-sufficiency that one normally expects from simple arithmetic where, once the result has been calculated, the equation itself becomes superfluous. Quite to the contrary, the resultant *Mischwort* is 'unintelligible in itself' (20), only making sense in the larger context of the joke. Furthermore, the 'zusammendrängende Kraft' (compressing force) that brings these two words together remains mysterious, be it called the principle of *Ersparnis* or not. And a purely quantitative understanding of *Ersparnis* cannot alone explain the laughter caused by jokes, for Freud realizes that not every laconic expression is funny. Freud begins with a technical approach both to introduce his topic and to demonstrate this approach's inadequacy, upon which he often remarks. To be sure, *Witz* makes use of *Ersparnis,* but in such an idiosyncratic manner as to continually call it into question. The shock effect of the *Mischwort* is designed to make us ask what is being said and why, to force us to search for the meaning that the joke's techne has made problematic. All this implies a rationality beyond the bounds of a purely quantitatively oriented *Ersparnis,* an economics that looks beyond the bottom line. Note as well that the ambiguous status of this joke as both representative and critical of formalism is shared by its fictional creator, Hirsch-Hyazinth. Under the tutelage of his master, Gumpelino, he learns to appreciate the works of the poet Platen by counting up the syllables in a given poem, checking to see that all the lines balance — a nice parody of the accountant's approach to aesthetics.

Famillionär is thus no arbitrary flight of fancy, but gives expression to the multifaceted nature of *Witz.* On the one hand it captures its cold and calculating side, but mixes it with something more mysterious and intuitional, the familiar. *Millionär* is coupled 'with the element of that sentence which is so much like it . . . "familiär"' (19). The unexplained *zusammendrängende Kraft* turns out to be *Ähnlichkeit,* which reappears on the scene in its traditional role of 'verkleidete Priester' to effect this mésalliance. Indeed, it seems that the vaguely defined similarities of *Ähnlichkeit* and its mysterious adhesive powers relied upon by traditional *Witztheorie* are replaced in Freud by relationships of 'famillionairity,' which encompasses and makes explicit both its erotic (in the widest sense) and financial components.

That the relationship between these components is at best a strained one, however, is thematized within the joke itself. In one sense the rule of money represents the realization of *Witz*'s attempt to destroy ossified social values, as most radically envisioned by Friedrich Schlegel. Everything is thrown into flux, resulting in an almost romantic confusion. 'Since money as the existing and active idea of the value of all things confuses, exchanges [*verwechselt, vertauscht*], so it is the general confusion and exchange of all things, therefore the world turned upside down, the confusion and exhange of all natural and human qualities' (Marx, *1844,* suppl. 566). *Verwechslung* and *Vertauschung* have of course been *Witz*'s stock-in-trade for many years now, and so it would appear to have quite a bit in common with money. But in the 'upside-down world' of money, *Witz*'s own topsy-turvy way of thinking can become a path back to more 'natural and human' relationships. Its ability to reinvoke traditional values in an antitraditional world is on the one hand a mark of cultural conservatism, but also has utopian potential in its demands for the recreation of genuinely human relationships. What may save this demand from being nothing more than romantic nostalgia for an irrecoverable past is *Witz*'s ability to work both with and against the new social order of money. If the problem of uniting Freud and Marx is one of bringing the former's theories of familial relations in touch with the latter's ideas on economics, then the joke book seems like a good place to start.

Heine proves to be an excellent mediator between these two thinkers. As Freud himself points out, the bitterness of Hirsch-Hyazinth's joke on Salomon Rothschild, its critical force, comes from Heine's own experience with his rich Uncle Salomon. In fact, Heine wanted to marry his cousin, but as a poor relation he had little hope of bringing this about as both cousin and uncle gave him the *famillionär* treatment.

A veneer of politeness, a familiar facade is maintained, but any attempt to form a genuine familial/erotic bond by marriage is thwarted by financial considerations. A Marxist revolution would remove these social barriers and thus also entail a liberation of Eros. 'If you posit people as people and their relationship to the world as a human one, then you can only exchange love for love, trust for trust' (Marx, *1844* 567). Heine as well, as we have seen, combined *Witz* and sensuality with a progressive political stance and Freud's selection of him to open this book would seem to place his own work on *Witz* within this framework.[8]

Heine's Uncle Salomon was not only connected by name with Salomon Rothschild, but also did business with his younger brother James, a relationship which afforded Heine access to the Rothschild house in Paris. Hans Mayer, in his discussion of the Heine-Rothschild connection, discovers the same ambiguities and tensions that we have come across in our analysis of the *famillionär* joke. The hidden aggression of the joke is there, for as Rothschild's guest, Heine maintained an air of civility, while at the same time missing no opportunity to mock his host behind his back. On the other hand, Heine declared Rothschild to be a greater revolutionary than Robespierre, for Rothschild represents the new economic order that will truly sweep away the last remnants of feudalism. Here Mayer identifies the basis for the cooperation between Rothschild and Heine, an alliance between progressive capitalism and progressive literature (359). Earlier I discussed Heine's acute awareness of himself as an entrepreneur in the literary marketplace, but that his identification with the Rothschilds and what they represented was not uncritical—quite the contrary—must also be stressed.

After this long exposition of a rather short joke in which I have tried to show what a perfect beginning for this book it really is, it comes as a bit of a letdown to hear Freud say that he only chose it 'by chance' (16). Is this the same Sigmund Freud who wrote the *Psychopathology of Everyday Life* where accidents never happen? Maybe so, but it does indeed seem that this joke is hopelessly tangled up in fortuitousness. For example, Freud himself had a chance connection with Heine from

8. And perhaps his theories of sexuality as well. Freud was in fact working on his *Three Essays on the Theory of Sexuality* at the same time as the joke book.

the very beginning, being born in 1856, the year of Heine's death. And it just so happens that Freud had an aunt who married into Heine's family and witnessed the condescending manner in which the poet was treated by his wealthier relations. This purely coincidental family tie breaks directly into Freud's theoretical discourse on page 141, where he raises the issue of what role the particular personality of the joke-teller should play in the theoretical analysis of the joke itself. But who is the teller of the *famillionär* joke—the fictional character who recounts it, the author who creates him, or the scientist who cites him? Hirsch changes his name to Hyazinth and boasts, 'there's the further advantage that I already have an "H" on my signet, so that I don't need to have a new one cut' (141). This allows Freud to see the poet, who made a similar leap from Harry to Heinrich, peeking out from behind his literary creation. But it is also the case that Sigmund used to be Sigismund until he decided to economize on his name by two letters. Can we see Sigismund-Sigmund standing behind Harry-Heinrich who in turn stands behind Hirsch-Hyazinth, all brought into alliance by the symbolic economy of *Witz* against the Uncle Salomons of the world? Freud himself started out with modest means and had to overcome economic hardship to win the woman he loved.[9] Though not an avaricious man, he certainly learned early on the value of thrift. So is his choice of this particular joke and his general affirmation of *Ersparnis* simply a sign of his own bourgeois ethos, which he tries to dress up in the finery of the struggles of the poet? Freud explicitly resists too great a personalization of *Witztheorie* with regard to Heine, which might also be taken as a defense against calling his own personality into question (Oring 24). We also see this defensiveness in the dream book, with several dreams being left only partially analyzed for fear of revealing too much about the dreamer.

This is not necessarily such a problem with jokes. Freud remarks that most jokes are anonymous, and thus that *Witztheorie* is forced to deal with them as social rather than individual phenomena. Even when the inventor is known, the fact that these jokes are taken up by a broader public makes *Witztheorie* resistant to being reduced to mere

9. For an account of Freud's early trials and tribulations see Jones, especially p.154ff.

psychobiography. Yet *Witz*'s traditional role as the defender of the individual against annihilation in the universal remains in play as well. Freud tells us that 'Hirsch-Hyazinth's remark made us laugh aloud' (17). The problem of what counts as a joke will dog Freud throughout this work. At times it seems as though the decisive criterion is what makes Freud laugh, binding his theory closely to accidents of his personality. This inherent fortuitousness, however, need not be seen as a fatal weakness, but as a vital element that keeps his theoretical framework open-ended and capable of further growth. The nexus of arbitrariness in which it is enmeshed in fact permits us to make connections through Freud's individual circumstances to the society and culture in which he lived. Furthermore, it stands as an invitation to all individuals to make such connections about their own lives, to make themselves an object of theory.

The need of the witty person for such a self-analysis is great, for, though Freud refuses to make a categorical pronouncement, it is often the case 'that the joker is a disunited personality, disposed to neurotic disorders' (142). Freud mentions George Christian Lichtenberg as an example of this. Lichtenberg's material is often cited by Freud and by other theoreticians, with one frequently repeated joke in particular both showing contempt for *Schulweisheit* (book learning) and conjuring up the image of Hamlet, the grandfather of all the neurotics in the Western world. '"There are more things in heaven and earth than are dreamt of in your philosophy," said Prince Hamlet contemptuously. Lichtenberg knew that his condemnation is not nearly severe enough, for it does not take into account all the objections that can be made to philosophy [*Schulweisheit*]. He therefore added what was missing: "But there is much, too, in philosophy that is not to be found in heaven or earth"' (72).

Despite Freud's hesitation in linking neurosis and *Witz*, it is clear in his theory that the sufferings of the individual are intimately tied up with the production of jokes. The words of the melancholy Dane appear again more prominently when Freud first announces the principle of *Ersparnis:* 'Thrift, thrift, Horatio' (42). The *Schulweisheit* of Horatio, both inadequate and superfluous, stands in sharp contrast to the rigorous efficiency of *Witz*, the soul of which is, of course, brevity.

Two pages later Freud presents us with Hamlet's next line, to give us an idea of what this thrift can really mean:

The funeral baked-meats
Did coldly furnish forth the marriage tables.

As Hamlet's friend, Horatio would like to help him, but his learnedness is completely disconnected from the realities of the world and the problems of the suffering individual. Hamlet assimilates the pragmatic principle of economy, but only to turn it against itself in bitter mockery of the inhuman extremes to which it has been carried in his mother's hasty remarriage. Again we see *Witz* responding to cold-hearted economic calculations as a sign of the breakdown of familial relations, leading to the breakdown of the individual itself in madness, perhaps feigned, perhaps not. Freud's reluctance to label all joketellers as neurotic never really prevents him from making the connection via *Witz* between individual suffering and society. I would argue that the examples he has chosen give him more than sufficient evidence on which to base such a claim.

That this crisis in relations of familiarity has very much to do with the new prominence of the millionaire is also made clear. Consider the following advice offered to the thrifty by Oliver Wendell Holmes: 'Put not your trust in money, but put your money in trust' (33). As Freud remarks, 'here there is promise of an antithesis but it does not materialize. The second part of the sentence cancels the antithesis.' The old moralistic stand against money and its corrupting influence has collapsed, and this passage into a new order is expressed in the transformation of the meaning of the word *trust*. In its initial meaning in the joke it expresses a personal relationship of confidence, ideally built upon the basis of long familiarity; the second meaning simply gives voice to a faith in the solidity of a large financial institution, which now incorporates the old bourgeois virtues of trust and thrift. The flip side of this joke is provided by Heine. 'Vile Macbeth does not rule here in Hamburg: the ruler here is Banko [bank money]' (36). The treacherous Macbeth, who came to power by betraying his personal allegiance to the king, has been replaced by the rule of the banks, where treachery disappears in its institutionalization. 'Iron foreheads

[*Stirne*] — iron cashbox — Iron Crown' (40) stands, courtesy of *Witz*, as the inscription in the coat of arms of the new *Geldaristokratie*. Freud offers the following interpretation of this motto: 'With the help of the necessary boldness and lack of conscience it is not difficult to amass a large fortune, and for such services a title will of course be a suitable reward' (43). In this iron age, obsolescent moral bonds are replaced by those of finance, and *Witz* is on hand to chronicle this development.

Which is not to say that *Witz* is merely a disinterested spectator. Nor does it always succeed in maintaining its critical purity; it too at times gets sucked into this swamp of venality, for even the wittiest man has got to eat:

> One day Saphir and Rothschild met each other. After they had chatted for a little while, Saphir said: 'Listen, Rothschild, my funds have got low, you might lend me a hundred ducats.' 'Oh, well!' said Rothschild, 'that'll suit me all right — but only on the condition that you make a joke.' 'That'll suit me all right too,' replied Saphir. 'Good. Then come to my office tomorrow.' Saphir appeared punctually. 'Ah!' said Rothschild, when he saw him come in, 'Sie kommen um Ihre 100 Dukaten [You've come about your hundred ducats].' 'No,' answered Saphir, 'Sie kommen um Ihre 100 Dukaten [You're going to lose your hundred ducats] because I shan't dream of paying you back before the Day of Judgement.' (38)

In this metajoke we find *Witz* thematizing the conditions of its own production. On the one hand it sells itself to the rich man, who demands the production of a joke as the condition for the loan. On the other hand it cynically abrogates the deal, proving that it has just as much 'boldness' as any other ruthless businessman. More, in fact, for it admits what the latter seeks to conceal. The joke lies in this moment of conformity that goes a little too far. Saphir plays court jester to Rothschild as a king of finance — he may speak the truth to him, but only in the form of a joke.

So as we see *Witz* become increasingly embittered against this economic rationality, it should come as no surprise that on the theoretical level the formalistic version of the principle of *Ersparnis* with which we have so far been dealing does not even survive until the middle of the chapter. After a short interlude in which puns are barely brought under its domain—their frivolity makes them slippery things to get hold of—Freud presents us with the following joke that just won't fit any of the previous explanatory models. 'The story is told of Heine that he was in a Paris salon one evening conversing with the dramatist Soulié, when there came into the room one of those financial kings of Paris whom people compare with Midas—and not merely on account of their wealth. He was soon surrounded by a crowd who treated him with the greatest deference. "Look there!" Soulié remarked to Heine, "Look at the way the nineteenth century is worshipping the Golden Calf!" With a glance at the object of so much admiration, Heine replied, as though by way of correction: "Oh, he must be older than that by now!"' (47–48).

What is it about this joke that breaks out of the theoretical edifice that Freud had so painstakingly erected? His technical explanation of this joke, to which we shall return, is fine as far as it goes, but is there not also something in the content of the joke itself that would explain this sudden disjunction? In fact the motif is nothing new; we have come across this transformation of man into beast before in the Cincinnatus joke and Freud gives us other examples as well. A younger brother, happy that his older, more clever sibling is suddenly having trouble in school, exclaims, 'Karl's going backwards on all fours [*geht auf allen Vieren zurück*]' (26). The possibility of such a regression was actually an important issue of the day. Max Nordau's prophecies of the biological degeneration of the human species rested on his analysis of the fin de siècle. In scientific circles the idea that mental illnesses and perversions resulted from physiological degeneration was still current, with Freud himself giving it qualified support in his *Three Essays on the Theory of Sexuality* (Sulloway 297). This process of bestialization is also a theme of some of the jokes of Herr N., who says of one man that 'I drove with him tête-à-bête' and of another that 'vanity is one of his four Achilles heels' (25). Stupidity and vanity, the mark of the uncivilized beast within us all, is an object of ridicule for the calculating and self-denying rationality of *Ersparnis*—the *tête* still controls the *bête* here without difficulty on both the level of content and of technique.

So what has changed with Heine's joke? For one thing, the foul beast has been transformed into a golden calf. No longer simply a sign of regression to the lower world of the animal, the man-beast now stands atop the social pyramid, symbolizing the omnipotent status that money has attained. We have come a long way from Heine's *famillionär* remark, where at least a vestigial human relationship was maintained. *Witz* is associated with clear-headed economic rationality, which used to provide at least some common ground with the rich man, but this link becomes tenuous as the venality and stupidity lurking behind the smiling face of the millionaire become more apparent. In the Saphir joke, the witty intellectual comes very close to joining this brotherhood of thieves, but here a clear break is made as the poets stand resolutely apart from the inhuman rich man and speak only among themselves, no longer attracted by his wealth. The mediating figure of Hirsch-Hyazinth has disappeared and *Ersparnis,* tainted with the money grubbing ethic of the well-to-do, is discarded.

This break is enacted for us within the joke itself. In fact, we have here two jokes in one. Soulié's joke does conform to the principle of *Ersparnis,* for it can be seen as a condensed version of the thought: 'Look at the way the people are crowding round the stupid fellow simply because he's rich' (48). Freud's analysis reduces the metaphor to its underlying thought, as in the *famillionär* joke, to show what has been 'saved.' But Heine's metametaphor forces Freud to leave the original untouched and so the best he can offer by way of reduction is, 'Oh, he's not a calf any longer; he's a full-grown ox.' Yet even in this form, it is still a joke, still funny. Heine's joke has embedded itself in an irreducibly metaphorical relationship that frustrates the formalist division of thought and word. *Witz* is no longer simply the more efficient, economical expression of a hidden thought, but develops its own independent principles of association and rationality, leaving the logic of *Ersparnis,* at least in the formalist sense, behind.

Which is not to say that *Witz* has slipped beyond the pale of reason into utter nonsense. It remains in contact with everyday rationality as the latter's breaking point. Freud describes the technique of Heine's joke as one of 'diversion of the train of thought' (51). According to Freud, the answer to Soulié's remark that one would have expected from Heine would be something like, 'Yes, such is human nature; thousands of years have made no change in it' (50). Cliché meets cliché in an exchange that would do little to credit the reputations of these two witty men. Heine's joke breaks free of this clichéd discourse by giving a new twist to the golden calf story. What makes this play on metaphor so impossible to reduce to 'normal' speech is its wealth of content. It would be a mistake to focus solely on the reproach of oxlike stupidity which it contains and which we saw in previous examples of man-into-beast jokes. Look rather at the process it describes: the calf has grown older, has changed. As a fetish object, the golden calf must seek to maintain an aura of immutability. Therefore the moralistic response expressed in the exchange of clichés simply plays into the hands of the ruling elite. Human nature remains the same, nothing has changed since biblical times, the calf is as young as ever. This sort of cultural pessimism gets us nowhere. Heine's diversion, his break with an ossified line of reasoning, takes us to a new level. Money as an object of worship needs to hide its unsavory character behind such shining and powerful imagery. *Witz,* as both reader and manipulator of metaphor, penetrates its fetishistic aura to get at the rot behind it. The golden calf need not be immortal; it too can grow old and die. Times do change—and perhaps history can still be made. It is this revolutionary gesture that shatters the formalistic theoretical framework that Freud has outlined for us and thereby permits him to deepen his analysis.

Freud gives several more examples of how *Witz* can be used to see through capital's defensive smoke screen. Here is a rather simple instance: 'A well-known stock-exchange speculator and bank director was walking with a friend along the Ringstrasse. As they went past a café he remarked: "Let's go inside and take [*nehmen:* to take, to get] something." His friend held him back: "But, Herr Hofrat, the place is full of people!"' (51). On one level this provocative misunderstanding is simply senseless. As a wealthy and respected member of the community, the bank director would certainly never think of stealing food. The remark only makes sense in connection with the financial dealings that made him what he is today. The apparent non sequitur is thus used as a transition to other perhaps less absurd thoughts. But now suppose that we actually do go into the coffee house. 'A gentleman entered a pastry-cook's shop and ordered a cake: but he soon brought it back and asked for a glass of liqueur instead. He drank it and began to leave without having paid. The proprietor detained him. "What do you want?" asked the customer. — "You've not paid for the liqueur." — "But I gave you the cake in exchange for it." — "You didn't pay for that either." — "But I hadn't eaten it"' (60).

In this confusing interplay of use and exchange value (what was consumed, what was traded for what) *Witz* reaches a new level of social criticism. Diversion is both the technique and the subject of this joke, thereby placing this bit of psychic chicanery in an explicitly economic, or perhaps antieconomic, context — the avoidance of payment, the concealment of a theft. The thematic link between the jokes we have just analyzed — ripping off a Viennese coffee house, the Austrian intellectual counterpart to the Parisian salon — makes a comparison between the two tempting. Now we see that to accuse the stock market speculator of outright larceny would be to do him an injustice; the man has much subtler means at his disposal. The complexity of modern economic relations renders the line between the thievery of the financier and the dealings of an honest businessman a fine one indeed, and we get a good idea of which party is going to lose out in this game of economic sleight of hand. *Witz* trains us to see how these tricks of financial wizardry are performed and who's getting away with the treats. Yet this joke also resembles others in which the poor use *Witz* to steal from the rich. One is reminded, for example, of the exchange between Saphir and Rothschild. Since the financial status of the gentleman sophist in the pastry shop is left unspecified, the question remains open as to whether *Witz* is here being used to expropriate the expropriators or the expropriated, an ambiguity that reflects *Witz*'s own indeterminate situation.

The malleability of money is such that it stretches itself far beyond the financial sphere proper. Consider the following story from America, the land of the nouveaux riches, where it seems that even respectability can be had if the price is right:

Two not particularly scrupulous business men had succeeded, by dint of a series of highly risky enterprises, in amassing a large fortune, and they were now making efforts to push their way into good society. One method, which struck them as a likely one, was to have their portraits painted by the most celebrated and highly-paid artist in the city, whose pictures had an immense reputation. The precious canvases were shown for the first time at a large evening party, and the two hosts themselves led the most influential connoisseur and art critic up to the wall upon which the portraits were hanging side by side, to extract his admiring judgement on them. He studied the works for a long time, and then, shaking his head, as though there was something he had missed, pointed to the gap between the pictures and asked quietly: 'But where is the Saviour?' (74)

The critic invokes both a religious and an artistic tradition that would have the crucified Christ depicted as hanging between two thieves. Rather than preaching against venality and corruption, a sermon that could only sound somewhat ridiculous and old-fashioned, critical *Witz* travels the indirect path of association and inference to reestablish contact with values that are not so easily found in the modern world. *Witz* cannot revive them by its own fiat, but can make their absence felt. Dirty money is trying here to launder itself with the cleansing aura of art, the cult value of which, as in the golden calf joke, can serve to hide more sordid dealings.[10] But art itself winds up getting sullied, becoming just another commodity. Art had long ago lost its religious function and *Witz* tears away its last shred of auratic dignity in order to keep it from falling into the hands of the highest bidder. Rather than bowing before the sheer technical excellence of these paintings, the critic uses *Witz* to force us to reflect on what has been lost: art's moral and religious significance.

And where is the Savior? Apparently he's gone into business for himself, at least according to Heine:

A Catholic cleric behaves rather like a clerk with a post in a large business house. The Church, the big firm, of which the Pope is

10. For a fuller discussion of the aura of art, see Walter Benjamin's *Das Kunstwerk im Zeitalter seiner technischen Reproduzierbarkeit*.

the head, gives him a fixed job, and in return, a fixed salary. He works lazily, as everyone does who is not working for his own profit, who has numerous colleagues and can easily escape notice in the bustle of a large concern. All he has at heart is the credit of the house and still more its maintenance, since if it should go bankrupt he would lose his livelihood. A protestant cleric, on the other hand, is in every case his own principle and carries on the business of religion for his own profit. He does not, like his catholic fellow-traders, carry on a wholesale business but only retail. And since he must manage it alone, he cannot be lazy. He must advertise his articles of faith, he must depreciate his competitors' articles, and, genuine retailer that he is, he stands in his retail shop, full of business envy of all the great houses, and particularly of the great house in Rome, which pays the wages of so many thousands of bookkeepers and packers and has its factories in all four quarters of the globe. (87)

What the reader should first notice about this joke is its inordinate length. The theme of the *famillionär* joke with which this chapter began — big businessman meets struggling entrepreneur — is developed for us now on a grand scale as personal confrontation is replaced by a conflict between two opposing economic creeds. A change in scale brings with it a change in the purpose of the joke, with the pointed remark directed at one person being replaced with a detailed account of a perceived correlation between certain economic and religious institutions and values. This is all matched by a new joke form, the *Gleichnis* (analogy, parable), which lends itself to extended analogy and thus extended analysis as well. Instead of racing towards the punchline (and there is none to be seen here), the humor of this *Gleichnis* rests in stretching itself out as long as possible. Of course, Heine was not Max Weber and was not trying to make a rigorously sociological argument. But neither should his remarks be dismissed as 'just a joke,' as having nothing to do with reality. This final joke provides the segue into the next chapter, on the tendentious character of jokes, where Freud confesses his fear that Heine's analogy will prove disturbing to many readers because of its controversial content. Whatever its sociological truth, this joke is dealing with real issues, which for Freud problematize its status as a joke and thus as a suitable object for *Witztheorie.* Yet even on a purely formal level, not just Heine's analogy, but the whole category of the *Gleichnis* presents Freud with immense problems. The 'certain feeling' that he has been relying on to tell him what is a joke and what is not fails him here; he is able to provide examples of some analogies that definitely are not funny, some that definitely are, and many that fall somewhere in between. Freud finds himself in 'doubt [*ein Schwanken*] as to whether they ought to be regarded as jokes at all' (81).

An interesting choice of words in light of the fact that the medieval *Schwank* was the forerunner of the modern *Witz.* Hermann Bausinger claims that 'there are few jokes [*Witze*] that cannot be traced back to an older *Schwank*' (702) and Lutz Röhrich goes even further: 'All jokes have at some time existed before' (28). Though Norbert Neumann is correct in pointing out that this focus on textual similarities tends to blur important cultural differences between early and later forms of these jokes, his own work also serves to demonstrate that one can indeed trace a line of development *vom Schwank zum Witz.* He discusses several common themes in jokes, illustrating each with an example from the sixteenth, eighteenth and twentieth centuries. In every case the joke becomes shorter and more densely packed with the passage of time. Freud's psychological theory of *Witz* as a process of condensation would thus seem to have historical validity as well. But what gets left by the wayside? Bausinger offers the following account of the difference between *Schwank* and *Witz*: '*Witze* are often told in the present tense: a situation is briefly presented. *Schwänke* are usually told in the past tense: the narrator gives himself over to reminiscence, takes his time in sketching out what happened, works in bits of proverbial wisdom (something unthinkable in *Witz*) and draws conclusions from the narration. The comic of the *Schwank* is easily accessible; it is usually developed in vivid imagery. *Witz* focuses on the punchline [*Pointe*], which I must understand. *Witz* is therefore more strongly anchored in the intellect' (703).

The lackadaisical, rambling pace of the *Schwank* is speeded up in the discourse of *Witz,* which always speaks to the *Pointe.* The logic is tighter in *Witz,* with no room for superfluities such as extensive scenic description or moralizing asides. This process of rationalization which takes place between *Schwank* and *Witz* robs the latter of much of its aesthetic and ethical richness. Its relationship with the world becomes less sensuous and direct. Bausinger remarks that *Schwank* is etymologically related to *Streich,* a type of joke with a marked practical bent, whereas *Witz* is related to *Wissen,* and we have seen that this highly intellectualized form of humor does indeed develop within a theoretical framework. The return then of this archaic forebear of *Witz* would understandably pose difficulties for Freud's own theory. *Gleichnis* itself can mean not only 'analogy,' as Strachey translates it, but also 'parable,' recovering the moralistic thrust of the *Schwank.* Heine's own *Gleichnis* touches on religious tensions which were favorite themes of the *Schwänke* of the Reformation (Neumann 26–27), and thus he carries on their tradition of engaged humor.

Freud the theoretician finds the whole business rather troublesome and gives voice to the fear that raising such issues can only arouse emotions that would disturb the calm analysis of the matter at hand (90). It seems that such ethical debates have no place in psychological theory and the rationality of the discipline must not be tainted by them. On the other hand, he admits in the chapter on tendentious jokes that such issues are inextricably bound up with the jokes themselves. The *Schwank,* as the returning archaic repressed, represents all these disturbing elements. Bausinger tells us that *Schwänke* were often products of the lower classes (703) and Neumann shows how they freely discussed sexual and scatological matters that today would be considered too crude to be funny (68ff.). We have seen in the history of *Witztheorie* that the tradition of the *Schwank* was never fully vanquished; the rationalization of *Witz* did not come easily and is even now by no means secured. Freud will seek to deal squarely with the problem of the *Schwank,* here represented by Heine and his *Gleichnis,* but even when he does occasionally find himself 'ins Schwanken geraten' (60), he will always try to regain his theoretical balance.

The concept of theory is a value-laden one, developed over a long period of time and Freud's debt to his theoretical predecessors should not be underestimated, despite the times when he calls their theoretical apparatus into question. Much more than the traditions of *Witz*-

theorie are in play here. Richard Simon links Freud's model of psychic economy with the ideas of Helmholtz and thermodynamics (214). However far Freud may have strayed from the reductionist psychology that dominated the late nineteenth century, his notion of psychodynamics remained grounded on the physicalist model that claimed that no matter how much energy is exchanged, it can never be created or destroyed. It is an economy of psychic determinism — nature makes no leaps and everything balances in the end. That this scientific paradigm has wide-ranging implications is clearly seen in Freud's later writings, where the creations of culture are only possible on the basis of instinctual repression — everything must have a sufficient reason, must be paid for one way or another. What makes the joke book interesting is the spectacle of the battle Freud must wage in order to make his scientific-bourgeois ethos prevail against *Witz*, which is not so easily adapted to this paradigm.

Let us examine what exactly it is that Freud the scientist has set out to do. To claim that the man just thought it would be fun to write a book on jokes would be far too modest. His discussion of the *Gleichnis* provides an opening for a much more comprehensive and ambitious explanation. For one thing, the *Gleichnis* leads Freud back to the already well-developed theories of *The Interpretation of Dreams*. 'Indirect representation — the replacement of a dream-thought by an allusion, by something small, a symbolism akin to *Gleichnis* — is precisely what distinguishes the mode of expression of dreams from that of our waking life' (89). We recover the principle *Ersparnis*, lost for a moment in the garrulity of the *Gleichnis*, on the level of the symbolic, where the underlying thought is replaced by something smaller, 'ein Kleines.' This psychic economy is mirrored on the theoretical level as the theories of dreams and jokes are merged together. Curious phrase though, this 'symbolism akin to analogy [*dem Gleichnis analoge Symbolik*],' for it would seem that the connection between dream symbolism and analogy is itself made through analogy, calling into question the rigor of the distinction that Freud makes at the end of the sentence between sleeping and waking thought. We have already seen enough examples of theories of *Witz* being swallowed by *Witz* itself that we should not be too taken aback by this. However it is made, the connection between dream and *Witz* is a significant one. Not only *Gleichnis,* but all previously discussed joke techniques are traced back to *The Interpretation of Dreams.* After a confused chapter in which all attempts at presenting a unified joke theory have been frustrated, Freud seems to be trying to reassure the reader, implying that he can still do for jokes what he did for dreams. Both are at first glance apparently senseless, but just as he was able to discover the hidden thoughts behind dream symbolism, we may analogously assume that he will be able to construct a theory of jokes that will uncover their submerged Logos.

But more is a stake here than the intellectual satisfaction to be gained from the interpretation of until now unintelligible phenomena. 'The use of absurdity and nonsense in dreams has cost them the dignity of being regarded as psychical products and has led the authorities to suppose that a disintegration of the mental activities and a cessation of criticism, morality and logic are necessary conditions of the formation of dreams' (88). Freud's theory has rescued dreams from imputations of immorality and degeneration. Such decadence was of course the problematic with which this analysis of the joke book began. I have argued that in his first chapter Freud portrays *Witz* as both the sign and the critic of a society given over to corruption and greed. But in this case disintegration is not just a matter of imputation and goes far beyond the individual psyche. The problem is posed in the first of a pair of analogies that Freud adduces as examples of nonwitty *Gleichnisse.* We are already familiar with it—it is 'the fine analogy between the tenderness in Ottilie's diary and the scarlet thread of the English navy' (82). It is the red thread that connects Ottilie's delicate feelings and the British Empire, Goethe and Napoleon, aesthetics and politics, which has snapped in this decadent age. Delicacy of inner feeling seems to have no place in the modern world, giving the aestheticist movement at the turn of the century its apolitical, unworldly bent. Freud's own theoretical enterprise, which has so far relied on his inner feeling of what constitutes a joke and what does not, is also threatened here with a lapse into a hermetic subjectivity. As *Witz* leaves the medieval world of the *Schwank* behind, it loses its own definite cultural and moral position. Freud must retie the red thread that leads back to this reality, in one form or another, if he wishes to save his own theory. It is therefore a genuine social problem that Freudian theory has set itself. Is it up to it?

Carl Schorske has forcefully argued that Freud's theoretical enterprise is in fact a flight from political engagement (181–207). Yet it is important to remember that with Freud the repressed always returns and so the question must still be asked: Is Freudian theory apolitical or does it pursue politics by other means? Schorske makes a good case for the claim that Freud was inspired to choose the motto of the dream book—*Flectere si nequeo superos, Acheronta movebo*[11]—by the left-wing politician Ferdinand Lassalle, who used it for his pamphlet *Der italienische Krieg und die Aufgabe Preussens* [The Italian war and the task of Prussia]. True, the revolutionary masses that Lassalle was threatening to stir up are replaced by Freud with the unruly forces of what he will later call the id, not generally known for its political (or any other) consciousness. The figure of Lassalle himself meets with an unhappy end in Freud's book, for in the 'Autodidasker' dream he comes to grief over a woman, whereas Freud is able to resist such temptations 'by his clinical understanding of neurosis. . . . Sex is stronger than politics, the dream seems to say, but science can control sex' (Schorske 201).

Which still leaves open the question as to whether science can control politics, if only in a mediated way through its understanding of the instincts. This possibility becomes an explicit problem for Freudian theory in his later writings such as *The Future of an Illusion* or *Civilization and Its Discontents.* Indeed, Freud was aware of the social implications of his sexual theories from the very beginning, as a work like '"Civilized" Sexual Morality and Modern Nervousness' demonstrates. Lassalle and the politics he represents are far from vanquished by just one dream and, in fact, he reappears in a much more positive light in the joke book in Freud's second nonwitty *Gleichnis,* which hints at the answer to the problem posed by the first. He tells us that it is an analogy 'which I am never tired of admiring and the effect of which I have not grown out of. It is the analogy with which Ferdinand Lassalle ended one of his celebrated speeches for the defence ("Science and the Workers"): "Upon a man such as I have shown you this one to be, who has devoted his life to the watchword 'Science and the Work-

11. 'If I cannot bend the higher powers, I shall stir up hell.'

ers,' being convicted, if it were his lot, would make no more impression than the bursting of a retort upon a chemist deep in his scientific experiments. As soon as the interruption is past, with a slight frown over the rebelliousness of his material, he will quietly pursue his researches and his labours"' (82).

Freud's enthusiasm for Lassalle's speech surely rests on more than a simple admiration of his rhetorical technique; a deeper sympathy for what Lassalle is saying is also present. Lassalle's argument is based largely on the claim that science and the scientist must be free to speculate and experiment if civilization is to continue to progress. Though this analogy is not witty per se, Freud includes it in the joke book as a point of contact between *Witz* and this ideology of rationalistic optimism, a creed which he would express programmatically in *The Future of an Illusion*. Lassalle's progressive philosophy of history offers *Witz* a way out of the decadent world in which it now finds itself. Science can reform society and *Witz* has its part to play, placing the idiosyncratic talents of the individual in the service of this greater cause. In the preface to his edition of Lassalle's speech, Eduard Bernstein praises Lassalle's *Witz* (206) and goes on to describe how many of Lassalle's friends 'from the realm of literature and science' were present at the trial in anticipation of 'an entertaining intellectual duel' between Lassalle and the prosecutor, the son of the philosopher Schelling. It appears that the scene of *Witz* has moved from the salon to the courtroom, where it is no longer a form of pleasant social intercourse but a weapon in the class struggle.

Lassalle employs wit to good advantage in his speech, using a heavy dose of sarcasm to rebut the charge that his 'science' is too tendentious to be worthy of the name. As already mentioned, the problem of science and *Tendenz* will arise for Freud in connection with Heine's *Gleichnis* concerning the Church. Though Freud treads carefully here, he does not back down; his science too will deal with matters of 'praktische Tendenz' (Lassalle 243). So in the end Freud is not so far apart from Lassalle after all. Both stir up an Acheron of lower forces (workers/instincts) which they seek to control through science. Both see science as something tendentious, as arousing volatile forces, but like the good chemist, both always seek to maintain their scientific objectivity and equanimity as well.

That this sort of objectivity can lend itself to political purposes is demonstrated by Lassalle, who at times uses it rather disingenuously to cover his political agenda. Freud, too, when analyzing civilization's discontents, could always pose as the clinically detached doctor. But the idea that scientists must be granted a measure of freedom of thought if they are to be able to do their work can indeed be subversive. The confrontation between science and political authoritarianism is the theme of the following joke. 'The King condescended to visit a surgical clinic and came on the professor as he was carrying out the amputation of a leg. He accompanied all its stages with loud expressions of his royal satisfaction: "Bravo! bravo! my dear Professor!" When the operation was finished, the professor approached him and asked him with a deep bow: "Is it your Majesty's command that I should remove the other leg too?"' (72–73). Freud's analysis makes it clear that the irony of this joke is based on the tension between the arbitrary authority of the king and the autonomous rationality of science. *Witz* serves here as a vehicle for both self-expression and self-preservation, avoiding a direct confrontation with the powerful monarch while still getting the point across.[12] The old connection of *Witz* with *Wissen* is here revitalized in its politically charged alliance with *Wissenschaft*.

That this brotherhood of science is open to more people than just the scientists is indicated by the following anecdote. 'A medical friend well-known for his jokes once said to Arthur Schnitzler the dramatist: "I'm not surprised that you've become a great writer. After all your father held a mirror up to his contemporaries." The mirror which was handled by the dramatist's father, the famous Dr. Schnitzler, was the laryngoscope. A well-known remark of Hamlet's tells us that the purpose of a play, and so also of the dramatist who creates it, is "to hold, as 'twere, the mirror up to nature; to show virtue her own feature, scorn her own image, and the very age and body of the time his form and pressure"' (36–37). Schnitzler, whom Freud once described as his *Doppelgänger*, provides an example of the merger of art and science. I

12. One is reminded of Freud's encounter with the Gestapo. Before he could leave Vienna, they demanded from him a statement that he had not been mistreated. Freud went even further and wrote that he could recommend the Gestapo to anyone.

have been arguing that Freud too has been holding up a mirror to his time in this work and so is not so far distant from the playwright. His individual feelings and experiences, like those of the artist, receive justification to the degree he is able to universalize them and show their correspondence to a larger reality. But we must also take note of the fact that much more than a passive act of reflection is being described here. This scientific aesthetic, as expressed above by Hamlet, has a definite moral and critical purpose. Suffering individuals, be they workers, neurotics, or even fictional characters, are themselves the mirrors which the poet, politician, and psychoanalyst can use to see the world and try to change it, united here in the project of the rational reform of society.

Our notion of science would be incomplete, however, if we were to think of it in purely intellectual terms. Another equally important element must be taken into account: work. It is no accident that Lassalle's speech is entitled 'Science and the Workers,' for the two shall be united, a marriage that Lassalle consummates at the end of his *Gleichnis*—after the explosion in the lab, the scientist goes back to work. Right before making this analogy, Lassalle had proposed the alliance of the bourgeoisie and the workers against their common aristocratic oppressors, thereby uniting head and hand. But Lassalle was no radical communist. He leaves the rights of private property untouched, seeking merely to combine bourgeois acquisitiveness with the spirit of cooperation and community represented by the workers. In Freud we have encountered the economic ethic of the bourgeoisie in the principle of *Ersparnis,* an ideal of individual thrift. But now Freud presents us with the notion of *Witzarbeit* (joke work), which, at the end of the first chapter, he connects with his previous formulation of *Traumarbeit* (dream work). *Witzarbeit,* however, in contrast to its dream counterpart, is an inherently social phenomenon. As Freud remarks, no one makes a joke purely for their private amusement. Thus Freud effects on a psychological level what Lassalle envisioned on the political: the unity of a social work ethic with the principle of individual economic rationality.

Though these bourgeois scientists may be very pleased indeed with the prospect of a state of thrifty and well-disciplined workers (Lassalle constantly assures us that violence and disorder are the farthest things from his mind), one may wonder how the workers themselves might have felt about the plan. Lassalle certainly had trouble keeping his comrades in line (recall the 'rebellious material' of the chemist) and we find Freud in similar difficulties. *Witz* never functioned solely as a principle of intellectual efficiency. Though this is an important part of it, it also contains anarchistic and playful elements which Freud, to a certain extent, must seek to suppress. In one passage, for example, he remarks that 'what is supposed by the authorities to show the character of jokes as a kind of "play" has been classified by us under the heading of "multiple use"' (36). Playfulness is jargonized out of existence; there is no room for it in the rigorous world of theory. On the next page we get to Schnitzler and the scientization of art; even the old refuge of the *Spieltrieb*[13] is no longer safe from the process of rationalization.

Not that the jokes don't put up some resistance. 'A man who had taken to drink supported himself by tutoring in a small town. His vice gradually became known, however, and as a result he lost most of his pupils. A friend was commissioned to urge him to mend his ways. "Look, you could get the best tutoring in the town if you would give up drinking. So do give it up!" "Who do you think you are?" was the indignant reply. "I do tutoring so that I can drink. Am I to give up drinking so that I can get tutoring?"' (52). Freud makes his disdain for this joke clear enough, declaring its technique to be so 'extremely scanty' that it is unable to cover the unabashed cynicism of the drunkard. This may be true, but could Freud's criticism also be motivated by the fact that the joke subordinates work to the purposes of pleasure? This would call into question the ethical categories, thrift and industry, that Freud wishes to use to interpret *Witz*.

He does his best to mobilize the power of *Witz* behind this agenda, but things do not always go as planned. 'A horse-dealer was recommending a saddle-horse to a customer. "If you take this horse and get on it at four in the morning you'll be at Pressburg by half-past six."— "What should I be doing in Pressburg at half-past six in the morning?"' (54). In Freud's analysis this joke appears to rest solely on the

13. 'Drive to play,' declared by Friedrich Schiller to be the basis of all artistic creation.

idiosyncratic fixation of the customer on the irrelevant and arbitrarily chosen point in time in the salesman's example, when in fact it is the overall 'capacity' of the horse that is at issue. But couldn't we then take a step further and claim that the cult of efficiency as a whole is being called into question by the consumer (Oring 8)? Why buy something just because it's faster? Is that necessarily better? The social nature of *Witzarbeit* raises the issue of the role of the recipient, the joke consumer, a perspective that has heretofore been missing from the psychic economy of *Witz*. Freud introduces the concept of *Witzarbeit* right before the Pressburg joke, where he makes clear that for now he is solely concerned with how the jokes are produced and will save the question of their reception for a later chapter. It appears that in this joke the issue of consumption is raised a little earlier than planned. From the point of view of production, *Witz* remains entangled in an economic logic which, as we have seen, has both emancipatory and repressive moments. Perhaps the new standpoint of consumption can help resolve this internal tension.

Before closing this chapter I should like to explore the notion of psychic economy a little more deeply. In its generally accepted meaning the word *economy* refers to a system of exchange. What is being exchanged in the psychic economy of *Witz*? The range of commodities we have so far encountered has been immense—from cakes and liqueurs, to horses and paintings, all the way up to salvation itself. On the level of content the marketplace of *Witz* seems to have something for everyone insofar as almost anything can be made the subject of a joke. But who is then responsible for their production? Here the range has not been so extreme; so far we have seen poets, professors, and other solid citizens as the major creators of jokes. This has suited my purposes very well, for in this chapter I have tried to focus on *Witz* as the product of intraclass tensions within the bourgeoisie. But these tensions will grow so great as to provide openings for other groups to appear on the scene and break the bourgeoisie's monopoly on *Witz*. Jews and women, some bourgeois, some not, as well as the threateningly amorphous force referred to as 'the masses' will invade the world of *Witz* with their own fresh perspectives, just as they were pushing their way onto the political scene.

Thus both political and psychic economy at the turn of the century begin to be marked by an increasing pluralism as the authoritative voice of the bourgeois male Christian is challenged by a chorus of others. While the bourgeois problematic that has so far been discussed is crucial to understanding the joke book, it cannot be interpreted solely by means of class analysis. But it would also be a mistake to try to explain this work simply on the basis of Freud's confrontation with his own Jewish heritage or to reduce *Witz* to the product of an unruly libido understood in a narrowly sexual sense. There is no gold standard in the psychic economy of *Witz*.

It is this realization that confronts us with the true radicality of *Witz*'s challenge to traditional notions of economy, psychic or otherwise. By undermining the claims of any privileged medium of exchange to be the sole source of value, *Witz* becomes the marketplace for a variety of values to meet and interact. It could be said to represent a shift from a money economy to a barter system. The formalist approaches which Freud has been discussing would seek to reduce the meaning of *Witz,* as well as individual jokes, to one primary explanation, the same underlying punchline in different guises. Freud dispenses with these theories one by one, but then comes up with his own in the all-encompassing principle of *Ersparnis.* But the change in levels of psychic energy will be seen to be no more adequate to explain the economy of *Witz* than the vagaries of the money supply are in explaining all the workings of capitalism. Many other forces are at work here, which both shape and are shaped by the dynamics of *Ersparnis* which Freud has begun to outline for us. The historical approach which I have chosen for my analysis of the joke book enables us to see the full complexity of *Witz* as an ideological construct, being used by groups with a wide variety of agendas. We shall examine one such constellation of forces within the social economy of *Witz* in the next chapter.

WITZ, WOMEN, AND JEWS

In the foregoing analysis of Freud's chapter on joke techniques we discovered that the concept of psychic economy has far more than a strictly psychological meaning. Freud himself felt that a purely technical analysis of *Witz* was inadequate and somewhat superficial, serving in fact only as a preface to the deeper explorations he would undertake in the area of tendentious jokes. The qualitative superiority of these jokes, which he considered to be the most important and interesting manifestations of *Witz*, rests upon their instinctual basis as expressions of aggression or sexuality. Yet it would be a mistake to imagine that this shift to the level of instinctual economy confines us to the ahistorical and apolitical world of the id. We must avoid the linear, one-way model of reasoning that would seek to explain jokes by reducing them to the allegedly primordial realities of sex and violence. Instead of limiting ourselves to talking about the instinctual basis of jokes, should we not also explore the witty nature of the instincts? The nature of both sexuality and aggression must be more precisely determined, and this can only be done with the very phenomena that they themselves were supposed to explain. Jokes again prove to be active partners and not just passive examples in Freud's theoretical enterprise. It is surely no accident that his discussion of the *repressed* instincts behind tendentious jokes centers around two of the most *oppressed* groups of his day, women and Jews; it is their plight that keeps his theory of the instincts firmly embedded in a social framework. Freud himself was well aware of the problems that this mixture of two levels of discourse would entail. We have heard him worry aloud in the case of Heine's *Gleichnis* that 'outside' issues might distract the reader from the scientific matters at hand. But the fact that he was unable to purify his text of these issues should indicate that they are not extraneous to the investigation. I therefore propose to add to the economic analysis of the previous chapter, which was centered largely around the bourgeoisie, a discussion of the problems faced by women and Jews at the turn of the century and how they are manifested in the joke book.

We shall begin by exploring the Jewish situation, for this is where Freud himself found the impetus to write the book. Freud's first significant reference to the topic of jokes comes in a letter to Wilhelm Fließ in June of 1897: 'Let me confess that I have recently made a collection of deeply significant Jewish stories' (Oring 3). We may assume the collection to be one of witty Jewish anecdotes, the likes of which one finds scattered throughout Freud's letters and works. How many, if any, of these jokes actually made it into the joke book is difficult to determine, for the manuscript is apparently no longer in existence. Still, it seems safe to say that this early collection was a source for the later work, the Jewish roots of which are still profoundly in evidence. Most of the prominent jokes are either explicitly Jewish, told by the assimilated Jew Heine, or originally had a Jewish form that has been Gentilized by Freud. The Jewish problematic is thus in many ways central to this work.

Elliot Oring has written an excellent study of the significance that Jewish jokes had for Freud. Through an analysis of these jokes he tries to explain Freud's troubled relationship to his own 'Jewish identity.' This can be very interesting and illuminating, but often suffers from a fault common to much psychobiography, which tends to exaggerate the importance of the personal at the expense of the larger context. For example, Oring raises the question as to why Freud refers to his first collection of Jewish anecdotes as 'deeply significant.' Their profundity cannot be a purely scientific matter, Oring argues, for that would have to lie for Freud in their connection to the theory of dreams, a connection which he only became aware of in September of 1899 after Fließ called his attention to it (Oring 4). More significant for Oring is the fact that, in the same letter to Fließ in which Freud mentions these anecdotes, he also makes what the editors take to be his first reference to his own self-analysis. As Oring puts it, 'the fact that Freud was collecting Jewish jokes in 1897 at the very time he was initiating his own self-analysis strongly suggests that these jokes contained personally meaningful messages. We could assume that significant discoveries about Freud's character might be made by scrutinizing these jokes closely' (4). This argument is more than plausible. We know that Freud's self-analysis revolved around his ambivalent reactions to his father's death, which had occurred just the year before. That his relationship to his father was also intimately connected to his sense of Jewish identity is clear as well. Jones contends that Freud got his sense of humor from his father (3). Jakob Freud was fond of telling Jewish anecdotes and his tragicomic narration of how an anti-Semite knocked off his hat and forced him into the gutter certainly made an impression on the young Sigmund. The deeply personal significance of these jokes for Freud remains above question.

But while it is certainly true that these jokes can tell us a great deal about Freud's character, I would also maintain that they have a great deal to say to us concerning his ideas. The elucidatory function that Freud assigns to them cannot be so easily ignored, for their profundity is marked from the very beginning by their intimate connection to Freud's theoretical enterprise. Returning to Freud's 1897 letter to Fließ, let us have a look at the sentence immediately preceding his admission that he has begun to collect Jewish stories: 'We will divide ourselves like the two *Schnorrer,* one of whom recieved the province Posen; you the biological, I the psychological.' In this carving out of intellectual turf, Freud puts both his own project and that of Fließ under the aegis of that popular figure of Jewish jokelore, the *Schnorrer,* the Jewish beggar. This image is by no means frivolous. It expresses very well the situation of the two Jewish outsiders from the Gentile scientific establishment and their grandiose, at this point still presumptively ludicrous, plans for the future. The profundity of the Jewish jokes that Freud discusses lies not only in their personal meaning for him but more importantly in the depth of the challenge they pose to 'Gentile culture.'

It is the challenging character of Jewish wit that I think is really missing from Oring's analysis. He tries to read them as signs of Freud's personal anguish over his desire to escape his Jewishness and assimilate the Gentile world, giving these jokes a rather introverted and defensive character. What he fails to emphasize is their aggressive and critical side. Freud's most important and sustained discussion of Jewish *Witz* comes in his chapter on tendentious jokes. He not only resisted but also identified with his Jewish heritage, and this identification was indeed prone to take pugnacious forms. Martin Freud relates a couple of anecdotes which show his father's willingness to confront anti-Semitism directly and energetically.[1] His 1926 letter to B'nai B'rith stands as a testament to his solidarity with the Jews as an oppressed and embattled minority. And as Oring himself points out, Freud's letter to Fließ was written just two months after the anti-Semite Karl Lueger was finally confirmed as mayor of Vienna. Michael Steinberg has suggested that Freud's personal crisis and thus the attendant discovery of psychoanalysis must be seen in the context of the sharp rise in anti-Semitic agitation between 1895–97.

Let us therefore look more closely at the challenge that these jokes posed to Gentile culture. As previously mentioned, Freud rather incongruously opens his chapter on tendentious jokes by apologizing for the blasphemous analogy from Heine with which he concluded the foregoing chapter on joke techniques. Yet his concern for the potentially wounded pieties of his readers only tells half the story—the real issue is who is doing the wounding. I believe that Freud wants to avoid giving the impression that two Jews, Heine and himself, are using *Witz* to defile the sanctity of the Christian religion by reducing it to nothing more than another branch of big business (an accusation, of course, which Christians had been making against Judaism for centuries). Freud tries to smooth over these religious tensions by retreating to the high ground offered by an impartial theoretical stance, the objectivity of which should remain unclouded by any sort of partisan sentiment. But both the untenability of this position as well as the true nature of his sympathies are soon enough made clear.

In an attempt to soothe the reader and to get back on theoretical track Freud initiates a discussion of 'harmless' jokes. He takes several examples from Lichtenberg, the final one of which runs, 'Not only did he disbelieve in ghosts; he was not even frightened of them' (92). He goes on to illustrate the deeper meaning of this joke, that the emotions

1. See Martin Freud, 'Who was Freud?' in *The Jews of Austria: Essays on Their Life, History and Destruction*, ed. Josef Fraenkel (London, 1967).

are not always subject to reason, with the words of Lessing: 'Not all are free who mock their chains.' These allegedly harmless remarks would thus seem to call into question the absolute sovereignty of rationality which Freud wishes to invoke in dealing with tendentious jokes. The ghosts of religious hatred from which Freud is trying to escape are perhaps not so easily exorcised by appeals to clear-headed objectivity. Let us pause a moment as well to consider who produced these aphorisms. Lichtenberg and Lessing were both important figures in the German Enlightenment. Lessing's words are taken from *Nathan der Weise,* a play in which he continued on the stage the polemic with Pastor Goeze that he had been forbidden by the authorities to pursue directly. It is difficult to believe that the connection of these remarks with a rather polemical side of the Enlightenment is just coincidental. To what degree is Freud smuggling in his own critical view of religion here? And is it not odd that in *Nathan* we are again confronted with a Jewish representative of this tradition, just where a Jewish subtext in Heine was beginning to prove troublesome?

The fact is that Jewish *Witz* was born in the Enlightenment. As Salcia Landmann has pointed out, the Jews did not always enjoy the reputation of having a quick and ready wit. The Old Testament is not particularly witty, especially when compared with the works coming out of classical Greece, and nobody reads the Talmud for laughs. Though Jews undoubtedly told jokes just like any other people, evidence of particularly Jewish jokes and the rise of their reputation for wit only appear at the end of the eighteenth century (Larsen 67). Landmann ties this directly to the Enlightenment critique of religion taking place at that time. It was their religion which had held the Jewish people together during the Diaspora and provided them with a system of beliefs that helped them make sense of the trials and tribulations they were suffering. The Enlightenment undermined this religious worldview and thus the justification for resigning oneself to a miserable situation. The anger that is the natural replacement for resignation was directed, according to Landmann, against Judaism itself, which had previously been sacrosanct. Add to this the Enlightenment's promises of toleration and emancipation, and one can understand why many Jews were tempted to discard old traditions for the faith in reason. Landmann is able to adduce quite a number of Jewish jokes which put the practices of Judaism in a ridiculous light. This brand of *Witz* therefore arose at least in part out of the Jewish Enlightenment's critique of religion and hopes for ultimate assimilation and acceptance in a new rational society.

Yet Jewish *Witz* reveals its tendentious character not only through *self*-critique. Landmann also recognizes its utility as a weapon in the hands of this oppressed minority which could have no hope of winning any direct fight. Contemporary evidence for this thesis is to be found in L. M. Büschenthal's 1812 work, *Sammlung witziger Einfälle von Juden, als Beytrage zur characteristik der Jüdischen Nation*. 'Büschenthal uses the eighteenth-century concept of *Witz* (humor) as the basis for his rationale in presenting this material. Humor calls upon the rational mind, and the Jews, Büschenthal comments, have long been noted for their rationality. It is this that the jokes reveal. But the Jews have been both damned as well as praised for this characteristic' (Gilman 257). That Jewish rationality must adopt the cloak of wit is only because, at least according to Büschenthal, they have so long been persecuted by their Christian neighbors. He tries to show how *Witz* can serve in both defense and counterattack. Thus this national characteristic is not really an inborn trait, but the product of the Jews' social situation and Büschenthal implies that 'the Jews' wit will soon vanish with emancipation and the Jew will become as dull and boring as the German.'[2]

But even if emancipation may ultimately mean the end of *Witz,* it was still an indispensable preface to emancipation. Its tendentious character sought to further the process of assimilation by hammering away at the traditional religious beliefs of Jew and Gentile alike, and was used for this purpose by representatives of both groups. In the first

2. Gilman 600. According to Landmann, this is indeed the case in modern Israel, where the Jews, whose arsenal now runs the gamut from rubber bullets to atom bombs, have little use for the old-fashioned weapon of wit. 'Greift man den Juden in Israel an, so kann er sich, statt mit dem Witz, wieder mit der Waffe wehren, genau wie sein Vorfahre in biblischer Zeit. Das neue Israel ist daher witzlos wie die Bibel' [If one attacks a Jew in Israel, he can defend himself, instead of with *Witz,* with weapons, like his forebear in biblical times. Modern Israel is therefore as witless as the Bible] (111).

two chapters I traced *Witz*'s connection with Enlightenment ideals of emancipation, and we now see why these ideals were particularly significant for the Jews. Freud draws heavily on the Enlightenment tradition of *Witz,* calling Lessing and Lichtenberg as accepted figures in German *Bildung* to the aid of Heine and himself, thereby making their own critical discourse on religion more acceptable to a Gentile audience.

That Freud still felt the need to cover himself with such authorities shows that the Enlightenment project of assimilation had so far been less than completely successful. Indeed, it had reached a critical stage in the Vienna of his time. To put things in perspective, we might recall that 1905, the year of the joke book's publication, saw terrible pogroms in Russia, while Lueger threatened the Austrian Jews with a similar fate should they throw their support to the socialists. This after a decade of anti-Semitic agitation and random asaults on individual Jews which, as Walter Weitzmann has argued (Oxaal 145), had driven Jewish self-consciousness to its prewar peak. The embattled situation of the Jews makes for a very plausible and immediate connection between them and Freud's discussion of tendentious jokes. It is clear that something has gone very much wrong with the grandiose plans of the Enlightenment, and *Witz* itself provides its own self-critique. 'Not all are free who mock their chains' becomes a commentary on the limitations of *Witz* as a vehicle of emancipation.

What exactly we are to be freed from still needs to be clarified. Freud, with reference to Lichtenberg's aphorism, seems to be focusing on the problem of freeing oneself from superstition. That ghosts have long been haunting the representatives of the Enlightenment is demonstrated in another joke. 'Frederick the Great heard of a preacher in Silesia who had the reputation of being in contact with spirits. He sent for the man and received him with the question "You can conjure up spirits [Geister beschwören]?" The reply was: "At your Majesty's command. But they don't come"' (70). Freud categorizes this joke as an example of 'representation by the opposite.' The priest says yes, but in a way that really means no, making this whole talk of spirits simply ridiculous. But Oring probably comes closer to the truth when he claims that in fact the joke leaves the matter open; the humor rests in the simultaneous assertion and denial of occult powers (80). The assumption that these spirits can be called in the first place implies that they do indeed exist, but hold themselves aloof from the court of the enlightened monarch and his absolute categories of yes or no, existence or nothingness. In some sense the ghost here may be identified with *Witz* itself, which throughout the history of *Witztheorie* has represented a mode of thought irreducible to narrowly rational concepts. *Witz,* positioned at the limits of rationality, makes us aware of the latter's limitations. Freud's set of ghost jokes are themselves revenants from the Enlightenment, serving as reminders that its problems have yet to be solved, that powerful irrational forces have yet to be dealt with.

Tendentious jokes are thus set up not only to pursue an Enlightenment agenda, but also to challenge it. Indeed, they could at times speak for the forces of anti-Enlightenment. We should recall that the 'not all are free' remark is not made by the enlightened Nathan, but about him by the Christian templar, who prefaces it so:

Der Aberglaub', in dem wir aufgewachsen,
Verliert, auch wenn wir ihn erkennen, darum
Doch seine Macht nicht über uns. (act 4, sc. 4)

The superstition, with which we grow up,
Does not therefore lose, even when we recognize it,
Its power over us.

The 'superstition' referred to here is of course Judaism, which remains as a mark of difference despite Nathan's attempts to wash it away through the baptism of reason. The fear of ghosts in Lichtenberg's aphorism could thus be read in the context of the anxiety of the assimilating Jew that his ethnic past, however distant, will always be there to haunt him. But fear is also present on the Gentile side of the line. The templar thinks he has identified a 'Jewish wolf in philosophical sheep's clothing.' This casts doubt upon Enlightenment rationality as being nothing more than a cover for nefarious Jewish intentions, precisely the impression which I have claimed that Freud wishes to avoid giving at the beginning of the chapter. These suspicions had become dangerously real in the irrationalist, antimodernist tendencies of turn-of-the-century anti-Semitism. The ghosts which haunt the Enlightenment thus arise in part from the incomplete project of Jewish assimilation. Freud's discussion of the relationship between theory and *Tendenz* takes on a much less abstruse meaning when placed in this context.

It therefore seems like a good idea to try now to gain a better understanding of this context with a brief look at the history of Jewish efforts to assimilate into Gentile society, focusing, of course, on *Witz*'s role within this process. In my first chapter I sought to elucidate the position of *Witz* within Habermas's concept of the bourgeois public sphere as it constituted itself in the Enlightenment. This sphere, it will be recalled, revolved on the axis between the poles of *Besitz* and *Bildung*. It is therefore not surprising to find the project of Jewish emancipation, as well as Jewish *Witz,* centered on achievement in these two areas. According to Hans Mayer (339–41) it is these two criteria upon which Lessing bases his portrait of emancipated Jews, both in *Die Juden* and in *Nathan der Weise.* Nathan is not only a wise man, he is also a wealthy man, a merchant whom we first encounter just coming home from a long and profitable journey. This connection between Jewish wealth and wisdom is more than just the product of poetic fancy. The Diaspora gave the Jews a ready-made network of international contacts, which for a long time permitted them to dominate trade between Christian Europe and the Moslem East (Kurt Schubart, in Drabek 20). Economic ties easily engender cultural ones, giving the Jews a cosmopolitan perspective that was denied to most of medieval Christian Europe. Such cosmopolitanism (at least within the Jewish mercantile class), combined with their own oppressed situation at home, would naturally provide fertile ground for the Enlightenment's ideals of universal tolerance.

Christian tolerance vis-à-vis the Jews was certainly not just a matter of pure humanitarianism, but was also shaped by economic conditions. During the Middle Ages, princes invited Jews into their realms because they knew that such a move would be good for business (Schubart, in Drabek 21). This bond between the Jewish merchant class and the aristocracy endured for centuries, with the rulers often protecting the Jews against the jealous wrath of their other subjects.

Joseph II's policy of toleration in Austria also rested on the consideration that it would be better for the economy if the Jews could be fully integrated, both financially and culturally, into Gentile society (see Wolfgang Häusler, in Drabek), thus avoiding unpleasant popular outbursts such as that which forced Leopold I to expel the Jews from Austria. Common economic interests thus brought the upper levels of Jewish and Gentile society together, which also led to mutually enriching cultural ties in this two-track project of assimilation.

Returning now to turn-of-the-century Vienna, it would seem that Jewish assimilation over the past century had been a great success, at least according to the critieria of *Besitz* and *Bildung*. The Jewish bourgeoisie was economically very prosperous and was disproportionately represented in the white-collar professions (Rozenblit 68). Though only 8 percent of the population, they made up 30 percent of the *Gymnasium* students, and this education opened the door to improved future economic and cultural status. And of course the list of Jewish artists and intellectuals then living in Vienna is as long as it is impressive. Yet despite these successes, Rozenblit has convincingly argued, no real assimilation ever took place. Though much was made of the fact that Vienna had the highest Jewish to Christian conversion rate in Europe, the actual number of converts remained small and never seriously threatened the integrity of the Jewish community. Jews tended to live among, work with, and marry other Jews. They remained apart and different, and this stubborn, haunting difference had very much to do with what was perceived as Jewish *Witz*.

Let us first examine the area of *Bildung*. Here the Jews remain true to *Witz*'s traditional association with aesthetic innovation. The importance of Jews to Vienna's avant-garde scene is indicated by the careers of men like Gustav Mahler, Arnold Schoenberg, and Arthur Schnitzler. And according to the latter's list, 70 percent of the writers of *Jung Wien* were Jewish (Steven Beller, in Oxaal 43). Jews were not only heavily represented among creative intellectuals, but they made up the backbone of the cultural scene in general, replacing the aristocrats in their traditional role as patrons of the arts. Wolfgang Häusler argues that the wives of Jewish bankers dominated the salon culture of the time, underlining again the link between *Besitz* and *Bildung*. According to Zygmunt Bauman, upper-class Jews became 'cultural fanatics,' taking culture more seriously than the Gentiles. This led paradoxically to its failure as a path of assimilation, with cultural mania instead becoming a mark of difference (53). Schnitzler remarks upon a similar phenomenon in his memoirs, *Jugend in Wien*. Here he recounts the history of his grandmother's family, which had been ennobled and was apparently completely successful in assimilating itself to the new aristocratic milieu, with one small exception: 'several of the younger and most recent descendants are distinguishable from the scions of old noble houses at the most through a bit more *Witz* and a racially typical [rasseneigentümlich] disposition for self-irony' (17). Or, as he describes one of his romantic rivals, 'a Jew to be sure, but the exact copy of an Austrian aristocrat, only favorably distinguishing himself by intellect and *Witz*' (226). On an intellectual and cultural level, *Witz* remains a mark of difference and of the failure of the emancipatory promises of *Bildung*.

This situation is mirrored on the economic level. The rationality of the Enlightenment envisions a society where status is accorded not upon the basis of tradition, caste, or religious belief, but solely upon considerations of individual merit. The Jews clearly had a great interest in taking up such ideas and on the whole they were rather successful, as we have already seen. Freud's own justification for the introduction of Jewish jokes into his text is particularly relevant in this regard. 'We do not insist upon a patent of nobility from our examples. We make no enquiries about their origin but only about their efficiency [Tüchtigkeit]—whether they are capable of making us laugh and whether they deserve our theoretical interest. And both these two requirements are best fulfilled precisely by Jewish jokes' (49). Freud touches on the heart of the matter here, for in the realm of *Tüchtigkeit* the Jews do indeed seem to be having the better of it. As Rozenblit demonstrates, turn-of-the-century Vienna did not offer all that much social mobility to the bulk of the population (68), yet many Jews were able to emigrate to Vienna and make better lives for themselves. *Witz*'s association with *Tüchtigkeit* thus transforms it not only into a mark of distinction but also, again, into one of difference. Though the Jews never dominated the economy to the extent imagined by the anti-Semites, they certainly provided prominent and easy targets for the jealous eyes of less fortunate Gentiles. The polemical distinction between 'schaffendes und raffendes Kapital' [productive and rapacious capital] which began circulating at this time sought to account for Jewish economic prosperity not through their industriousness but through cunning and trickery. The Jews's reputation for sharp-wittedness easily became synonymous with such a deceitful, money-grubbing character.

Witz, therefore, insofar as it is identified with the project of Jewish assimilation as conceived in the Enlightenment, had reached a critical stage by the turn of the century. Peter Pulzer has maintained that the anti-Semitism that was prevalent at this time was in fact a form of anti-Enlightenment (32). Jewish identification with an aesthetic and economic modernism led many anti-Semites to embrace an explicitly romantic ideology that looked fondly back to the pristine world of the Middle Ages.[3] It is therefore important that Freud would sound these Enlightenment themes to begin his chapter on tendentious jokes, for this tradition and the social program it represented were very much at issue. *Witz* proved to be a mark of difference not only in the stereotype of the witty Jew but also in the commitment to cultural modernity which it embodies.

Keeping all this in mind, I should like to turn now to two jokes which deal with the problem of Jewish assimilation. Both are set on trains, a significant fact in and of itself. That the train as the bearer of modernization could be the ideal vehicle to bring one into the Gentile world was symbolized by the career of a figure we have already become acquainted with in the joke book, Salomon Rothschild, who financed Austria's first railroad, the *Nordbahn.* Rothschild's ability to buy respect among the Gentiles made him somewhat of a legendary figure in the Jewish community. But that the freedom train had been derailed had also become clear, for the fight over the renewal of Rothschild's *Nordbahn* franchise provided an important impetus for the growth of political anti-Semitism in Austria.

The first train joke I want to deal with is in fact not found in the joke

3. The careers of Karl von Vogelsang and Georg von Schönerer provide the two most striking examples of this radical antimodernist and anti-Enlightenment tendency.

book at all, but in *The Interpretation of Dreams,* coming up in connection with Freud's third Rome dream. In this dream Freud asks a Herr Zucker for the way to Rome, later associating this dream event with two jokes. 'Here is the first one: the "constitution" story. An impecunious Jew had stowed himself away without a ticket in the fast train to Karlsbad. He was caught, and each time tickets were inspected he was taken out of the train and treated more and more severely. At one of the stations on his *via dolorosa* he met an acquaintance, who asked him where he was travelling to. "To Karlsbad," was his reply, "if my constitution can stand it"' (4:195).

As Freud himself explains, the name *Zucker* (sugar) is connected to Karlsbad because it is this spa where doctors often send people 'suffering from the constitutional complaint of diabetes.' And of course the very act of asking Herr Zucker the way connects Karlsbad with Rome, to which all ways lead. Oring has given an excellent analysis (56–60) of the subtext of Jewish assimilation contained in both dream and joke, the main points of which I should like to summarize here. According to Oring, the 'constitutional disease' at issue is actually Judaism, and indeed Jews were considered at the time to be particularly susceptible to diabetes. This turns the spa at Karlsbad into a metaphor for the baptismal waters that Rome has to offer. The poor Jew's *via dolorosa* is leading him to a conversion to Catholicism and thus the dissolution of his Jewish constitution, which indeed will not be able to survive the trip. Oring also sees this joke playing upon Heine's famous remark that baptism was 'the entrance ticket to European culture.' The poor Jew remains a stowaway without such a ticket until he can reach Karlsbad/Rome. He also cites a poem of Heine's in which Judaism is described as 'that family disease a thousand years old,' against which medical science is powerless. The suggestion seems to be that, where a doctor fails, a priest must be called. What Oring is attempting to do here is get a peek behind the mask of Doctor Freud, proponent of the Enlightenment, to discover a hidden desire within him to go over to the camp of the Catholics, who were the traditional enemies of progressive liberalism in Austria. Oring goes on to develop this thesis, claiming that Freud's problems with his Jewish identity and thoughts of assimilation are tied up with repressed religious desires on his part

(89–90) and attempts to explain away Freud's attacks on religion as simply expressing his need to clear the ground for the founding of a new one, namely, psychoanalysis (121–22). The enlightened unmasker stands himself unmasked, with his hermeneutics of suspicion having become irredeemably suspect of ulterior motives. Though this argument is at times very suggestive, it can also be rather misleading. Let us return to Karlsbad.

Jokes, like dreams, can be overdetermined. Though there is an undeniable assimilatory motif present in this joke, it is more than balanced by other tendencies. Oring brings Heine into the discussion but fails to emphasize the difference between Heine's and Freud's respective situations. The Karlsbad joke is not merely an extension of Heine's 'entrance ticket' remark, but a commentary upon it—indeed, its *reductio ad absurdum*. If one must have a (train) ticket to obtain the (entrance) ticket, then the poor Jew without any ticket at all is out of luck and his *via dolorosa* is a road without end. In fact the end itself, the idea of redemption through baptism, proves to be a mirage. Oring makes the right connections between Rome and Karlsbad, but he makes them in the wrong way. The constitutional disease of diabetes is not just a veiled reference to Judaism as a religion; more important is the fact that Judaism itself had become a constitutional disease that no baptism could ever wash away. The late nineteenth century had witnessed a shift from a religiously motivated hatred of the Jews to a racial anti-Semitism. Since religion had proven to be a porous barrier, the distinction between Jew and Gentile was refounded and absolutized in a specious science of race. Jewish attempts at assimilation, including religious conversion, were being met with increasing violence, just as was the poor Jew in the joke. What this joke is really telling us is that Heine's ticket is no longer good, assimilation through religious conversion no longer possible.

But if it's impossible, why is the Jew going to Karlsbad in the first place? The answer is to be found in Freud's identification with Hannibal, which he sees as the basis for the Rome dreams:

> Hannibal . . . had been the favorite hero of my later school days. Like so many boys of that age, I had sympathized in the Punic

> Wars not with the Romans but with the Carthaginians. And when in the higher classes I began to understand for the first time what it meant to belong to an alien race, and anti-semitic feelings among the other boys warned me that I must take up a definite position, the figure of the semitic general rose still higher in my esteem. To my youthful mind Hannibal and Rome symbolized the conflict between the tenacity [Zähigkeit] of Jewry and the organization of the Catholic church. (196)

Clearly, then, an encounter with an explicitly racist anti-Semitism was an important element motivating both dream and joke. Seen in this light, Rome/Karlsbad are not longed-for refuges of conversion/healing, but instead represent two types of a much hated anti-Semitism, religious and racial. Hannibal and the poor Jew on the train, united by their constitutional *Zähigkeit,* are on the way to these cities not as supplicants but as would-be conquerors.

That the enemy to be dealt with goes beyond anti-Semitism is indicated by Freud's above description of the Catholic church as an 'organization.' This takes us back to our starting point, the comparison in Heine's *Gleichnis* of Catholicism to a large business, with the attendant imagery of hierarchy and bureaucracy. Freud has opened up a war on two fronts here, with Rome now representing both an irrational anti-Semitism and an overrationalized modernity. The Jew remains caught in the middle as the partisan of a rugged individualism that continually frustrates all attempts to crush it. Take, for example, another Jew-on-a-train joke. But this time, instead of the direct violence of anti-Semitism, we see a subtler form of repression:

> A Galician Jew was travelling in a train. He had made himself really comfortable, had unbuttoned his coat and put his feet up on the seat. Just then a gentleman in modern dress entered the compartment. The Jew promptly pulled himself together and took up a proper pose. The stranger fingered through the pages of a notebook, made some calculations, reflected for a moment and then suddenly asked the Jew: 'Excuse me, when is Yom Kippur (the Day of Atonement)?' 'Oho!' said the Jew, and put his feet up on the seat again before answering. (80–81)

John Murray Cuddihy has also analyzed the conflict between Freud's Jewishness and modernity. In his reading of this joke, the forces of social discipline represented by the 'gentleman in modern dress' only hold up until his question reveals a shared ethnicity, permitting a regression to the manners of earlier, less formal times back in the ghetto. Freud takes a somewhat different tack, claiming that this joke 'is meant to portray the democratic mode of thinking of the Jews, which recognizes no distinction between lords and serfs, but also, alas, upsets discipline and co-operation' (8:112), an explanation which Cuddihy describes as a 'lumberingly apologetic "interpretation" written with the Gentile reader in mind' (21). He finds it illegitimate of Freud to translate the ethos of the rough and tumble world of the *Shtetl* into the rhetoric of modern democracy. Cuddihy seems so intent on maintaining the barrier between the ethnic reality of the Jew and modern society that he misses the point of Freud's overall project here, which is to break down the ghetto wall and bring these worlds into productive interaction. True, in the end, the modern world must absorb the ethnic; as far as Freud and other assimilated Jews were concerned, there was no going back. But though Freud may have no desire to return to what he sees as the inefficient anarchy of the *Shtetl,* he is more that willing to use its traditions to remind us of the freedoms we have lost and to provoke critical reflection on the conflict between the disciplinary and democratic tendencies of modernity.

Another key figure in Freud's critical mobilization of the traditions of the Jewish joke, and one he has already identified himself with, is that of the *Schnorrer,* the beggar who lives off the largesse of the Jewish upper classes. Most of these jokes revolve around the complete lack of deference or humility with which the *Schnorrer* makes his demands. 'A *Schnorrer* on his way up a rich man's staircase met a fellow member of his profession, who advised him to go no further. "Don't go up today," he said, "the Baron is in a bad mood today; he's giving nobody more than one florin."—"I'll go up all the same," said the first *Schnorrer.* "Why should I give him a florin? Does he give me anything?"' (113).

The root of the *Schnorrer*'s shamelessness is his treatment of the rich man's money as his own, and in a sense he is within his rights. Freud tells us that the Jewish religious law commands the rich to give to the poor and moreover to be thankful for the chance of doing a good deed. The conflict between religious duty and the 'ordinary, middle-class view of charity' (113), which is not so crazy about giving money away, creates the tension upon which these jokes are based, as well as giving them a political edge. The democratic spirit which Freud identified behind the two-Jews-on-a-train joke becomes radicalized in the anecdote where the *Schnorrer* demands money from the rich man for a trip to Ostende, one of the most costly spas, because nothing is too expensive for his health. The poor Jew avoids a repetition of the Karlsbad experience by securing what seems to be the real 'entry ticket' to Gentile culture, money. In another joke the arrogant 'famillionairity' of the Baron finally meets its match in the fresh familiarity of the *Schnorrer,* who, invited by the Baron to dinner as an act of charity, brings along his new son-in-law because he had promised him room and board for the first year. Though this invocation of the traditions of religion and family has some critical power, Freud is quick to remind us of its limits. The privileged class's 'view of charity' rebels 'in the other story of the Baron who, deeply moved by a Schnorrer's tale of woe, rang for his servants: "Throw him out! He's breaking my heart!"' (113). *Witz* covers the violence that is about to occur, the forcible ejection of the beggar, with a facade of humor. The *chutzpah* of the *Schnorrer* in the end provides no real defense against the sheer superior power of the wealthy man who is prepared to ignore considerations of religion and compassion. Though some of these *Schnorrer* jokes might be useful in helping the poor maintain their self-respect, they show them no way out of their dependent relationship.

What *Witz* might have to offer the lower classes in this regard is indicated by the following *Schnorrer* story, the first one Freud tells and the one he most often makes reference to:

> An impoverished individual borrowed 25 florins from a prosperous acquaintance, with many asseverations of his necessitous circumstances. The very same day his benefactor met him again in a restaurant with a plate of salmon mayonnaise in front of him. The benefactor reproached him: 'What? You borrowed money from me and then order yourself salmon mayonnaise? Is that what you've used my money for?' 'I don't understand you,'

replied the object of the attack; 'if I haven't any money I can't eat salmon mayonnaise, and if I have some money I mustn't eat salmon mayonnaise. Well, then, when am I to eat salmon mayonnaise?' (49–50)

The joke arises in the context of the discussion of Heine's 'Golden Calf' remark, the point at which we saw the breakdown of the principle of *Ersparnis*. Here as well the joke technique is that of diversion. The answer of the 'impoverished bon vivant' has the appearance of logic but is in fact a smoke screen. 'His benefactor is not reproaching him with treating himself to salmon precisely on the day on which he borrowed the money; he is reminding him that in his circumstances he has no right to think of such delicacies at all.' By the logic of bourgeois economics, one's fantasy should not extend beyond one's means, thereby confining the poor to bread-and-water dreams. *Witz*'s diversionary tactics subvert this logic of *Ersparnis,* opening up other possibilities for the imaginations of the downtrodden.

Freud claims that this joke is only superficially Jewish in nature, that in fact 'the core belongs to humanity in general' (49). He at first can see only cynicism at its heart, but later transfigures its message into the poet's invocation of *carpe diem,* seize the day (109). This, he claims, may sound like cynicism from the ascetic standpoint of religion, but he reminds us that we have all felt the desire to break out of our cycle of daily renunciations at least once in a while, and that the religious promises of a Great Beyond where everything will be made good have become less than believable. What keeps Freud's interpretation of *carpe diem* from dissolving into an insipid warning against the dangers of all work and no play is his reminder that the allegedly universally human core of this joke is very much class conditioned. For the poor, the morality of renunciation is not a matter of ethical choice, but of brutal necessity.

The critique of religion remains of central importance here. We have already seen how religious injunctions to charity come into conflict with the hard-headed economics of *Ersparnis.* The next logical step is that if the rich no longer feel themselves bound by a sense of religious duty, then the poor are free as well to renounce the morality of renunciation, finally realizing 'that this morality is only a selfish regulation laid down by the few who are rich and powerful and who can satisfy their wishes at any time without postponement' (110). The recognition of the ideological character of religion transforms *carpe diem* from a vaguely universal poetic gesture into a weapon in the class struggle. That the salmon mayonnaise joke comes up in the context of Heine's golden calf witticism is not just because they apply the same joke technique; they also participate in a common fight against the social dominance of the rich, centering their attack on religion, whether it takes the form of the worship of money or the preaching of a highly ideological asceticism. Freud himself is no detached observer here. He would later refer to Heine as his 'Unglaubensgenosse' (fellow unbeliever), an appellation which Heine himself used with reference to Spinoza. Freud follows this with Lichtenberg's cry, 'we, by the ungrace of God, day-labourers, serfs, negroes, villeins' (77). The atheistic solidarity of these Enlightenment thinkers is extended to include the most wretched members of the underclass in this liberation antitheology.

Freud has built a strong case for the intimate connection between religious and economic critique within *Witz*; hence the hesitancy with which he treated Heine's analogy at the beginning of the chapter on tendentious jokes is replaced with a resounding affirmation of the redemptive powers of blasphemy. Heine is again used as the mouthpiece for these views, and this time there is no apology for any ruffled feelings on the part of the reader. 'Heine is said to have made a definitely blasphemous joke on his death-bed. When a friendly priest reminded him of God's mercy and gave him hope that God would forgive him his sins, he is said to have replied: 'Bien sûr qu'il me pardonnera: c'est son métier' [Of course he'll forgive me: that's his job]' (114).

Heine reduces God to the level of a tradesman, whom he summons to perform a certain task, in this case the absolution from sin, and can dismiss at his pleasure. The implicit message is that God is in fact man's creation. 'What was supposed to be the created being revealed itself just before its annihilation as the creator' (114). The insight that God is simply a projection of man, a projection of his better self which he must take back within himself if heaven is to be realized on earth, was a standard feature of German left-wing radical thought from Ludwig

Feuerbach on. Freud's attempt to keep his discussion of tendentious jokes on a neutral level has been an utter failure; *Witz*'s critique of religion infects Freud's theoretical discourse itself, embedding his conception of tendentiousness within the context of an engaged, progressive political stance.

What has enabled Freud to shake off his previous timidity and now speak so openly in these terms? I made the claim that his reservations concerning Heine's *Gleichnis* were in large part due to a reluctance to get involved in an explicitly Christian-Jewish confrontation and the resultant anti-Semitic passions this would arouse. Only after a reworking of the traditions of the Jewish joke, translating ethnic and confessional conflicts into the language of class struggle, is Freud prepared to take a definite stand. This brought him very close to the contemporary socialist position on the Jewish question, which also avoided a direct confrontation with anti-Semitism, viewing it as a side issue that would simply disappear once the fundamental question of class relationships had been decided.[4] But whereas Marx and other prominent Socialists often seem to share the anti-Semite's stereotype of Judaism as the religion of avarice, Freud reverses the cliché, using Heine's analogy to depict Christianity as the religion of big business, while at the same time mobilizing elements of the Jewish tradition for a critique of capitalism and bureaucratic modernity.

Which is not to say that Freud denies any Jewish complicity with the System. We have seen in the conflict between *Schnorrer* and Baron, that Jews were on both sides of the class battle lines, perhaps giving some sense to Freud's attempt to make the Jewish situation paradigmatic for the human condition (the 'universally human' of the salmon mayonnaise joke). Marx makes a similar move in his *Zur Judenfrage*. He also takes the situation of the Jews as a metaphor for that of society as a whole. For Marx, the struggle for Jewish political emancipation has entailed a split between the Jews' personal religious lives and their public participation in the (at least theoretically) religiously neutral realm of the state. But this split between private and public is in fact the condition of all members of the modern liberal state, where one's pri-

4. See Wistrich, *Socialism and the Jews*, for an excellent analysis of the relationship between the two.

vate economic life remains untouched by considerations of the greater good. This double life of public and private leads to what Marx refers to as a sophistic relationship to the state. Judaism is identified with a utilitarian outlook which reduces everything to a commodity, but Marx is quick to add that Christianity is no better and that, as depicted in Heine's golden calf joke, the truly dominant cult in society is that of money. It is this egoistic religion of avarice that must be destroyed if society is to be saved. Freud seems to be following a similar line, but is not so quick to abandon the cultural and religious traditions of Judaism, instead seeking to turn them to critical advantage.

Let us now meet another character from this tradition, the *Schadchen*. The *Schadchen* is the Jewish version of the marriage broker and the subject of innumerable jokes. Freud groups these jokes around two types of 'faulty reasoning,' the sophistic and the automatic. Here is an example of each:

> The *Schadchen* was defending the girl he had proposed against the young man's protests. 'I don't care for the mother-in-law,' said the latter. 'She's a disagreeable, stupid person.'—'But after all you're not marrying the mother-in-law. What you want is her daughter.'—'Yes, but she's not young any longer, and she's not precisely a beauty.'—'No matter. If she's neither young nor beautiful she'll be all the more faithful to you.'—'And she hasn't much money.'—'Who's talking about money? Are you marrying money then? After all it's a wife that you want.'—'But she's got a hunchback too.'—'Well, what do you want? Isn't she to have a single fault?' (61)

> A *Schadchen* had brought an assistant with him to the discussion about the proposed bride, to bear out what he had to say. 'She is straight as a pine-tree,' said the *Schadchen*.—'As a pine-tree,' repeated the echo.—'And she has eyes that ought to be seen!'—'What eyes she has!' confirmed the echo.—'And she is better educated than anyone!'—'What an education!'—'It's true there's one thing,' admitted the broker, 'she has a small hump.'—'And what a hump!' the echo confirmed once more. (64)

The breaking down of the woman in question into selling points is a common device of the *Schadchen* jokes; five of the seven examples Freud gives employ it. Marx also comments on the commodification of women, which was certainly not restricted to the Jewish community. In his *Die Frau und der Sozialismus,* Bebel criticizes what he refers to as the *Ehebörse* (marriage market) as well as the related, if even less savory, industries of prostitution and the white slave trade; all were flourishing in the Gentile society of the day. The *Schadchen* pays lip service to the norms of rational discourse, but cannot keep from lapsing into sophistry. Freud's account of sophistry shows interesting parallels with that of Marx. Freud's *Schadchen* is caught in the plight of Marx's *Privatmensch,* 'who views other people as means, reduces himself to a means and becomes the plaything of alien forces' (1:355). Freud, too, recognizes that reason is perverted here in the name of economic interest. The *Schadchen,* however, is also a victim of the system, and thus a sympathetic figure for Freud. The breakdown of his sophistry in the 'automatic pieces of faulty reasoning' in which the truth finally comes out is no accident. Freud draws on his theory of parapraxis to explain this as a sign of internal resistance on the part of the *Schadchen,* who at heart is happy to break through the tissue of lies he has wrapped himself in. Freud claims that the *Schadchen*'s nearness to the system puts him in an excellent position to critique it, but also recognizes that his critique must be muted because he also lives off it. This is perhaps why the moment of truth, be it sophistic *reductio ad absurdum* or Freudian slip, comes only after it is clear that the sale is a bust, that the damaged goods cannot be moved. 'The popular mind, which created these stories, and others like them, is torn by a similar conflict; for it knows that the sacredness of marriages after they have been contracted is grievously affected by the thought of what happened at the time when they were arranged' (106–7). The *Schadchen* symbolizes the double bind in which society as a whole finds itself. The utilitarian rationality of modern society, which treats everything as a commodity, threatens to come apart as it undermines moral institutions, such as marriage, which provided for social cohesion. *Witz,* like the *Schadchen,* is caught in the middle of this dialectic of the Enlightenment, attempting to criticize the system while still remaining for the most part trapped within it.

If modernity's double edge has left Jewish *Witz* and its hopes for emancipation in a precarious position, perhaps it might find a natural ally in the 'commodity' itself, women. The eroticization of economic relationships that has occurred within these *Schadchen* stories would indicate that the fate of both these oppressed groups is intertwined. Büschenthal recognizes this in his 1812 collection of Jewish jokes, which, according to Sander Gilman, was the first collection of its kind to appear in Germany. 'We ascribe the fact that the Jews are in general so witty to the repression they have suffered for centuries. Need and weakness—as the female sex teaches us—give birth to cunning, and cunning is the mother of *Witz*' (Büschenthal iv).

One of the first jokes Büschenthal recounts demonstrates just how potent this alliance can be. 'A young Jewess sat in a loge in the theater in B——. A young rake entered and approached her in a familiar and aggressive manner. "Sir," said the young girl, "you evidently take me for someone else." "God forbid," he replied, "I can see very well that you are a young girl." He then became ever more impolite and finally brazen. The young girl, very upset, used her tongue as only a young girl can. "Now, now," the rake cried, "don't eat me up!" "Sir, have no worries," she quickly replied. "I am a Jewess, and we are not allowed to eat pork"' (quoted in Gilman 257).

A truly remarkable exchange, especially when read against Freud's theory of the *Zote,* the dirty joke. For Freud the *Zote,* at least in its original form, is directed by a sexually aroused man at a particular woman with the purpose of arousing her as well—basically the situation of the young man in the theater. Should the man succeed in his intentions, then the *Zote* is quickly dropped as words pass over into deeds. More likely, however, the woman will simply stand there, silent and ashamed. Such embarrassment, according to Freud, is in fact 'only a reaction against the excitement and, in a roundabout way, is an admission of it' (97). This also affords a degree of pleasure to the man who, like Freud, can see the repressed desire behind the woman's superficial defensiveness and knows that deep down she really wants it. Freud's apparent support for this fundamental tenet of the rapist's credo not only does him little credit personally, it also limits his theoretical vision.[5] The scenario described in Büschenthal's joke, where the Jewish woman uses *Witz* to strike back at and silence her masculine antagonist, seems to have been simply beyond his powers of imagination. It is true, much had changed since Büschenthal's day. Hans Mayer identifies a process of counter-enlightenment that runs through the nineteenth century which systematically rolled back previous gains made by women. This wave of misogyny had reached a high point by the turn of the century, and Freud's theory of the dirty joke certainly does little to stem it—quite the contrary.

Nonetheless, elements of a potentially subversive coalition between Jews and women are still present within *Jokes and Their Relation to the Unconscious.* The following joke provides perhaps the best example. 'This girl reminds me of Dreyfus. The army doesn't believe in her innocence' (40). Keeping this in mind, let us return to Freud's theory of the dirty joke. For Freud, the *Zote* functions as 'an exposure of the sexually different person' (98)—read: the woman, since only men seem to be capable of making dirty jokes. Though a man can enjoy this sport on his own, the ideal situation occurs when another man is present. Here the first man finds an 'ally' against the woman, perhaps in case she should prove to be as uppity as the Jewess in the theater. 'Through the first person's smutty speech the woman is exposed before the third, who, as listener, has now been bribed by the effortless satisfaction of his own libido' (100). Thus a male group constructs itself based upon an aggressive sexuality directed against the excluded female.

Karin Huffzky has given a very interesting account of the dynamics of the sort of male-bonding that takes place here. She points to the 'militancy' of such *Witz,* which indeed often expresses itself using martial imagery (33–34). 'And when Freud speaks of 'smutty intercourse' [*Zotenverkehr*], the homosexual phantasy shines through.' Suppose we applied this model to the army of the Dreyfus joke—a patriarchally organized and aggressive group of men that constitutes itself over and

5. This is made even more explicit in *The Psychopathology of Everyday Life,* in which Freud speaks of sexual assault on women, 'where the man's attack cannot be repelled by her full muscular strength because a portion of her unconscious impulses meets the attack with encouragement' (6:181).

against suspicious outsiders such as women and Jews. But, of course, suspicion and fear go hand in hand. What threat is being posed here by women and Jews?

According to Freud's analysis, this joke depends upon the double meaning of the word *innocence,* the lack of which can refer to both sexual and criminal misbehavior. Within the context of the Dreyfus case, the notion of crime becomes of course highly politicized and charged with anti-Semitic overtones. Freud finds it impossible to determine which meaning of *innocence* is predominant here, confronting us with the inextricable intermingling of sex and politics. He was later often to remark that one of the roots of anti-Semitism was the disdain felt for the circumcised Jew, who was perceived as having been castrated.[6] He puts this perception as well at the heart of men's low opinion for women. Jews too become the 'sexually different person' and thus the objects of a *Zotenverkehr* that is now revealed to be both misogynist and anti-Semitic. In his history of *Die Juden in der Karikatur,* Eduard Fuchs tells us that the nineteenth century was especially inventive in creating anti-Semitic jokes of a pronouncedly erotic nature (290ff.). For example, the stereotypically large noses of the Jews were often caricatured as immense penises, which served both to mock their legendary prodigious sensuality as well as to soothe the anti-Semite's own fears of castration by fetishistically replacing the lost organ. In line with this it should also be noted that two of the most prominent castrating female figures in the art of the time—Judith (Klimt) and Salome (Oscar Wilde / Richard Strauss)—were also Jewish. The active sexuality, the lack of 'innocence' on the part of what was to have been the passive victim of aggression, threatens to place the aggressor himself into an objectified / passive / castrated state. Fear for one's own masculinity is thus the most likely basis of the *Zotenverkehr,* driving the army of misogynists and anti-Semites ever tighter together against the castrational threat posed by Jews and women.

The chief contemporary theoretician of misogyny and anti-Semitism was Otto Weininger. The rather prudish Weininger was certainly not interested in defending, much less in telling, dirty jokes,

6. See his analysis of 'Little Hans,' as well as his essays on Leonardo da Vinci and *Moses and Monotheism.*

but was very much concerned with the dangers posed by *Witz* in the hands of the other side. True, he does maintain that the Jew is 'after sexuality, the most fruitful object of *Witz*' (427), but it is the Jews themselves who make these jokes as a form of self-understanding and self-expression. The sensuality of the Jews brings them into a natural alliance with women, and the preferred weapon of both against the patriarchal order is the negativity of *Witz*. 'Jews and women are humorless [*humorlos*], but sarcastic [*spottlustig*]' (428). *Humor* supposedly strengthens social bonds, whereas the critical voice of *Spott,* which is equivalent to tendentious *Witz,* has the opposite effect. 'The Jew never really holds anything to be true and incontrovertible, holy and sacrosanct. Therefore he is everywhere frivolous, mocking everything [*alles bewitzelnd*]' (431). If a woman can at times be tamed by her love for a man, the sexuality of the Jewish female still remains ominously anarchic. Weininger asserts that 'no woman in the world so fully represents the idea of woman as the Jewess' (429) and cites Franz Grillparzer's 'Jüdin von Toledo' as an example. In this play the Jewess distracts the monarch from his military responsibilities and almost costs him his kingdom until he is finally able to free himself from her influence. Just as in the Dreyfus joke, the Jew(ess) appears as the desired and feared disturber of army discipline.

As we know from the *Schadchen* stories, the Jews are also 'true matchmakers,' an activity that Weininger equates with 'the blurring of boundaries [*Grenzverwischung*].' This has not only a sexual but also political and economic dimensions. 'The principle of all aristocracy is the strictest maintenance of all borders between people. The Jew is a born communist' (417). The boundary which Weininger was most concerned to uphold was that between men and women. But the paradoxically both castrated and oversexed Other, be it Jew, woman, or both, refuses to stay on its side of the line; indeed, it does its best to turn the lines and boundaries that make up the social order into nothing but a joke. The army of Christian soldiers pledged to uphold this order is hard pressed indeed, for the spirit of the age has turned against them. Weininger speaks glumly of 'our age, which is not only the most Jewish, but also the most effeminate of all ages' (441). Modernity itself becomes the enemy here, a modernity marked by an alliance of women and Jews under the banner of a critically tendentious *Witz*. It is they who represent the leveling forces of sexuality,[7] the relative social mobility offered by capitalism, and the ideal of a classless society in communism.

We can now perhaps better understand the suspicions of the 'army' (taken in the broad sense as representing heirarchical social organization in general) against these two groups. The fear of their subversive influence is well-founded, for the stability of a society that bases its identity upon the excluded Other is tenuous indeed. Let us again return to the model Freud offers in his discussion of the *Zote*. The *Zote* is not only a mark of sexual difference, but also of class difference. According to Freud, the lower classes remain on the crudest level of the *Zotenverkehr* as previously described, directing their lewd remarks at a physically present woman. But as one climbs the social ladder, one finds that the presence of a woman, far from arousing such comments, acts as an inhibiting factor. The men now wait until they are alone, *unter sich*. 'So that gradually, in place of the woman, the onlooker, now the listener, becomes the person to whom the smut is addressed' (99). We shift from a female to a male audience, from a heterosexual to homosexual bond. The woman in her absence simply provides the excuse, a hetero cover for pleasurable intercourse within a strictly male group. Whose innocence is to be doubted now? The Colonel Redl case, which combined treason with homosexuality, would soon provide the Austrian counterpart to that of Dreyfus.

Even more confusion arises when we trace the *Zote* back to its primordial beginnings. The *Zote* is based upon a fundamental component of the libido, 'the desire to see the organs peculiar to each sex exposed . . . The libido for looking and touching is present in everyone in two forms, active and passive, male and female' (98). This original bisexuality threatens to throw the whole *Zotenverkehr* into chaos. If men possess both active and passive tendencies, then they too would be proper objects for the aggressive exposure of the *Zote* and secretly enjoy it just as much as Freud claims women do. He asserts that men can be just as exhibitionistic as women, though the basis for

7. Recall here the 'moral' of Schnitzler's *Reigen* in which all classes are joined in the same erotic dance.

his characterizing only female exhibitionism as passive remains unclear.[8] This element of male exhibitionism suggests the following reconstruction of the *Urzote.* The sexually aroused male shows his erect penis to the female in an attempt to provoke similar desires. But this is just the opposite of the situation in the *Zote* we first discussed, which was based upon the exposure of the woman as the sexually different person. What is in fact being exposed in the *Zote* is the penis, both here in this stone age scenario as well as within the cultured milieu of the gentleman's club, as the men swap blue anecdotes to demonstrate their virility. The insecurity lying at the root of this exhibitionism is later recognized by Freud in a footnote added to his *Three Essays on the Theory of Sexuality* in 1920: 'The compulsion to exhibit, for instance, is also closely dependent on the castration complex: it is a means of constantly insisting upon the integrity of the subject's own (male) genitals and it reiterates his infantile satisfaction at the absence of a penis in those of women' (7:157). The problems of bisexuality and castration are dealt with through the ostentative reaffirmation of genital difference.

The trouble, of course, is that civilization tends to frown upon openly displayed penises. Even the *Zoten* themselves undergo a process of refinement that in the end leaves not only women out of the picture, but very little trace of the original sexual desire, which has also become socially inadmissible. The joke technique most often used to satisfy these cultural demands for subtlety and sublimation is that of 'allusion — that is, replacement by something small' (100). Culture has replaced the original erect male penis and the sexual aggression it represented with 'something small'; the male group which sought to exclude the castrated other through the *Zotenverkehr* can only do so at the price of its own castration. As the cultural hierarchy of patriarchy becomes ever more rigid, as women and the sexuality they represent become ever more distant, then the male identity constructed within this framework itself becomes ever more insubstantial. *Witz* plays a nasty joke on the men who had sought to exploit it for their own purposes.

8. For an excellent analysis of the contradictions of Freud's use of the dichotomies of active/passive, masculine/feminine, see Sarah Kofmann, *The Enigma of Woman.*

Of course, this is all complete nonsense. Men are not really castrated, and neither are women and Jews. The castrational and repressive logic of phallocentrism proves to be nothing more than a bad joke. Its attempts to construct a social hierarchy of sublimation are demonstrated to be fruitless with every guilty guffaw at a dirty joke, however subtle: 'When we laugh at a refined obscene joke, we are laughing at the same thing that makes a peasant laugh at a coarse piece of smut' (101). This could be viewed as nothing more than interclass chauvinist solidarity, but its democratic character must also be recognized. The *Zote* and its degrees of refinement help in constructing class boundaries, but they also serve as a reminder of how fragile those boundaries can be. The veneer of upper-class *Bildung* proves liable to be swept away at any moment. 'We can observe how men of a higher class are at once induced, when they are in the company of girls of an inferior class, to reduce their smutty jokes to the level of simple smut' (101). The 'army's' suspicions as to the young girl's innocence are really a mark of its own uncertainty in the face of the leveling force which sexuality here represents, a tendency revealed in the analysis of the Dreyfusard Freud.

The tension between the Jews and the army displayed by the Dreyfus joke goes back a long way. Fuchs documents the fact that the Jews had long been caricatured as making bad soldiers (153ff.). They in fact had little opportunity to prove their valor, having lost the right to bear arms early in the thirteenth century (Drabek 39). Though they fought bravely in the revolution of 1848 and continued to serve in the Habsburg army of the restoration, they still faced discrimination and mockery. In his autobiography, Schnitzler describes the disparaging attitude the rest of the army held for the 'Mosesdragoner,' the dragoons of Moses (137). The most striking example of the Jewish exclusion from the Gentile brotherhood of arms was the *Waidhofener Prinzip,* adopted by many fraternities, which declared Jews to be incapable of giving satisfaction in a duel. Acceptance within male society was thus conditional upon one's perceived right and ability to handle a weapon. This theme is taken up in another joke of Freud's, the story of Itzig the Artillerist. 'Itzig had been declared fit for service in the artillery. He was clearly an intelligent lad, but intractable and without any interest in the service. One of his superior officers, who was friendlily disposed to him, took him on one side and said to him: "Itzig, you're no use to us. I'll give you a piece of advice: buy yourself a cannon and make yourself independent!"' (56).

For Freud, *Witz* is here on the side of the army. The apparent absurdity of the officer's suggestion is in fact designed to unmask Itzig's own stupidity. What the officer is really saying is, 'Itzig, I know you're an intelligent man of business. But I assure you it is very stupid of you if you can't see that it is impossible to behave in the army in the same way as in business life, where each person acts for himself and against others. In military life, subordination and co-operation are the rule' (58). We have already seen that the Jews were able to achieve an impressive degree of social mobility through their entrepreneurial spirit and they indeed were stereotyped as the bearers of the egoistic ethic of economic liberalism. That this was a threat to the traditional social hierarchies that are epitomized by the army should be clear enough. But to find Freud treating this thinly disguised anti-Semitic joke with some approval is perhaps somewhat more surprising.

In keeping with the parallelism between women and Jews that I have been developing, we find that female sexuality can also have a subversive economic meaning similar to that accorded to Itzig's Jewishness. Immediately following the Dreyfus joke, Freud recounts a 'diabolically ingenious joke' of the Viennese humorist Daniel Spitzer. 'Mr. and Mrs. X live in fairly grand style. Some people think that the husband has earned a lot and so has been able to lay by a bit [sich etwas zurückgelegt]; others again think that the wife has lain back a bit and so has been able to earn a lot' (33). Unlike the Dreyfus joke, however, which maintains its political and sexual ambiguity, Freud finds that in this joke the sexual overtones of 'sich zurücklegen' drown out its standard meaning, to save. In my view, this interpretation only serves to obfuscate the interaction between its sexual and economic levels. The joke presents us with two roads to success; the long and difficult one of *Ersparnis,* which the man takes, and the quick and easy path to riches open to the beautiful woman who is willing to sell her body.[9] The

9. That prostitution was in fact a miserable occupation is beside the point. What is in play here is the widespread myth of the carefree and wealthy courtesan. See Fuchs, *Die Frau,* 398.

'army's' suspicion of Jewish economic activity becomes heightened in the case of women. Both pursue an entrepreneurialism that promises quick success and results in the undermining of authority figures (army/husband). This individualization and eroticization of the economic realm carries with it the threat of anarchy, and Freud takes this threat seriously. Though a Dreyfusard and a sexual pioneer, he criticizes as 'stupidity' activities that would lead to the collapse of social and sexual discipline. This is not the last time we will find Freud on the side of the army.

Freud expands upon his analysis of the Dreyfus joke later in the book, this time considering its topicality (*Aktualität*). He admits that most jokes within a work on *Witz* cannot deal with topical events, for the circumstances soon fall into oblivion, making long footnotes necessary to explain the now-incomprehensible examples. Even the Dreyfus joke, despite its theoretical interest, has paled with age. The following example as well has lost its punch for Freud. 'At the end of a meal in a house to which I had been invited as a guest, a pudding of the kind known as a "Roulard" was served. It requires some skill on the part of the cook to make it; so one of the guests asked: "Made in the house?" To which the host replied: "Yes, indeed. A home-roulard"' (94). That 'Home Rule' is no longer 'a standing head-line in the political columns of our daily papers' (122–23) may rob this joke of its immediate impact, but it remains a fit subject for analysis.

Freud determines that the success of the 'home-roulard' joke rests on the '*Ersparung* of a long detour in thought, from the circle of ideas of the kitchen to the remote one of politics' (123). He takes it for granted that this 'Denkumweg' is a one-way street, that the pleasure of the joke turns on the abandonment of the dull life of the kitchen for the fascinating world of newspaper politics. That this is a strictly masculine world is clear; it is the male host (Hausherr) and not the female cook (Köchin) who speaks, as if the homemade dessert were of his own making. This expropriatory authority of the patriarch remains unchallenged, either by the cook or by Freud. That the question of home rule could turn into one of who rules the home, that domestic issues could themselves be capable of politicization, is ignored.

Still, it is interesting to note that all of the examples Freud chooses for his discussion of topicality deal with women. Women are the point at which politics could be made real, bringing this 'remote' realm out of the comfortably mediated framework of the newspaper directly into the home. The characterization of women as something timely and constantly changing has already been established by Lichtenberg's remark concerning '"a girl scarcely twelve *Moden* [modes] old." This sounds like "twelve *Monden* [moons]," i.e. months' (76). The portrayal of women as creatures of fashion is of course an old sexist cliché, but it must also be remembered that the tyranny of *Mode* was coming under attack by the feminists of the time with their rejection of the corset and their introduction of a more comfortable and practical style of dress. This is a good example of one area in which the early feminists attempted to politicize everyday life. As Fuchs tells us (*Die Frau* 263ff.), the controversy surrounding this issue was a hot topic in the contemporary jokelore, though Freud himself seems to have taken no direct notice of it.

The final topical joke he offers is based on the story of Crown Princess Louise of Saxony. Because the events behind the joke were of a very recent nature, Freud gives us little by way of explanation and later editors refer the reader to Louise's autobiography. Her account of her life is at times self-serving but nonetheless fascinating. According to her, she was happy in her marriage to the prince, but was driven from court because of her modern ideas and sympathy for the common people. Her chief antagonist was her father-in-law, who as king threatened to have her committed to an insane asylum for her alleged hysteria (a good example of the repressive uses to which the ideology of the hysterical female could be put). One of the many conflicts concerned Louise's desire to take up the at the time fashionable sport of bicycle riding. The bicycle had become a symbol of women's emancipation, offering them both needed physical exercise and freedom from restrictive clothing. But royal disapproval soon ruined even this small pleasure for her.

In her chapter entitled 'J'accuse' (again we are led back to the Dreyfus afair), she fingers Baron Georg von Metzsch as being the principal architect of the machinations that finally drove her from Dresden. At first she was attracted to von Metzsch as an 'intelligent, witty and pleasant man, an exception at the court of Dresden' (201). But von Metzsch would soon give her a very disagreeable taste of his wit. Inviting Louise and her husband to dinner, he serves his royal guests two thin slices of cold ham, mocking Louise's reputedly simple and folksy tastes. Louise is enraged by the joke, but is able to counter with one of her own. She throws a lavish dinner for von Metzsch, who is naturally surprised and asks her why she has gone to the trouble. Her reply: 'Excellency, this is my revenge for the two pieces of ham that you recently served me. Later, when I as queen sit at the political table . . . you will receive only two thin slices of political influence' (204).

Two very different forms of *Witz* have come into conflict here. That of von Metzsch represents the class discipline of the old courtly tradition. Louise presents herself as a would-be reformer of courtly life; she would like to raise its intellectual level with modern ideas and so her *Witz* is allied with the forces of democratization and women's liberation. Perhaps what von Metzsch and his fellow courtiers found so disturbing in her joke was that it revealed her as a *Machtweib,* a woman not afraid to make use of political power. Because of this she is declared to be hysterical and driven away from court, her husband, and her children. These were the events that lay behind the following joke. 'The Crown Princess Louise approached the crematorium in Gotha with the question of how much a *Verbrennung* [cremation] costs. The management replied: "Five thousand marks normally; but we will only charge you three thousand as you have been *durchgebrannt* [literally 'burnt through,' slang for 'eloped'] once already"' (123). Cremation itself was at the time growing in acceptance while being fiercely resisted by the church, and so Louise's interest in it in the joke types her as a woman of modern ideas. And what is the fate of the woman with such newfangled notions who disquiets the king and abandons her natural place at the side of husband and children? Annihilation by fire. In these three topical jokes, the topicality of women has been exposed as a threat to the patriarchal order of army, *Hausherr,* and husband/king. The exterminatory gesture of the final example may be seen as a desperate effort to stop the flow of time and progress that women represent in the timelessness of death.

That the basis of patriarchy, the institution of marriage, is in trouble and that *Witz* is partly to blame for this, is also made clear in the joke book, as marriage turns out to be the favorite target of cynical jokes. But now we find Freud getting rather defensive. The utopian and revolutionary aspect of *carpe diem* that he previously accorded to *Witz*'s cynicism gives way to his concern for the integrity of the social fabric. Though aware that society's attempts to satisfy individual desires, particularly in the sexual sphere, have been less than successful, he is convinced that change can only come slowly, if at all, and that repression will always be a fact of life. The morality of renunciation, once it has been refounded on this pragmatic basis, is affirmed, and therefore the *Witz* that would overthrow it remains tarred with the perjorative epithet 'cynical.'

Freud proposes no detailed reform program of his own, but does cite the work of Christian Ehrenfels in this regard, and would return to Ehrenfels as the basis of his 1908 essay *'Cultural' Sexual Morality and Modern Nervousness.* Ehrenfels's theories put Freud's own in a very interesting light. Ehrenfels believed that the restrictive sexual morality of monogamy, though possibly acceptable for the weaker sex drive of the female, could never prove satisfactory for the male. In the healthy state of nature, men used to have to fight for sexual access to women, providing the 'virile selection' that kept the species strong. The winner would have not just one but many wives. This was the natural state of affairs since one man can get many women pregnant, and the strongest man should beget as many children as possible.[10] On the other hand, the 'cultural' sexual morality of monogamy offers the advantage of social stability since the men aren't constantly fighting over women. Ehrenfels's problem, then, is to recover the vitality of natural selection while maintaining a viable social order.

Ehrenfels is highly critical of attempts, especially on the part of a small faction of the women's movement, to loosen the strictures of monogamy through an ethic of free love, which he feels can only lead to degeneracy. Though he does not completely dismiss the efforts of such reformists, he feels that this woman-led movement should be brought under male control. Procreation must remain the chief pur-

10. A situation somewhat reminiscent of the primal horde in Freud's *Totem and Taboo.*

pose of sex, not pleasure. Ehrenfels thus proposes the establishment of women's collectives, in which the women could assist each other with the duties of tending to the children. Men would be allowed access to these women based on their ability to pay, guaranteeing the reproduction of the economically fittest. The lower classes would have their women's collectives as well, with the only difference being that admission would be cheaper and that these women would be prevented through birth control from having children. The need for such reforms is all the more pressing in Ehrenfels's view because of the competition of the Mongols who are on the verge of outbreeding the Europeans. As for the future, Ehrenfels envisions the merging of these two races in a society with a (mostly Aryan) managerial class and a (mostly Mongol) industrial proletariat.

As ludicrous as this theory may sound, Freud and the jokes he tells share some of its basic assumptions. That marriage is the natural state that all young girls desire (and that their failure to attain it is an appropriate object of ridicule) was made clear early on in the joke book. '"More *Hof* [courting] than *Freiung* [marriage]" said a witty Viennese about a number of pretty girls who have been admired for many years but had never found a husband. "Hof" and "Freiung" are the names of two neighboring squares in the center of Vienna' (36). But what is depicted as the natural destiny of the female is conversely seen as an imposition of the freedom of the male. 'A young man who had hitherto led a gay life abroad paid a call, after a considerable absence, on a friend living here. The latter was surprised to see an *Ehering* [wedding ring] on his visitor's hand. "What?" he exclaimed, "are you married?" "Yes," was the reply, "*Trauring* but true." The joke is an excellent one. The word "Trauring" combines both components: "Ehering" changed into "Trauring" and the sentence "traurig aber wahr" [sad but true]' (21).

Freud's enthusiasm for the joke may indeed betray his own discomfort within the confinements of marriage (Oring 34). But whereas he may have been able to sublimate his sexual energies in his intellectual labors, most men take another way out. 'A wife is like an umbrella—sooner or later one takes a cab' (110). The 'insight' contained within this joke is nothing new. A wife provides inadequate shelter against the storm of sensuality faced by the man, who takes refuge in a public vehicle, that is, a prostitute. For Freud, marriage is so vulnerable to attack because it fails to satisfy 'a man's sexuality' (111); it is this inadequacy which the cynical joke exploits. The undifferentiated pleasure of *carpe diem* has now been made gender specific; it is the pleasure of men that is at stake. In the same passage, Freud praises Ehrenfels's 'love of truth and eagerness for reform.' Yet the reform he proposes with his two types of women's collectives is nothing more than the radicalization of the split between mothers and whores. For Freud, this was apparently no joke.

Religion is naturally the guarantor of the sanctity of marriage, and it was the critique of religion with which we began our discussion of the tendentious joke. The religious critique of the Enlightenment also had an impact on the sphere of sexuality, as we may recall from Schlegel's attempt in *Lucinde* to found a new religion of love and the important role *Witz* played therein. Lichtenberg makes an even more direct connection: 'Eine zweischläfrige Frau—Ein einschläfriger Kirchestuhl' [a woman who sleeps two—a church pew that puts one to sleep] (86). The increasing lack of interest in traditional religion, indicated by the soporific effects of the church, is paired with growing sexual freedom. But the possibility that a woman might use this freedom to take more than one lover, as suggested by the *zweischläfrig* remark, is denounced by Ehrenfels as *Hetärism* (courtesanism) and the jokes Freud chooses that deal with this theme agree, depicting such women as prostitutes. Whereas the demands of male sexuality are taken as an appropriate basis for social critique, signs of such desires on the part of women are met with suspicion (Dreyfus joke), their social implications are ignored (*zurücklegen* joke) and, should the woman actually break the marriage bond like Louise, she becomes the object of fantasies of a fiery death. Freud's acceptance of the idea that the male sex drive is naturally stronger than that of the female makes marriage look like a trap that women spring upon men, just as Ehrenfels described it to be. If the husband in the umbrella joke is dissatisfied with his wife, apparently he has good, scientific reasons for it. Freud also goes along with Ehrenfels in seeing male sexuality as being naturally aggressive, leaving men trapped in the macho domains of the army,

Zotenverkehr and 'virile selection.' Freud was simultaneously working on his *Three Essays on the Theory of Sexuality* and the joke book, and we can see here how deep the connection runs between *Witz*- and *Sexualtheorie* of the time. Freud often seems to recognize the challenge posed in the politicization of sexuality by the women's movement, but is quick to bring the project for reform back under male control, which, as for Ehrenfels, entails the assertion of the primacy of procreation. Gender hierarchy is thereby maintained, women remain divided according to their sexual functions into mothers and whores, and the critique of this order offered by *Witz* is effectively suppressed.

The weak point in this hierarchy is the prostitute, who defies the injunctions of procreation. Innummerable attempts were made to solve the 'problem' of prostitution, but Freud's analysis uncovers why it proved to be so intractable. The threat posed by the prostitute to the social order has a deeper biological basis—that of human, but especially female, sexuality's inherent polymorphous perversity. 'Prostitutes exploit the same polymorphous, that is, infantile, disposition for the purposes of their profession; and, considering the immense number of women who are prostitutes or who must be supposed to have an aptitude for prostitution without becoming engaged in it, it becomes impossible not to recognize that this same disposition to perversions of every kind is a general and fundamental human characteristic [*das allgemein Menschliche*]' (*Three Essays* 191).

Not only the obvious streetwalker but a 'huge number' of other women have a bit of the prostitute within them. The army's suspicions and Ehrenfels's efforts to divide the good girls from the bad ones would thus seem to be justified if one is bent on preserving 'normal' sex for procreation from the seductive wiles of these androgynous perverts, who only recognize the imperatives of bodies and pleasure. Freud blurs these dividing lines with his postulation of an original polymorphous perversity, but then hurries to set them up again, making it clear that in the *Three Essays* his purpose is not to affirm perverse sexuality but to explain our susceptibility to it that we might better keep it under control.[11] This ambiguity is present in the joke book,

11. See Davidson's analysis of Freud's concept of perversity in his article on the *Three Essays,* as well as Freud's later moralistic condemnation of such activities in '"Civilized" Sexual Morality' (vol. 9).

being reflected in *Witz* itself, which is just as often used to speak for the perverse as it is a tool in repressing it.

Freud takes up Heine's attacks on Platen's homosexuality right after his first mention of the umbrella joke (78). The intricacies of Heine's Platen polemic have already been touched on in chapter 2, where I attempted to demonstrate that, despite his best intentions, Heine enters into a sublimated homoerotic, sadomasochistic relationship with Platen through the medium of *Witz*. We also explored Heine's ambiguous position with regard to women. In spite of his reputation as a proponent of healthy sensuality, he seems to have a low opinion of the women who actually make use of it. Freud cites the following remark of Heine's concerning a woman of easy virtue. 'She could *abschlagen* [refuse, urinate] nothing except her own water' (41). This comes interestingly enough right after the Dreyfus and *zurücklegen* jokes. In the first, Freud allows female sexuality to mingle with political issues against the army of reaction. In the next joke he represses any connection with the economic sphere, preferring to keep it on the level of spicy double entendre, and finally concludes with Heine's disparaging remark, which Freud himself acknowledges to be little better than the crudest *Zote*. After being called into question in the first joke, the *Zotenverkehr* of the army takes on a refined form in the second and reappears in all its hostile vulgarity in the third. Not only is promiscuity being assailed in Heine's remark, but, because of the excremental associations, female sexuality is again condemned as perverse. This motif also appears in his polemic against Platen in Hirsch-Hyazinth's 'Venus Urinia' (79), 'a malapropism for "Urania," the heavenly, homosexual love of Plato's symposium' (79). Freud, who has used Heine to lead the attack against religion, now sets him up as a defender of traditional sexual morality against the homosexuals and prostitutes.

That this project has little chance of success is suggested by Freud's own theory of the erotics of *Witz*. According to Freud, tendentious jokes operate on the 'fore-pleasure principle' (137). The relatively innocent pleasures that *Witz* offers through simple wordplay and nonsense are used to put our internal censors off their guard, allowing the critical message concealed within the tendentious joke to be smuggled past them into the public sphere of *Witz*. This temporary overthrow of censorship leads to the release of even greater pleasure. In the *Three Essays,* Freud adapts the principle of fore-pleasure to his sexual theories (210ff.). Fore-pleasure is important insofar as it leads to intercourse, but it can also serve to undermine the primacy of the genital zone. One may easily become fixated on fore-pleasure, lingering there instead of moving on to copulation, a hesitation which leads to any number of perversions. This explains Freud's obsession that jokes must be meaningful, for without a deeper message we remain, as it were, fixated on the fore-pleasure of wordplay. But *Witz*'s susceptibility to perversion has already been demonstrated in the psychodynamics of the *Zote.* Originally designed to prepare the way for sexual intercourse, the *Zotenverkehr* becomes an end in itself.

This turn away from the 'real' sexual object offered by women into the sublimated homoeroticism of the *Zotenverkehr* can be taken a step further to the autoeroticism of masturbation. If 'civilized sexual morality' has made the achievement of sexual satisfaction with another person so difficult, why not abandon the attempt altogether? Karl Kraus's cynical remark seems right on target: 'Copulation is no more than an unsatisfying substitute for masturbation' (*'Civilized' Sexual Morality* 200). Freud is clearly alarmed by this aphorism, which wittily turns the accepted notion of genuine and perverse sexuality on its head. Freud had just condemned masturbation as an act which weakens one's character by making it too easy to attain pleasure, possibly leading to neurosis and psychosis. In the struggle against such degeneracy, which was at the time viewed as a serious social problem, *Witz* seems to have gone over to the side of the perverts.

Freud counterattacks by exploiting *Witz*'s connection to onanism for his own purposes. He recounts a joke common 'in medical circles': 'If one enquires from a youthful patient whether he has ever had anything to do with masturbation, the answer is sure to be "O na, nie" ["Oh no, never"—*Onanie* is the German word for masturbation]' (31). What might have been a joke on the doctor becomes one on the patient as *Witz*'s defense of perversion turns into its betrayal—provided that the doctor knows how to take a joke. That the doctor's question is not an innocent one is clear from Freud's above remarks; masturbation is a problem which the medical men must strive to keep in check for the good of society. The doctors' attempts to get at this problem can be aided by an understanding of the sexual basis of *Witz*, permitting them to drive perversion from its hiding places behind apparently innocent remarks.[12] *Witztheorie* takes its place within the edifice of what Michel Foucault has described as the sexual science/sexual discipline developed in the late nineteenth and early twentieth centuries.

The position of the doctor here is an ambiguous one. At the end of *'Civilized' Sexual Morality,* Freud remarks that while it is not the place of the doctor to make detailed proposals for social reform, he hopes that his work can support that of reformers such as Ehrenfels. Freud is aware of the social implications of his theories, but stops short of thinking them through. He instead abdicates responsibility for their practical implications, turning himself into the stooge of Ehrenfels and his sexist and racist schemes. Yet there is more to Freud than this and the difficulty of his position may be indicated by the following joke. 'A doctor, as he came away from a lady's bedside, said to her husband with a shake of his head: "I don't like her looks." "I've not liked her looks for a long time," the husband hastened to agree' (37). In the 'Civilized Sexual Morality' essay and elsewhere Freud gives excellent and thought-provoking analyses of the suffering women undergo due to the sexual repression demanded by society. But his sensitivity to the plight of women expressed in his scientific work as a doctor all too easily passes over into support for the husband/patriarch. Freud simply shares too many misogynist, pseudoscientific premises with Ehrenfels and other sexual researchers of his day.

But to return now to the parallelism between women and Jews that I have been drawing, we must ask ourselves where the latter fit in this regard. That 'modern nervousness' is not purely the result of sexual problems is hinted at by Freud at the beginning of the essay. 'Occasionally a nervous patient will himself draw the doctor's attention to the part played in the causation of his complaint by the opposition between his constitution and the demands of civilization and will say:

12. We see Jones successfully apply this technique in the *Psychopathology of Everyday Life,* diagnosing a patient's 'masturbation complex' on the basis of a joke he tells (249).

"In our family we've all become neurotic because we wanted to be something better than what, with our origin, we are capable of being"' (182).

Constitution has previously been shown to be a code word for Jewish ancestry in connection with the Karlsbad joke and is here made even more explicit in the problem of the family's 'ancestry' and their attempt to be something they are not. The subtext of this essay on the problems imposed by culture's sexual discipline is the similar problematic of Jewish assimilation (Cuddihy 40). We recall from the two-Jews-on-a-train joke that Jewish ancestry, like sexuality, is something not so easily repressed. Freud's view of this issue in the joke book is once again fraught with ambiguity. While admiring the 'democratic mode of thinking of Jews,' he laments the fact that it tends to disturb 'discipline and co-operation' (112), which was of course exactly the reproach the officer made against Itzig. In the salmon mayonnaise joke, Freud claims that 'it is only the setting that is Jewish, the core belongs to humanity in general [allgemein menschlich].' The core was the idea of *carpe diem,* a hedonistic ethic that seems not unrelated to the previously described *allgemein Menschliches* of the prostitute, polymorphous perversity. Both reassert the right to pleasure and are subjected to social repression. Freud's tendency to wring a universal message out of the Jewish jokes he uses shows his commitment to the project of assimilation, but that this plunge into Gentile culture is not an uncritical one should also be clear. Reforms must be made, but in the end both women and Jews, as the chief victims and critics of modernity and its nervousness, must drop their most radical demands and make their peace with the army of patriarchal/Gentile culture.

The question Freud does not answer is whether this 'army' itself is in the mood for peace. What he systematically fails to deal with are the problems raised to his vision of reform and reconciliation by the irrational hatred expressed in misogyny and anti-Semitism. He acknowledges male aggression towards women in the *Zote,* but is content to leave women in the passive role of silent victim. Jews find themselves in a different, though at times analogous, situation. They too are often the object of hostile *Witz,* as Fuchs documents in his history of the anti-Semitic caricature. This type of humor found a home in the nineteenth century in the popular anti-Semitic *Witzblätter,* the first of which was the Viennese *Kikeriki.* Freud was certainly aware of such jokes, but was able to ignore them through a bit of finesse. The best Jewish jokes, he claims, are those 'created by Jews and directed against Jewish characteristics. The jokes made about Jews by foreigners are for the most part brutal comic stories [*brutale Schwänke*]' (111). Freud relies on the *Witz/Schwank* distinction to exclude openly anti-Semitic jokes from consideration and thus keeps Jews from being placed in the same position as women as the objects of what we have seen to be a highly sexualized form of 'witty' aggression. Anti-Semitism is associated with the anachronistic character of the *Schwank,* a mere leftover from a premodern time that we can only hope will soon whither away. This is clearly whistling in the dark on Freud's part, but it may help to explain his hostility to any form of psychological or cultural regression. A return to the past not only poses the threat of anarchic sexuality, but also of irrational aggression like that found in anti-Semitism. Both must be kept in check by the progressive modernity *Witz* represents.

We may nonetheless doubt the success of his endeavors to repress anti-Semitism by banning it to the realm of the archaic. One might examine, for example, to what extent anti-Semitic clichés have simply been internalized in the allegedly constructively self-critical *Witz* of the Jews. That Jews might indeed succumb to some sort of self-hatred under the pressures of assimilation was remarked upon by the witty Herr N.: 'He heard a gentleman who was himself born a Jew make a spiteful remark about the Jewish character. "Herr Hofrat," he said, "your antesemitism was well-known to me; your antisemitism is new to me"' (33). That Freud himself is not immune to this is shown in his discussion of the 'bath jokes.' 'Two Jews met in the neighborhood of the bath-house. "Have you taken a bath?" asked one of them. "What?" asked the other in return, "is there one missing?" If one laughs at a joke really heartily, one is not in precisely the best mood for investigating its technique. Hence some difficulties arise over making one's way into these analyses' (49). Freud laughs so hard at this rather pathetic joke that his powers of analysis are temporarily lamed, which may explain why he lets this anti-Semitic stereotype pass without comment. Indeed, he seems to share it, speaking of 'the Galician Jews' aversion to baths' as if it were an accepted fact. Since both his parents were Galician Jews, Freud's exaggerated reaction may well be based on his own assimilation anxieties and desire to show that he has left his ancestral past behind by laughing at it.

But other factors as well are at work here. As Zygmunt Bauman has pointed out, tensions between assimilated Viennese Jews and the new Eastern immigrants were also conditioned by class considerations, and it is on this level that Freud would prefer to deal with the problem. In a footnote to the bath joke (51) Freud remarks that the word *nehmen,* to take, because of its many meanings lends itself to such jokes and then goes on to offer the example of the thievish stockmarket speculator which was discussed in the previous chapter. In contrast to the bath joke, Freud describes this as 'ein reines Beispiel' (a pure example). I would suggest that the 'purity' of this joke lies in the fact that the 'dirty Jew' has been replaced as the object of mockery by the squeaky-clean and nondenominational financier. As a matter of fact, the speculator was usually identified as Jewish in the jokes of this time (Fuchs 138), but not so here. Freud has washed away his Jewish character, transforming the religious and racial prejudices of the bath joke (and he is dealing with the joke technique of displacement here) into the issue of class conflict—the alleged rapacity of the capitalist becomes the real dirt.

Freud takes this purification process a step further. Immediately following the footnote we read: 'Let us go back to the "Salmon Mayonnaise," since it is the most pure example [*dem reinsten*].' The poor Jew is here completely cleaned up and rehabilitated, transformed into the figure of the *Schnorrer* whose universally human claims to *carpe diem* lead the assault against religion as the ideology of the rich and powerful. Freud reacts to anti-Semitism the same way the socialists of the time did (see Wistrich)—he ignores it, along with his own occasional indulgence in anti-Semitic stereotype, and would much rather talk about class issues. It was supposed by Socialists of the time that once these issues were satisfactorily resolved, anti-Semitism, the 'socialism of fools' as Bebel called it, would disappear. The poor Eastern Jew was in fact often despised for his backwardness, here represented by his supposedly primitive sense of cleanliness, and receives respect only to the degree that he can be recast as a revolutionary, or at least progressive, subject.

In his analysis of the joke book, Sander Gilman also accuses Freud of harboring latent anti-Semitic tendencies. Gilman places Freud's work within the wider context of the production of Jewish joke books at the turn of the century, showing how they were cleaned up for a Gentile audience by having their racy content toned down and in being purged of, for the Gentile reader at least, unintelligible Yiddish. Freud goes along with this trend, leaving at best only a hint of Yiddish in some of the punchlines of his jokes. Worse still, all these jokes are embedded in a rationalistic discourse, reducing the Jewish character of these jokes to a mere object of scientific investigation. It is spoken about, but never allowed to speak, reminding us of the fate of the woman in the triangle of the *Zote*. 'The Jew in the structural presentation of the "Jewish" joke in Freud's retelling thus becomes the woman and vanishes in the presence of the idealized German self' (267).[13]

This analogy is tempting but not fully accurate. Neither women nor Jews 'vanish' in the joke book, and both, despite attempts to silence them, have much to tell us. But whereas the attempts of women to participate within the economic and political discourse of *Witz* meet with repression on the part of Freud, he is more than willing to draw on Jewish elements here.[14] This is where the parallelism I have been drawing between women and Jews breaks down. Gilman, like Cuddihy and Oring, sees Freud's resolution of Jewish jokes into something *allgemein menschlich* as a repression of his own Jewish heritage. While Freud certainly faced the assimilatory anxieties common to many Jews, to say he was just fighting off the Yid within here (as Cuddihy puts it) is too simple. We must remember that the Jewish tradition extends far beyond the boundaries of the *Shtetl*—the tradition of the Jewish En-

13. Gilman goes on to assert a fundamental similarity between Freud's conception of *Witz* and that of Weininger, in that both allegedly exclude women and Jews from this strictly male discourse. I have argued that, on the contrary, Weininger saw *Witz* as a tool of women and, especially, Jews. I think Gilman has been led astray here through a misunderstanding of the distinction between *Humor* (which only men have) and *Spott* (the tendentious wit of women and Jews).

14. See Estelle Roith, *The Riddle of Freud,* for an interesting discussion of the relationship between the misogyny of Freud's Jewish heritage and his own sexist views of women.

lightenment that Freud draws on must also be reckoned with. What these critics fail to deal with is Freud's argument that Judaism, like all religion, is simply not tenable in the modern world. Leaving the ultimate truth of this proposition aside, I have tried to demonstrate that Freud finds a natural ally in *Witz,* whose modernist drive mocks religion and tends to flatten out ethnic particularities, as well as any other extraneous elements, in order to get as efficiently as possible to the punchline (see my discussion of the progress from *Schwank* to *Witz*). That enlightenment can pass over into genocide has been demonstrated by history, but no such exterminating gestures (at least with regard to the Jews — women are a different matter) are to be found in Freud, who does his best to show the contribution of the Jews to modern society and to put the resultant loss of ethnic identity in as progressive and hopeful a light as possible.

Freud is admittedly a little optimistic here, and the jokes themselves paint a grimmer picture of the consequences of a general loss of religious faith. The *Entzauberung* (demystification) of the world that this entails raises the threat of an existential loss of meaning, best revealed in the element of nonsense (*Unsinn*) that creeps into *Witz.* Recall that in the Itzig joke Freud was able to enlist *Unsinn* to serve a higher rationality; the apparent nonsense was an imitation of and a rebuke to stupidity, representing in fact the voice of social order and common sense. But later in the book Freud acknowledges that such edification is not the primary function of nonsense in jokes and gives two further examples. 'A man at the dinner table who was being handed fish dipped his two hands twice in the mayonnaise and ran them through his hair. When his neighbor looked at him in astonishment, he seemed to notice his mistake and apologized: "I'm so sorry, I thought it was spinach." Or: "Life is like a suspension bridge," said one man. — "Why is that?" asked the other. — "How should I know?" was the reply' (138–39).

What is remarkable about both examples is that they were originally Jewish jokes. Landmann retells the first in the form of a *Schnorrerwitz* (93–94). The apparently senseless behavior of the guest in fact has its roots in Jewish custom. 'Very poor Jews from the East liked to maintain the shine and durability of the curled hair at their temples by rubbing it with sugar water.' The loss of the specifically Jewish character of this joke reflects the general collapse of Jewish traditions, leaving only nonsense behind. Similarly, the insight that life is like a suspension bridge was originally offered by a rabbi. Again, the religious element has disappeared, but the questions as to the meaning of life which religion failed to answer remain.

This vacuum of meaning opens up space for nihilistic pessimism. '"Never to be born would be the best for mortal men." "But," adds the philosophical comment in *Fliegende Blätter*, "this happens to scarcely one person in a hundred thousand"' (57). This joke too has a Jewish version (Schnitzer 119). Coming right after the Itzig joke, Freud uses it as an example of the positive application of *Unsinn*. Such a pessimistic attitude is ridiculed as nonsensical, for the solution it offers is obviously unattainable. But after the critique of religion in the chapter on tendentious jokes, Freud is no longer so sure of his rationalistic optimism. He tells the story of the man who, because of his excessive drinking, is losing his hearing. Upon giving up the bottle he recovers, only to relapse into his old habits with the justification that 'so long as I didn't drink I was able to hear. But nothing I heard was as good as the brandy' (114). Freud places this joke among the 'borderline cases [*Grenzfälle*] of *Witz*' not only for technical reasons, I would suggest, but because it deviates from the ideology of progressive optimism contained in Freud's view of *Witz*. That this is a Jewish joke is recognizable by the hint of 'jargon' within the punchline. Freud himself poses the question, 'May not the man have been right in his choice? It is on account of the allusion made by these pessimistic stories to the manifold and hopeless miseries of the Jews that I must class them with tendentious jokes.' As Landmann has pointed out, Judaism not only served to hold the Jewish community together during the Diaspora, it also helped them to make sense of the sufferings and persecutions they faced. But now, even after the process of assimilation is well under way, persecution and anti-Semitism seem only to increase and the comforts of religion are no longer to be had. A despairing withdrawal from the world like that of the deaf drinker appears to be the only way out.

Freud follows these reflections with the figure of the dying Heine and his *métier* joke in what can be seen as an attempt to demonstrate that it is possible for the assimilated Jew to keep his courage and wit in the face of a meaningless death. Heine is depicted here as a hero of the Jewish Enlightenment, denying God to the very end. But Heine was also the poet who just before his death wrote an ode to morphine which concluded on the following note:

> Gut ist der Schlaf, der Tod ist besser—freilich
> Das beste wäre, nie geboren sein.
>
> Sleep is good, death better—truly
> It would have been best never to have been born.

The dying Heine affirms the pessimism of the *Fliegende Blätter* as well as encouraging the substance abuse of the deaf drinker. Freud shows that he is aware of the fundamental challenge these jokes pose to his hopes for the progressive character of *Witz,* but his attempt to give Heine's life an upbeat ending does not quite convince. The rationality of the Enlightenment has always had difficulty in dealing with intractably irrational forces such as anti-Semitism or the apparent meaninglessness of the universe after the loss of religion, and Freud himself has so far avoided confronting these issues head on. Does he have a more serious answer to the discontents of civilization manifested within these jokes?

The best he can offer is probably to be found in his final formulation of the psychology of *Witz* in his chapter on 'The Motives of Jokes.' The reformist tendencies we have seen him exhibit earlier are here brought to full fruition. Freud closes the chapter with a discussion of *Ersparnis,* the concept with which he began his investigation. But we have come a long way from the *Ersparnis* of the word game, which was simply a matter of saving a few words, or even letters. The exertion of our intellectual faculties in the *Witzarbeit* would hardly be justified if this were the only result. But with his discussion of tendentious jokes, Freud has brought other factors into play. In its subversive activities as the speaker of the unspeakable, *Witz* uses the innocent facade of the word game and its attendant forepleasure to lift, if only for a moment, the barriers of censorship. This relaxation of internal discipline, and the consequent saving of the energy required to maintain it, turns

Ersparnis into *Erleichterung* (relief). The release of pressure is only temporary, of course, for *Witz* does not result in the revolutionary overthrow of the internalized constraints of civilization; it simply makes their burden a little easier to bear.

The triumph of *Ersparnis,* after having been so fundamentally challenged by *Witz* itself, now seems complete. Again we find Freud exploiting the literal meaning of this concept, comparing the psychic economy of the individual to a 'business enterprise' (156). As long as this psychic enterprise is a small one, such as that in the word game, then savings on every word and letter makes sense; the small businessperson must pinch every penny. But in the big business of instinctual economy, where the psychic capital is far greater, the role of what Freud terms the 'administrative cost' (157) declines in the face of the massive turnover and profit. Still, there is always room for localized savings. 'The mind of the manager, if it is inclined to economy, will now turn to economy over details' (157). The avaricious capitalist, previously the object of *Witz*'s hostility, has been transformed into a smart and frugal manager. The anarchistic entrepreneurialism of women and Jews is surrendered for assimilation into what Heine has portrayed as the Catholic religious order of big business. *Witz* becomes just a tool to help the system run more smoothly and efficiently through tactical savings and to act as a safety valve for the release of built-up pressure. Freud goes on to compare the pleasure one has at the savings that *Witz* offers to that felt by the person who has recently replaced their gas lighting with electric; one remembers the difficulties involved in the former system and rejoices in the convenience of modern appliances. This is one way to rebut the nihilistic challenge offered by pessimistic *Witz:* co-opt it with an optimistic ideology of progress driven by the engines of corporately organized big business.

But a second alternative can be discerned as well, for the chapter is also dedicated to 'Jokes as a Social Process.' Freud points out that we do not make jokes for our own amusement, but that they are designed to be shared with others. Expanding the tripartite model of the *Zote,* we find that a teller, an object (either a person or an institution), and a listener are required for all successful jokes. Freud quotes Shakespeare to substantiate his claim that the success of the *Witzarbeit* can only be judged by a third person. 'A jest's prosperity lies in the ear of him that hears it, never in the tongue of him that makes it' (144). The inherent intersubjectivity of the joke becomes essential in the process of *Erleichterung*. One does not laugh at one's own joke because the exertions of the *Witzarbeit* more than balance the savings of the resultant temporary escape from repression. The release of laughter is enjoyed by the third person, who is happy 'that he has bought the pleasure of the joke with very small expenditure on his own part. He might be said to have been presented with it' (148). This 'might be said' blurs a very important distinction here. The idea that the first person does all the work while the listener sits back and enjoys the fruits of the other's toil at a bargain price smacks of exploitation and alienated labor. But if the pleasure of *Witz* is truly a gift, then the calculative rationality of *Ersparnis* seems to have broken down completely. This is all complicated by the fact that the laughter of the third person enables the teller himself to laugh, bringing on a state of 'general relief' (157). Freud would like to depict this as a relationship of mutual exchange in which each party gets something from the deal, but he's at a loss to provide a clear explanation of how the first person, the original joke teller, is able to laugh, falling back on vague notions of the infectious power of laughter or laughter 'par ricochet' (156). The intersubjective psychology of this hilarious process of mutual liberation seems to be beyond the grasp of the utilitarian rationality of economic liberalism. At the moment, we can only surmise what the actual reasons for this phenomenon may be. Perhaps the teller laughs because of the discovery he or she is not alone in the struggle against repression. If such repression is based on the internalization of social norms, then the teller must indeed fear the other as a potential representative of the social order. But should the listener ratify the *Witzarbeit* with laughter, then this restraint is removed and the teller is free to respond in a similar fashion. Society, as represented by the other, has ceased for the moment to be an object of fear. The cultural discipline represented in *Ersparnis* is used to defeat itself and passes over into its opposite, celebratory expenditure in the solidarity of laughter. But let us draw back from such speculations, saving them for the next chapter where I will be able to present more solid evidence of *Witz*'s utopian tendencies. Important for now is simply the realization that the intersubjectivity of *Witz* could offer an alternative both to the corporate community of cogs in the machine as well as the despair and retreat into isolation of the drunkard.

Freud is aware that not all jokes can be told at all times to all people. A certain 'psychical accord' (151) between listener and teller is required for the intersubjective relationship of the joke to be possible in the first place. Both must have the same inhibitions against which the joke can operate. Freud accentuates the restrictive character of this requirement of each joke for a 'public of its own,' pointing out, for example, that the members of one class cannot be expected to appreciate the jokes of another. What he fails to see is that solidarity in the face of repression can also act to overcome such boundaries. Coalitions can be formed to defeat the common enemy, an enemy which Freud describes in very suggestive terms. 'This readiness for inhibition, which I must regard as a real expenditure, analogous to mobilization in military affairs, will at the same moment be recognized as superfluous or too late, and so be discharged *in statu nascendi* by laughter' (151). We are back to the confrontation described in the Dreyfus joke, only now the hostile army is vanquished without firing a shot. I have argued that the similar positions of women and Jews as objects of repression promotes the formation of an alliance against the 'army' of patriarchy and anti-Semitism. *Witz* is the weapon that unites them and laughter is their cry of victory.

But victory does not really come so easily, and more mournful cries are also to be heard.

> The doctor, who had been asked to look after the Baroness at her confinement, pronounced that the moment had not come, and suggested to the Baron that in the meantime they should have a game of cards in the next room. After a while a cry of pain from the Baroness struck the ears of the two men: 'Ah, mon Dieu, que je souffre!' Her husband sprang up, but the doctor signed to him to sit down: 'It's nothing. Let's go on with the game!' A little later there were again sounds from the pregnant woman: 'Mein Gott, mein Gott, what terrible pains!'—'Aren't you going in, Professor?' asked the Baron.—'No, no. It's not time yet.'—At last there came from next door an unmistakable cry of 'Aa-ee,

aa-ee, aa-ee!' The doctor threw down his cards and exclaimed: 'Now it's time.' (81)

As Theodor Reik has shown, this was originally a Jewish joke, with the Baroness's final cry in fact being 'Oy vay iz mir.' The triumphal 'Oho' of the Jew on the train, the joke immediately preceding this one in the Freud, is echoed by the cry of pain of the (Jewish) woman in labor. In both cases the Jew/woman is shown breaking out of the strictures of society, be they expressed in refinement of manners or of language, and revealing a primal level of ethnicity/suffering. The juxtaposition of the cry of triumph in the first joke and the cry of suffering in the second reflects a deeper split in the nature of *Witz*. As in the case of the *Schadchen*—the figure in which the problems of women and Jews come most closely into contact—*Witz* can criticize the system, and indeed bring it to the point of a temporary breakdown, but remains entangled within it, unable to effect radical change and left simply to cry for help.

Help comes in the form of the doctor. It is he who understands the incomprehensible cries of the woman, just as Freud has taught us to hear the deeper meanings of *Witz,* the forbidden criticisms and desires it harbors. As with dreams and hysteria, Freud replaces incomprehension in the face of *Unsinn* with understanding and an attempt at amelioration. Yet the doctor in this joke remains cold and detached from the woman's suffering. Is the purpose of the analyst then to help people with their pain or to help the system keep this pain under control? Freud, I have argued, often seems to tend to the latter alternative, but he was also intelligent enough to recognize the deeper challenge posed by *Witz* and did his best to meet it. That he was unwilling to permit this radical questioning to pass over into the development of radical solutions is clear—for Freud we have reached the limits of *Witz* and now must proceed into the realm of the *Komik*. From the Enlightenment on we have seen that this act of limiting, of determining what counts as a joke and what does not, has always had political implications; Freud is no different. His bourgeois-liberal worldview set certain boundaries for him, beyond which he may have been able to see, but never to go. In the next chapter we shall examine for ourselves what he saw on the other side of *Witz*.

AT WITZ END

Freud concludes his investigation into the nature of *Witz* with a chapter on its relationship to various forms of the comic. He has already outlined in his chapter 'Jokes as a Social Process' (144) the basic differences in interpersonal psychology between *Witz* and *Komik,* which he now expands upon. Whereas *Witz* operates on a tripartite model of joketeller, listener, and butt of the joke, the comic is of a binary nature. Here one laughs at a feature that strikes one as funny in another with no particular need to communicate the source of merriment to a third person. It would be misleading, however, to conceive of the distinction between *Witz* and *Komik* in the purely quantitative terms of one person more or less. Freud in fact tells us that in the case of nontendentious *Witz* the object or butt of the joke may drop out of the picture, leaving just a two-person relationship as in the comic. And, of course, I can as well share my comic observations with others, which may strengthen the comic process, 'but adds nothing new to it' (181). Nonetheless, a definite change has occurred, for we find 'that socially the comic behaves differently from jokes.' As we know, *Witz* is inherently communicative, its jokes are made to be told, thereby establishing a subject-subject relationship. The comic, on the other hand, can dispense with the listener, and so its essence remains defined on the level of subject-object. Put simply, and so perhaps not completely accurately, it is the difference between laughing with and laughing at.

We can already see Freud at work setting up a subtle hierarchy between *Witz* and *Komik.* Though, as Freud admits, the former is usually perceived as a subgenre of the latter, he will reverse this relationship, defining the comic through what we have learned about *Witz.* 'A joke is made, the comic is found.' *Witz* is associated with activity, whereas *Komik* has something irredeemably passive about it.

The source of pleasure in *Witz,* 'one's own thought processes,' shifts in the comic over to 'outside people,' a foreign otherness that is relegated to an inferior position through a laughter tinged with ridicule.

Nonetheless, the comic remains menacingly opaque, daunting, Freud tells us, the best efforts of his predecessors to fully fathom it. He confesses his own trepidations when confronted with the task. The issue has already been raised several times before as Freud has sought to justify his choices of jokes as examples of *Witz* by distinguishing them from the merely comic. I wish to suggest that more is a stake here than the simple question of theoretical tidiness. *Komik* will prove to be the breaking point of the bourgeois subjectivity represented in *Witz* which Freud has been doing his best to support. That the comic is indeed 'socially different' is demonstrated not only in its different psychology but also by the different social groups with which it is associated. The liberal ego seeks to defuse the threat to its own integrity posed by these 'outside persons' by transforming them into objects of ridicule, but is in the end only just able to save itself from being completely overwhelmed.

The first form of the comic which Freud takes under consideration is that of the naive. The naive is in fact not purely comic, but 'a marginal case of the joke' (185). 'The naive (in speech) agrees with jokes as regards wording and content. . . . But the psychical process in the first person, who produces it, which raised so many interesting and puzzling questions for us in regard to jokes, is here completely absent' (185). So even though the naive utterance may sound like a witty remark, what differentiates the two is that the former is made by a person free from the repression that the fascinating and mysterious psychological processes of the *Witzarbeit* must overcome to produce the latter. Recall that this overcoming of repression was the basis of the intersubjectivity of *Witz,* bringing two consciousnesses with the same inhibitions together in a shared experience of liberation. The third person validates the *Witzarbeit* of the first and thus, I have suggested, permits the first person to laugh along in a relationship of intersubjective mutual recognition.

The naive consciousness is something radically different. Because it has no inhibitions, its production of witty remarks is apparently 'without any effort' (185). Indeed, one must use the term *production* rather loosely here, for no work seems actually to be done. 'The complicated technique' with which the subject expresses itself in *Witz* is absent here, leaving a psychological vacuum, a *tabula rasa* as it were. This lack of technical sophistication means that the naive remark is often of low quality when viewed objectively as a joke. Why then are we so prone to laugh at it instead of reacting with indifference or even outrage should it prove to be too provocative? This all depends upon our belief in the genuine naiveté of the speaker. 'Only when this is certain do we laugh instead of being indignant. Thus we take the producing person's psychological state into consideration, put ourselves into it and try to understand it by comparing it with our own. It is these processes of empathy and comparison that result in the economy of expenditure which we discharge by laughing' (186).

This alleged attempt to understand the other is really nothing more than a charade. By labeling them as naive, we disqualify the 'outside person' as an intellectual and moral subject. We are only able to place ourselves 'inside' of the other after having gutted their psyches. Now confronted with such hopelessly primitive psychological conditions, we find the formation of a critical judgment of indignation to be simply superfluous, and so the psychic energy which would have gone into this is released in laughter. The laughter aroused by this comparison (*Vergleich*) has very much to do with feelings of superiority on the part of the 'sophisticated' listener, who finds the naive other literally beneath contempt. This sort of invidious comparison will become symptomatic for the comic as a whole.

Having established the existence of a not-so-subtle hierarchical relationship between *Witz* and *Komik* on the theoretical level of the psychological models which Freud has offered us, let us turn to more practical implications. The inferior status of the comic is seen in its objects, in the types of people who 'produce' it. Since Freud begins with the naive, his first examples all come from children, investing the comic as a whole with an aura of immaturity. Kids may indeed say the darndest things, but Freud makes a rather peculiar Art Linkletter, particularly since he was at the time busy demonstrating in his *Three Essays on the Theory of Sexuality* that children are anything but the naive innocents which adults take them to be. In his 1907 work *On the Sexual Enlightenment of Children,* he tells us that 'the new-born baby brings sexuality with it into the world' (133) and goes on to explain that 'a child's intellectual interest in the riddles of sex, his desire for sexual knowledge, shows itself accordingly at an unexpectedly early age. If it has not been possible to make observations such as I am now going to put before you more frequently, that can either be because parents are either afflicted with blindness in regard to this interest on the part of their children, or, because, if they cannot overlook it, they at once take steps to stifle it' (134).

So who's really being naive here: children, adults, or Freud himself? How can he speak of childish lack of inhibition in the joke book when elsewhere he admits that sexual curiosity is from the very beginning met with repression? He does indeed alert us to the fact that 'we may assume in the child an ignorance that no longer exists; and children often represent themselves as naive, so as to enjoy a liberty that they would not otherwise be granted' (184). But while cautioning against being deceived, he fails to warn us against the possibility of self-deception; that the projection of naiveté by adults onto children more often serves the interests of the former than the latter. Let us have a look at the gems of childish wit that Freud discusses and see how genuine they really are.

> A three-and-a-half-year-old girl gave this warning to her brother: 'I say, don't eat so much of that pudding or you'll get ill and have to have some "Bubizin."' '"Bubizin?"' asked her mother, 'What's that?' 'When I was ill,' answered the child in self-justification, 'I had to have some *Medizin.*' The child thought that what the doctor prescribed was called 'Mädi-zin' when it was for a 'Mädi' [little girl] and concluded that if it was for a 'Bubi' [little boy] it would be called 'Bubi-zin.' (183)

> A brother and sister—a twelve-year-old girl and a ten-year-old boy—were performing a drama composed by themselves before an audience of uncles and aunts. The scene represented a hut by the sea-shore. In the first act the two author-actors, a poor fisherman and his honest wife, are complaining about the hard times

> and their small earnings. The husband decides to cross the wide seas in his boat to seek his fortune elsewhere, and, after tender farewells between the two of them, the curtain falls. The second act takes place a few years later. The fisherman has returned a wealthy man with a big bag of money; and he tells his wife, who awaits his arrival outside the hut, what good fortune he has met with in foreign lands. His wife interrupts him proudly: 'I too have not been idle.' And thereupon she opens the door of the hut and reveals to his eyes twelve large dolls lying asleep on the floor . . . At this point of the drama the actors were interrupted by a storm of laughter from the audience, which they were unable to understand. (183–84)

> A Frenchwoman was engaged as governess for a little girl, but did not meet with her personal approval. Scarcely had the newcomer left the room when the little girl gave voice to loud criticism: 'That a Frenchwoman? She may call herself one because she once lay beside a Frenchman!' This might have been a joke—even a tolerably good one—(double meaning or allusion, with *double entendre*) if the child had had the slightest notion of the possibility of the double meaning. In fact she had merely transferred to the stranger she disliked a facetious way of describing a thing as ungenuine which she had often heard: 'That genuine gold? It may once have lain beside gold.' (184)

It is interesting that in all three cases the allegedly naive person is a young girl. Freud always had difficulties with female sexuality, admitting in the *Three Essays* that his theories were based solely on observing the male of the species, 'for their erotic life alone has become accessible to research. That of women—partly owing to the stunting effect of civilized conditions and partly owing to their conventional secretiveness and insincerity—is still veiled in an impenetrable obscurity' (151). He is nonetheless willing to generalize on his conclusions to cover both genders. Freud tells us that infantile sexuality reaches a high point around the age of four, whereupon it begins to succumb to the repression of the latency period (176–77, 189). The exact age at which the latency period begins is left undetermined, but Freud does assert that 'the development of the inhibitions of sexuality (shame, disgust, pity, etc.) takes place in little girls earlier and in the face of less resistance than in boys' (219). We might even be able to assume that this process had begun in the aforementioned three-and-a-half-year-old girl. In all three of the young women we could reasonably postulate, based of Freud's theories, an interest in sexuality, the repression of this interest, as well as a gender-specific tendency to deceitfulness precisely in these matters. That most adults project naiveté onto their children in order to avoid confronting their nascent sexuality is perhaps understandable, but why does Freud go along with it here when he really should know better?

His motives become clearer when we realize that, though his theories allow for an early childhood interest in sex, these young women are not going about it in the right way. For the early Freud, both boys and girls should be chiefly interested in where babies come from and not in the nature of sexual difference. It is only much later in his 1925 essay *Some Psychological Consequences of the Anatomical Distinction between the Sexes* that he corrects this view and admits that young women especially are interested in just this problem. Indeed, sexual difference is the subject of all three of the above 'naive' remarks. Its appearance in the Bubizin joke is certainly clear enough. In the second case, the young actress is not so much concerned with where the babies came from as in using them to assert her equal status with her make-believe husband. It is this intergender rivalry that I would identify as the true basis of the comic in this remark, a tension which appears again in the third example. Women like the Frenchwoman, who permit themselves to be defined by the gold standard of the male (Frenchman), are here the objects of contemptuous rejection. Thus we are witnesses not only to an early awareness but also a critique of sex roles insofar as the female is in danger of being subordinated to the male. But this is precisely what Freud's theories do. Since female sexuality remains shrouded in impenetrable obscurity, he defines it through that of the male, and so it is logical and expected to hear him surmise that 'the sexuality of little girls is of a wholly masculine character' (*Three Essays* 219). All this will lead to his infamous hypostatization of the phallus. Freud puts all women in the position of the Frenchwoman, typing them as second-class men, and dismisses their protestations of a more fundamental gender difference as simply naive, all in all a fascinating example of how the projective powers of the comic can be used to annihilate the subjectivity of the Other.

Projection is just the beginning of the comic process, which in fact turns on the *Vergleich* (comparison). We have seen above that this comparison is to be made in terms of the expenditure of energy. Confronted with the naive effortlessness of the child, whose supposed innocence renders his or her utterances proof against reproach, the energy of our critical faculties is transformed into laughter. This model works fine on the mental/moral level, but is apparently reversed on the physical. Here childishness loses its effortless character and appears to us as 'extravagant and inexpedient,' as involving too much effort. For example, it strikes us as funny 'when a child who is learning to write follows the movements of his pen with his tongue stuck out; in these associated motions we see an unnecessary expenditure of movement which we should spare ourselves if we were carrying out the same activity' (190). Yet even though the surplus energy now seems to stand on the other side of the equation, I still have the power to laugh at it. Where does the energy for this come from?

Freud identifies within us a *Drang zur Nachahmung* (impulse to imitate), which is aroused as we observe the actions of the other. 'But actually I do not carry the imitation through, any more than I still spell words out even if I learnt to read by spelling' (191). Though I do not actually imitate the other's clumsiness, small amounts of energy do go into innervating the muscles necessary for such an action, energy which is then released as laughter when we realize that the efforts of the other stand all out of proportion to the intended results. This is all dependent upon the ability to sublimate the *Drang zur Nachahmung* from direct physical imitation to the intellectual level where the comic *Vergleich* is made.

Unfortunately not everyone is capable of making this leap. 'If a child or a man of the common people, or a member of certain races, narrates or describes something, it is easy to see that he is not content to make his idea plain to the hearer by the choice of clear words, but that he also represents its subject-matter in his expressive movements:

he combines the mimetic and the visual forms of representation' (192). The social hierarchy of the comic begins to take on more definite shape as women and children are joined by the lower classes and 'certain races' on its bottom rungs. That last category could refer to 'savages' of various exotic realms, but we should also remember that Jews stereotypically gesticulate while they speak. Freud may well have had his unassimilated brethren, the Eastern Jews, in the back of his mind.

On the top of the hierarchy then are those who have overcome mimesis—those who speak without gesture, read without noticing the physical presence of the letters on the page, and write without the aid of their tongues. At stake is the discipline of symbol and abstraction. It is really the old mind-body distinction that is at the heart of the matter and Freud tells us as much. In the comic we laugh at too much physical exertion, but at too little mental/moral effort. 'But this peculiarity, which at first sight confuses our judgement, vanishes when we bear in mind that a restriction of our muscular work and an increase of our intellectual work fit in with the course of our personal development towards a higher level of civilization. By raising our intellectual expenditure we can achieve the same result with a diminished expenditure on our movements. Evidence of this cultural success is provided by our machines' (195).

The discussion of the process of cultural and social rationalization at work in the transition from *Schwank* to *Witz* in chapter 4 showed us what problems Freud had with the *Gleichnis* and its stubbornly nonrational elements—moralizing, tendentiousness, and a rambling lack of closure. Freud used Lassalle to enlist the *Gleichnis* for his faith in scientific progress, which is now extended to the comic *Vergleich* as a whole. Though *Gleichnis* and *Vergleich* are by no means identical, Freud seems to be doing his best to assure that, as soon as comparisons of any sort start being made, the forces of scientific modernism come out on top.

While this sounds fine in theory, the fact is that the laugh is not always on the side of the technocrats, and Freud admits as much. He tells us 'that analogies are capable of a use which brings with it a relief of intellectual work—if, that is to say, one follows the usual practice of comparing what is less known with what is better known or the abstract with the concrete, and by the comparison elucidates what is more unfamiliar and more difficult' (210). Thus the *Gleichnis* can be an aid to intellectualization, but it can also be used by the comic *Vergleich* to reverse the process 'if something serious and unfamiliar, especially if it is of an intellectual or moral nature, is brought into comparison with something commonplace and inferior' (210). The comic here results from the savings of energy demanded in the rigors of abstract thought. The same principle of comparison and analogy which helps sustain the world of abstractions is also capable of breaking it back down into its original concrete elements. In such a case the comic *Vergleich* becomes a process of 'degradation.' When we are confronted with the sublime, Freud claims that we experience an increase in internal tension, 'not very different from what I should adopt if I were to enter the presence of an exalted personality, a monarch, or a prince of science' (200). By removing this oppressive aura of the sublime, the comic undermines as well the authority of both these political and intellectual aristocrats. Two groups, by the way, which Freud had earlier depicted as enemies within the realm of *Witz*, but who now find themselves in the same foxhole in the face of the onslaught of the comic.

Those who before had been passive objects of ridicule now rise up against their oppressors. 'One can make a person comic in order to make him become contemptible, to deprive him of his claim to dignity and authority.' The notion that people can be made fun of in this way would seem to contradict the rule that the comic is found and not made. Some effort certainly goes into the finding, at any rate, bringing new factors into play. 'The discovery that one has it in one's power to make someone else comic opens the way to an undreamt-of yield of comic pleasure and is the origin of a highly developed technique' (189). The naive subject, supposedly a psychic blank with no access to 'the complicated technique' of *Witz*, is replaced by an aggressively comic subject armed with technically sophisticated weaponry. The comic proves to be as Janus-faced as we have found *Witz* itself to be, capable of both supporting and of undermining the social order of things.

This fundamental similarity may help in explaining Freud's difficulties in keeping the two distinguished. This question, which has been haunting him throughout the book, is taken up once again. According to Freud, both *Witz* and *Komik* make use of the technique of 'comparison,' but in *Witz* this lacks the comic element of 'degradation.' He attempts to support this thesis with examples discussed earlier on in the book. Lichtenberg's aphorism—'it is almost impossible to carry the torch of truth through a crowd without singeing someone's beard'—proves to be 'purely in the nature of a joke [*rein witzig*]' (211). Even though the abstraction 'truth' is being brought down to a concrete level, the torch which now embodies it remains possessed of 'a certain distinction [*einer gewissen Vornehmheit*]' which makes it a suitable representative in Freud's eyes. The joke itself could be read as a figurative representation of the theoretical 'truth,' the distinction between *Witz* and *Komik,* of which Freud is attempting to convince us. *Witz* must assert its own individualistic integrity against the leveling tendencies of the comic, burning a path for itself through the 'crowd' of the masses. The comic, of course, lacks all distinction, and Freud has already explicitly identified it with the common folk (182, 192).

The integrity of both the individual and of *Witz* is at issue in the next example, taken from Johann Nepomuk Nestroy's play *Einen Jux will er sich machen.* The shop clerk Weinberl compares his memory to a 'warehouse,' a metaphor that combines *Witz* and *Komik.* The comparison is witty for Freud insofar as it establishes 'a quite unexpected unification' (211) between Weinberl's psychology and his profession, but comic since his mental life is degraded to the commercial level. The distinction between witty 'unification' and comic 'degradation' seems to be simply a matter of emphasis, for both are making basically the same connection between the psychological and the economic. *Witz* cannot easily pretend to be too noble for the latter, for we have already explored the role it plays in the internalization of the economic ethic of *Ersparnis.* Weinberl is a good example of the results, a model of orderliness and efficiency, who is on the verge of becoming a partner in the firm where he works. It is this prospect of success which triggers the warehouse remark, for Weinberl is afraid that the cupboards of his memory are bare. Because he has been so intent on making his career, he has never found the time to get out and really live, and so now fears that he will have nothing worth remembering as he grows older. Thus he decides to go out and have his *Jux*, to be a 'verfluchter Kerl' (confounded fellow) at least for a day before settling down in the sediment of solid citizenry. This witty/comic remark is in fact a critique of his slavish internalization of the business ethic and directly paves the way towards the emancipatory act of the *Jux*—the lark, the spree, the *practical* joke. The purely intellectual moment of liberation that we have identified in *Witz* now passes over into the praxis of the comic. The two work well together here. *Witz*'s ability to critique its own economic foundations, though offering little hope of a radical break with this order, does help open up space for the more radical challenge posed by the comic. The lines between the two are by no means clearly defined, but an intensification of the struggle with repression in the latter is definitely noticeable.

The comic's tendency to burst through the restraints that *Witz* still respects is further demonstrated in a passage Freud quotes from Heine's *Romanzero:* 'till at last all the buttons burst on the breeches of my patience.' It is significant that this is taken from the section 'Hebräische Melodien,' where Heine returns, to a certain extent, to his Jewish roots. The scene leading up to the above verse runs as follows. The poet, who is searching for the etymology of the word *Schlemihl,* has turned for help to the assimilated Jew (H)itzig, who proves rather reluctant to blow his cover:

> Viel Umschweife nahm der Heilige
> Konnte sich nicht recht erinnern,
> Eine Ausflucht nach der andern,
> Immer christlich—bis mir endlich.
>
> The saint made many circumlocutions
> Could not quite remember exactly
> One evasion after the other
> Always Christian—till at last.

The restraint being broken here is that imposed by Jewish assimilation to Gentile society's standards of decorum (see Cuddihy). But Heine's impolite outburst is not without effect. After losing his patience he begins 'gotteslästerlich zu fluchen' (to curse blasphemously), which so unnerves the 'pious Pietist' that he finally retells Schlemihl's story. Schlemihl is the archetypal innocent, passive victim of violence and Heine identifies him as the father of all Jewish poets. If it is true that those who forget history are condemned to repeat it, then in his comic loss of patience Heine, like the neurotic, frees himself of the tyranny of the past by recovering it. By digging back into his Jewish heritage, he simultaneously breaks both with the strictures of Gentile society as well as with the Jewish passivity which he sees as complicitous in its silence. The comic can thus be helpful in the development of a critical ethnic consciousness by battling against the forces that would prefer to simply repress such issues. Freud has shown a willingness to permit *Witz* to take up Jewish elements in this fashion, but only so far as they can be reassimilated back into the 'universally human.' This more intractably ethnic subtext of the 'Hebräische Melodien' remained unexplored by him.

Freud does see a witty side to Heine's 'breeches of patience' metaphor in its allusive power which generates a certain 'pleasure in the obscene.' Why the connection of the higher mental faculty of patience with the obscene is not simply a case of comic degradation is left unclear. He has already remarked (196) that the comic enjoys playing upon uncontrollable physical needs, which seem to be erupting here. The picture becomes even more muddled when we recall that Freud first comes upon Heine's metaphor only after discussing a similar one by Lichtenberg: 'Everyone has his moral backside, which he does not show except in case of need and which he covers as long as possible with the breeches of respectability' (84). Freud clearly identifies this as an example of *Witz*, but if the *Vornehmheit* (nobility) of the comparison is to be the standard as was the case in Lichtenberg's *Fackel* joke, then at the very least we must accuse him of inconsistency.

We are thus faced with the choice of either explaining this contradiction away or explaining why Freud had to be inconsistent here. He is well aware that his arguments are by no means conclusive and constantly bemoans the fact that he has been forced to rely on his subjective feelings in differentiating between *Witz* and *Komik*. Heine's 'pleasure in obscenity' has hopelessly entwined the source of pleasure at the heart of these two forms of humor, and Freud confesses that he is unable to disentangle them. 'However tempting it may be to follow up these more intimate determinants of the yield of comic pleasure, the author must bear in mind that neither his education nor his daily occupation (*Beruf,* profession) justify his extending his enquiries far beyond the sphere of jokes; and he must confess that the topic of comic comparisons makes him particularly aware of his inability' (211–12).

Freud cannot explain the comic because of the challenge it poses to the aforementioned twin poles of his identity—*Beruf* and *Bildung* (an interesting transformation of the *Besitz/Bildung* constellation we have previously dealt with). In Nestroy we witnessed the subversive effect the pleasure offered by the comic can have on one's professional discipline. We see the restraints of *Bildung* under similar assault in Heine, both in terms of social etiquette as well as in regard to which cultural traditions an educated person can be expected to be familiar with. Freud himself finds the prospect of pursuing the pleasure of the comic 'tempting,' but still wishes to cling to the more respectable *Witz,* for if *Witz* collapses into the comic, then an important bastion of his own identity falls with it.

Freud is thus forced to try once again to firm up the distinction between the two, offering us two fresh examples for the purpose. The first comes from Heine's *Harzreise:* 'Speaking generally, the inhabitants of Göttingen are divided into students, professors, philistines and livestock [*Vieh*]' (69). Freud finds his second example in Lipps: "Mit einer Gabel und mit Müh' / zog ihn die Mutter aus der Brüh [With a fork and much effort / his mother dragged him from the stew].' Both use the same technique, 'joking enumeration,' but whereas Heine's list is 'exquisit witzig,' the conjunction of *Gabel* with *Mühe* makes only a comic impression on Freud. What he still fails to give us is a precise definition of the standards involved here; the definition remains purely ostentive. We are left to wonder why Heine's bringing together of professors with livestock is not considered a case of comic degradation and why the nonsensical connection of 'effort' with 'fork' remains comic and not witty. We have, after all, seen cases of witty nonsense.

The basis of the distinction is perhaps to be found in the subject matter of the two jokes. Heine's concerns the old university town of Göttingen, thus placing it for Freud on a different cultural level from that of the mother in her kitchen (recall his discussion of the 'home roulard' joke). A slip on Freud's part reveals his own underlying obsession with questions of hierarchy. His initial citation of Heine (see above) is accurate, but in his second recounting of Heine's joke, he changes the word order to read: 'professors, students, philistines and livestock' (212). By restoring the professors to the top of the list, he leaves no doubt as to the true order of rank. It is precisely this sort of intellectual and social hierarchy that is at stake here in the distinction between *Witz* and *Komik*. The emphatic tone that creeps into Freud's discourse betrays his desperation, made all the greater since the joke he has just unwittingly corrected still calls the legitimacy of such a hierarchy into question. Earlier Freud gave us Heine's sardonic commentary on his own list: 'and these four classes are anything but sharply divided' (69). Whether viewed as an example of *Komik* or *Witz,* the joke turns on its ability to violate these social boundaries.

The pleasures of devolution may help explain the comic of the fork/effort joke. Heine's Göttingen quip demonstrated that every hierarchy contains the seeds of its own destruction, for every attempt at differentiation opens the door to the invidious comparisons of the comic *Vergleich.* Heine's blurring of social/species distinctions provides a natural segue into the undifferentiated 'stew' of mother's melting pot. Freudians in the audience will have already remarked that the description of the mother with the fork dragging the child out of the pot is rather suggestive in its imagery, bringing us back to the matriachal world of phallic women and primordial chaos. Though Freud only cites Lipps here, the joke actually comes from Wilhelm Busch, famous as the creator of *Max und Moritz.* Busch's work often centers on the pranks of bad boys and the horrible punishments that befall them. 'Der hinterlistige Heinrich,' from which the *Gabel/Mühe* verse is taken, is just such a story, which shows how the comic blends anarchy with authoritarianism, both entertaining and terrifying the young.

The hierarchy upon which Heine's joke is playing is of course that of *Bildung,* which we have seen to be an essential constituent of *Witz.* Problems with *Bildung* are touched upon in a second list joke of Heine's that immediately followed his remarks on Göttingen. He speaks of the school he attended where he had to put up with 'so much

Latin, caning and Geography.' In chapter 3 we saw how *Bildung* had gradually in the course of the nineteenth century lost any claim to be intellectually (and socially) challenging and had become simply a matter of rote memorization and brutal discipline. Stefan Zweig attests in his autobiography to a similar state of affairs in turn-of-the-century Vienna (46ff.). Heine is aware of the politically repressive forces driving this development. In *Deutschland, Ein Wintermärchen,* he gives us the following description of a group of Prussian soldiers:

> Sie stelzen noch immer so steif herum,
> So kerzengrade geschniegelt,
> Als hätten sie verschluckt den Stock,
> Womit man sie einst geprügelt.
>
> They still strut so stiffly about,
> So upright and trim,
> As if they had swallowed the cane
> With which they were once beaten. (Heine 1:435)

Freud briefly discusses the educational practices of the day in the joke book, but makes no mention of corporal punishment and its political ramifications. The internalization of discipline which Heine has so vividly described becomes for Freud a purely intellectual process designed to lead the young from infantile nonsense to adult rationality. This is, of course, not accomplished without a fight, and even after its successful completion Freud recognizes that it still meets with sporadic resistance. Older students and professors turn to alcohol to recover a bit of the intellectual freedom they have lost—hardly making them stable pillars in the edifice of *Bildung*. Young boys (the girls apparently remain passive) often evince a tendency 'to do absurd or silly things' (126), showing just how tough the infantile 'pleasure in nonsense' can be to get rid of. 'In pathological cases we often see this tendency so far intensified that once more it dominates the schoolboy's talk and answers. I have been able to convince myself in the case of a few boys of secondary school age who had developed neuroses that the unconscious workings of their pleasure in the nonsense they produced played no less a part in their inefficiency than did their real ignorance' (126).

Neurosis and nonsense can be strategies, if for the most part self-defeating ones, used to fight back against the system. Freud has shown little patience for nonsense and his determination to use psychiatry to help neurotic people back to 'normalcy' puts him again in a highly questionable position. His recognition and support of the disciplinary nature of *Bildung* gives him another incentive to suppress the *Komik,* which he has already discovered 'beim ungebildeten Erwachsenen' (uneducated adults; 182) and whose roots in the infantile pose a serious threat to the stability of the social order. If in the process Heine's critique of this order has to be abandoned and his words rearranged to suit the purpose, then so be it.

The schoolroom is not the only place where children are subjected to social discipline—even the playground offers no real refuge, as children's games also become tools in the hands of the forces of civilization. Relying on the work of Karl Groos (121), Freud claims that the principle of 'recognition' lies at the root of most of these games. Since the recognition of something familiar is intellectually easier to deal with than the confrontation with something completely new, by artificially bringing this about the children experience a pleasurable relaxation of psychic tension while they play. This pleasure of recognition is most often evoked by children through repetition. For example, while learning to speak, children will repeat the words of their elders, not so much with regard to their meaning, but depending upon similarities of rhythm or rhyme. This simple game is not long tolerated by the adults, who gradually begin to insist that the child use the vocabulary that has been learned through play in a sensible fashion (125). *Witz* is developed in the attempt to recover this lost pleasure while still passing the muster of the internalized censorship of reason. Play is thus the 'first stage of *Witz*' (128), turning *Witz* into 'developed play' (179).

For the moment this does little to resolve the question at hand, the differentiation between *Witz* and *Komik,* because, following Bergson (222–23), Freud traces the comic as well back to children's games, specifically the comic of mimicry. It is this form of repetition that Freud sees as the driving force behind most children's games (227). The objects which the child chooses to copy are naturally enough the grown-ups, and so this drive can be seen as useful to the child's own maturation. Their games help children appropriate the norms of the adult world which they will need later on in life. This is all in line with the developmental process which we saw in the case of *Witz.* But whereas *Witz* offers us only a faint echo of earlier childhood spontaneity, the pleasure of the comic goes much further. The playful imitations of children not only bring them closer to the adult world, but can also be seen as attempts to get the adults to loosen up a little. 'There is little that gives children greater pleasure than when a grown-up lets himself down to their level, renounces his oppressive superiority and plays with them as an equal. This relief, which gives the child pure pleasure, becomes in adults, in the form of degradation, a means of making things comic and a source of comic pleasure' (227). Imitation then can be an invitation to the adults to play along — an invitation to imitate their childish imitators. The adults, in becoming complicitous in their own 'degradation,' release their own long repressed *Drang zur Nachahmung* and thereby bring childish playfulness and the physicality of mimesis back into their own lives. Here we can see an important difference between *Witz* and *Komik,* for whereas the former remains restricted to the intellectual level, the latter opens up possibilities of direct physical expression.

Like *Witz,* however, the comic tries to beat society with its own logic. Social discipline is based on recognition and repetition, the basic elements of the game. Groos tell us that 'recognition is always, unless it is too much mechanized . . . linked with feelings of pleasure' (121). That this pleasure is indeed soon lost in the discipline of civilization is recognized by Bergson, who sees the modern world in the throes of what he calls the 'mécanisation de la vie' (209). Freud likes Bergson's formulation, but fails to go into its socially critical implications, seeing it as just another comic technique.[1] Little wonder, I suppose, since he

1. In chapter 3 I discussed Bergson's view that laughter functioned as a means of keeping deviants in line through the dicipline of ridicule. But he also credits it with the power of saving people from a fate of mechanized uniformity and preserving their organic individuality. 'The comic is that side of a person which reveals his likeness to a thing, that aspect of human events which, through its peculiar inelasticity, conveys the impression of pure mechanism, of automatism, of movement without life. Consequently it expresses an individual or collective imperfection which

previously went to such trouble to enlist the comic for the cause of mechanistic modernism. The comic's affinity for these trends permits it to turn the repetitiveness of the mechanized world back against itself through mimicry. Parodied uniformity serves to remind us that life is not supposed to be like that, that its multiplicity and spontaneity have somehow gotten lost. These vital forces protest against the order that oppresses them by pretending to conform to it. The targets of this form of the comic include 'professional habits' (*Gewohnheiten*) (209) — and we have already seen Freud remark that his profession kept him from understanding the sources of comic pleasure. We can now identify two distinct, if also intertwined, ones: the pleasure of laughing at someone considered to be inferior in the social/cultural hierarchy, but also the pleasure in expressing the forbidden desire to return to (or drag someone else down to) just such a 'lower' state of existence. In the latter case, the comic of mimicry and degradation is not directed so much at external authority figures as at the internalized discipline they represent. Both techniques could be important tools in a psychotherapy which sought to free people from repression and not just teach them how to accommodate themselves to it.

To what extent the comic can break with the forces of social discipline is demonstrated by the set of examples Freud takes from Julius Stettenheim and his character Wippchen. Wippchen is a would-be war correspondent, who in fact never goes near the front, and so, in order to write his reports, falls back on the powers of his imagination. This suits him just fine, for as we learn from his account of his childhood, which Freud draws upon for many of his examples, he is in fact a frustrated poet. 'While I was still young, Pegasus stirred within me.' Freud explains: 'If we put back "the poet" instead of "Pegasus" we find an autobiographical cliché well-worn by frequent use. It is true that "Pegasus" is not a suitable substitute for "the poet," but it has a conceptual relation to it and is a high-sounding word' (214).

Stettenheim constantly gives such new twists to the hackneyed chronicle of the Pegasus as a young man. While Wippchen's mother is

calls for an immediate corrective. This corrective is laughter, a social gesture that singles out and represses a special kind of absentmindedness in men and in events' (117).

supportive, his father is opposed to his son's literary ambitions, and so does his best 'mir Papier und Tinte höher zu hängen [to hang paper and ink higher for me]' (213). (The standard figure of speech used when one person places obstacles in the way of another is 'einem den Brotkorb höher hängen [to hang his breadbasket higher]'). His teachers are hostile as well and show him little compassion. 'Thus I lived through the thorny shoes of childhood.'

All three examples are based on clichéd expressions which Stettenheim has freshened up with the addition of new elements. The joke techniques he most frequently makes use of are amalgamation and modification—yet his creations are not *Witze* but mere 'joke-like productions' (215). They remain nonsensical, lacking the deeper punch necessary for true *Witz*. As we saw in Freud's discussion of tendentious jokes, *Witz*'s depth is based on its expression of repressed drives. Wippchen's jokes have no basis in the unconscious, this reservoir of forbidden meaning, and so are simply comic and can at best appeal to the preconscious level. Freud has previously identified this psychological distinction as the chief difference between *Witz* and *Komik* (208).

This hypothesis strikes me as particularly dubious when made with regard to Wippchen. Putting a fictional character on the couch is always a problematic undertaking, but in this case not without interest. For Freud, the unconscious is the product of repression, and Wippchen certainly seems to have experienced enough of this in his childhood. Furthermore, we have evidence in his biography, upon which Freud is drawing, of an Oedipal situation in his account of his loving mother and tyrannical father. The struggle with his father is projected onto his later editor, as Wippchen must subordinate his creative drives to the exigencies of earning a living. Wippchen's productions are thus both a compromise with the patriarchal Logos of banality and subversive of it in his imaginative additions to its stock of clichés. So if the psychological preconditions for *Witz* are all in place, what then is the deeper message that Wippchen is trying to get across to us?

Here is the first Wippchenism that Freud relates: 'Turkey has money like hay by the sea.' This is an amalgamation of the expressions 'money like hay' and 'money like sand by the sea.' Why then does he not simply use one of these accepted figures of speech to describe the financial state of the Turks? What Wippchen has added here is the element of absurdity, which is important in the context of his overall report. Turkey has just lost a battleship but, because of its allegedly fabulous wealth, will have no trouble replacing it. Money, machines, and, incidentally, lives are all just so much hay to be washed away in the senseless ebb and flow of the war. 'For hours the battle went back and forth until at last it remained undecided.' Stettenheim's nonsense, as tendentious as *Witz* ever was, is the perfect tool for lampooning the meaningless waste of war.

In contrast to witty tendentiousness, however, Stettenheim's humor does not take the side of any one party but, like his fictional correspondent, remains well away from the fray and so is able to offer a metacritique of the institution of war itself. Wippchen, over the protests of his sensation-hungry editor, is constantly trying to declare peace and go home. These pacifist tendencies should make us aware of the utopian moment contained within his imagery. His fantastic and wildly improbable accounts of the war are not simply mimetic reproductions of the bloody orgy of battle, but the mockery of such reports. Freud describes Stettenheim's style as relying upon a 'fast überreichlich quellende Komische der Rede [almost overabundantly flowing comic of speech]' (212). This is a long way from *Witz*'s austere ethic of *Ersparnis* and may help explain why Freud refuses to see any deeper meaning behind Wippchen's remarks. Their playful richness makes a mockery of *Witz*'s psychic stinginess and calls into question the demand for repression it represents. There is a point at which frugality devalues itself through its own success. Too much stockpiled wealth is indeed as valuable as mere hay if it is never spent. One is reminded of Max Weber's *Protestant Ethic and the Spirit of Capitalism* (published, like the joke book, in 1905), where the thrifty and industrious are depicted as creating a state of wealth that they must forbid themselves from enjoying. War is one way to dispose of these seductive surpluses, a wild release of pent-up tensions that nonetheless takes place within the framework of martial law. Wippchen, the unabashed pacifist and hedonist, offers us another way out.

In 'The Economics of *Witz*,' above, I argued that Freud's concept of psychic economy was shaped not only by strictly psychological considerations, but that materially economic as well as cultural factors come into play. This latter component comes to the fore in Freud's comparison of Wippchen to Gustav Freytag's character Schmock, 'one of those uneducated people who misuse and trade away the nation's store of culture [*Bildungsschatz*]' (212). *Witz*'s efforts, as one of the guardians of *Bildung*, to preserve cultural capital are allegedly being undermined by comic figures like Wippchen, who grind up the pearls of Western culture into the journalistic slop they serve to the masses. Journalists of the time did indeed frequently try to give themselves an air of authority through learned references, especially by citing classical literature (Senoner 192). Impressive as they may have appeared, such references were more often than not used incorrectly, empty of meaning and served more to obscure than to elucidate the matter at hand. Freud recognizes that Wippchen was originally intended as a satire on this sort of journalism, but claims this praiseworthy intention has gone astray in a swamp of 'all kinds of insipidities' (213). The 'comic nonsense' upon which Wippchen relies renders his productions just as empty of meaning as the journalistic bombast that he is trying to parody.

Yet here again Freud misses the deeper level of critique that Stettenheim/Wippchen has to offer us. We have already encountered the crisis that *Bildung* in general was going through at the time. Having been left to stagnate in the prison of various cultural institutions (schools, museums, and so on), it was badly in need of revitalization. Wippchen experiences this situation directly. Having been forced to abandon his artistic aspirations in order to earn a living, he voices the following lament. 'I am no more than a column stripped of its leaves [entlaubte Säule], which bears witness to vanished glory.' The antique column, symbol of Western civilization, has become *entlaubt*, has lost its bloom and is on the verge of dying. What is the cause of this? James Strachey gives us a clue in his translation of the joke book, pointing out that *entlaubte Säule* resonates with *entleibte Seele*, a disembodied spirit. Freud has previously described the process of civilization as one of the replacement of physical effort by the powers of the intellect, and here we have the end result, a falling out of touch with the body. The comic, which had directed its scorn against those who lagged behind in this process, now comes to regret it. The implication is that culture will blossom once again only when the mind/body hierarchy has been overcome. We should also recall that this hierarchy is paradigmatic of many others; especially relevant here is that between intellectual elite and uncultured masses. Stettenheim both satirizes a journalism that seeks to exploit the hierarchical, authoritarian status of culture, turning *Bildung* into bombast, while at the same time providing an alternative model of how these traditions could be more playfully and productively appropriated.

The desolate state of culture in the *entlaubte Säule* remark brings us to the following question. 'Where is the thread of Ariadne which will lead me from the Scylla of this Augean stable?' Admittedly quite a mythological mishmash, but by no means as incomprehensible as Freud would have us believe, particularly given the context provided by our discussion of the previous two Wippchenisms. The cleaning of the Augean stables was of course one of the labors that Hercules was forced to perform. Scylla was the monster that ate seven of Odysseus's sailors, a loss that he was forced to accept in order to avoid complete destruction in the whirlpool of Charybdis. Thus we could say that Wippchen is trying to escape from a world of forced labor and necessary sacrifice.[2] Ariadne, who rescued one classical hero, is presented as a potential savior for us all. She has already made an oblique but telling appearance in the joke book. In Freud's discussion of *carpe diem* he cites the line "di doman" non c'è certezza [there is no certainty about tomorrow]' (109), taken from Lorenzo de' Medici's *Il Trionfo di Bacco e di Arianna*. Ariadne, as the companion of Bacchus, whose triumph puts an end to all want and suffering, would be the perfect one to lead us out of the 'Scylla of this Augean stable,' otherwise known as the iron cage of modernity (see Weber).

Part of the pleasure offered by both *Witz* and *Komik* would thus seem to involve a certain degree of utopianism. Freud gives us a hint of just how essential it is in a footnote regarding the physiology of laughter. Laughter characteristically involves the muscular action of the smile. 'So far as I know, the grimace characteristic of smiling, which

2. See Horkheimer/Adorno's reading of the Odysseus myth in their *Dialectic of Enlightenment* (New York, 1972).

twists up the corners of the mouth, appears first in an infant at the breast when it is satisfied and satiated and lets go of the breast as it falls asleep. Here it is a genuine expression of the emotions, for it corresponds to a decision to take no more nourishment, and represents as it were an "enough" or rather a "more than enough"' (146–47).

The 'thread of Ariadne' would thereby be transformed into an umbilical cord leading us back to the infantile paradise of enough and more than enough. Before condemning this as a hopelessly regressive desire to return to the womb, we should recall the context of the two Wippchenisms which preceded this one. Not just Turkey, but all the countries of pre-1914 Europe seemed to have had more than enough money when it came to building the weapons of war. On the other hand, culture is left to whither and the great majority lead lives of misery and poverty. Stettenheim makes the 'thread of Ariadne' remark in attempting to sort through the complex causes of the Russo-Turkish War. The cutting of this thread is later used as a metaphor for lives cut short in battle, and could thus be seen as a vitalistic principle striving to find a way out of the militaristic nightmare that had descended over Europe.

That a woman is depicted as the savior of civilization reminds us of the feminine character that opposition to the army took in the Dreyfus joke. The comic here not only mobilizes the oppositional potential of femininity, but also draws upon infantile memories of utopia in order to further its political ends. This gives the comic a basis in the unconscious (previously denied by Freud), which is the object of fierce repression by a society committed to an ideology of scarcity and the necessity of hard labor and constant individual sacrifice. As is well known, Freud, like Odysseus, also accepts the necessity of sacrifice for the good of the whole. But unlike his classical forbear, he does not even pause to listen to the siren song of Wippchen, drowning it out with protestations that it's all just a lot of nonsense and clinging tightly all the while to the mast of the *Witz/Komik* hierarchy—a position which his own discoveries had hopelessly undermined.

The utopianism latent in Wippchen's remarks is not simply a matter of principle, but reflects a shift from the entrepreneurial bourgeois individualism we have previously seen expressed in *Witz* to a different economic ethos. By the end of the nineteenth century we find ourselves confronting a nascent mass-market consumerism, which, as Lawrence Birken demonstrates in his book *Consuming Desire,* had an impact on more than just people's shopping habits. The 'emergence of a culture of abundance' between 1871 and 1914 was intertwined with the development of the science of sexuality, and so with Freud's own work.

> How far ideology had shifted in the last quarter of the nineteenth century is well illustrated by a comparison of Marx's productivist and Freud's quasi-consumerist philosophy. If Marx exemplified the importance of production in the classical epoch by his vision of work as an end in itself, Freud exemplified the shift toward consumption by his conception of production as a necessary means toward the ultimate goal of consumption. For Marx, work was a positive force that was both objective and creative. For Freud, in contrast, work was merely a negative deferral of play. In this sense, the reality principle was not a production principle but a substitute for a production principle. Still, Freud did not completely embrace this consumerist complex of values. Again and again he reasserted the importance if not the primacy of work, linking (like the marginalist economists) the ability to defer pleasure to the development of civilization. Freud had a negative definition of work, but it was still a definition. If Marx stood at the end of the productivist, Freud stood at the beginning of the consumerist tradition. (121–22)

I think we have to be careful about ascribing an overly negative concept of work to Freud, particularly given its emancipatory character in the 'working-through' of neuroses as well as the creative and playful forms it can take in the *Traum-* and *Witzarbeit.* Still, the basic insight that Freud was caught between productivist and consumerist values seems correct and helps explain some of the dynamics of his confrontation with Wippchen. The superficial rejection of this type of humor cannot conceal the fact that the economic subtext of his own theories was leading him inexorably into Wippchen's whirlpool.

The shift from *Witz* to *Komik* can thus be seen as part of a broader historical transition from bourgeois to mass public sphere. In Habermas's terms, we move 'from a public that reasons about culture to one that consumes it' (193). The comic, insofar as it is found and not made, proves ideal for this new breed of consumer. The subversive potential of the comic goes hand in hand with the danger that the utopia of the mother's breast may simply prove to be a mask for the friendly fascism of the culture industry. The infantile roots upon which the comic bases its oppositional stance are also capable of being co-opted by a social order that rests on the passivity, the *Entmündigung,* of its members. Freud's attempt to cling to the critical subjectivity of *Witz* in the face of the prospect of its dissolution, though perhaps romantic, is certainly not unambiguously reactionary.

Despite his laudable intentions, however, I believe he is confronting us with a false dilemma. I have tried to demonstrate that the attempt to draw a fundamental distinction between *Witz* and *Komik* is untenable. Rather, we can see the latter developing naturally out of the former as cultural conditions change. The situation parallels *Witz*'s own relationship to the older *Schwank,* with no obvious point at which a decisive break between the two was effected. Both *Witz* and *Komik* can be mobilized by reactionary forces; there is nothing ontologically superior to the form of subjectivity of *Witz* as compared to that of the *Komik.* The latter's tendency to degenerate into mindless name-calling is balanced by the potential militancy of its critique of power structures and the utopian prospects it unveils by breaking with the discipline of 'making sense.' Like *Witz, Komik* can open up many new 'senses.' Critical reflection on the part of both joketeller and listener remains the key element, and Freud's theories can certainly make a contribution to this.

We have also seen how close Freud unwittingly came to the anti-Semites and misogynists of his day because of his failure to reflect on the political implications of some of his jokes. His culturally conservative hostility to the new mass public leads him into similarly compromising positions. The dominant form of mass media at that time was undoubtedly the daily newspapers and Stettenheim/Wippchen's comic essays were written for dissemination through the press. Freud has described Wippchen as a modification of Freytag's Schmock, taken from his play *Die Journalisten* (1853). *Schmock* would live on through the turn of the century as a term of abuse for less-than-ethical journalists—who, in the popular mind, constituted the majority of the profession. Freytag portrays Schmock as having no opinions of his own, but simply out to sell his pen to the highest bidder. Though not explicitly identified as such, Schmock's idiomatic syntax is designed to make it clear that he is a Jew. Jews were indeed heavily represented in the journalistic profession, a fact used by anti-Semites to propagate the myth of a Jewish conspiracy which allegedly dominated the mass media (Häusler, in Drabek 105). Far from combatting this cliché, Freud contributes to it. His characterization of Schmock as 'one of those uneducated people who misuse and trade away the nation's store of culture' (212) takes on a much more sinister meaning when viewed in this light. Though certainly not his intention, Freud leaves one with the image of the venal Jewish journalist, parasitically squandering the cultural capital earned by the sweat of various Aryan intellectual brows. The word *Schmock* itself came from Prague ghetto slang and meant 'Narr' or 'Spaßvogel' (fool or buffoon; Senoner 29). As in Weininger, we see Jewish humor portrayed as undermining Christian culture. By bringing Wippchen into association with Schmock, Freud puts himself into dangerous proximity with the anti-Semitic critique of the mass public sphere as outlined above.

As we learned in the previous chapter, when Jewish issues are raised, the woman question cannot be far behind. The object of Freud's scorn this time is Friederike Kempner, a minor poet who is today only remembered for the storm of ridicule her works aroused. Freud takes her as an example of 'involuntary comic of speech' (216). According to Freud, her demand to be taken seriously as a poet is so completely undermined by the miserable quality of her work that all we can do is laugh; her writings are simply beneath all critique and contempt. It is not my goal here to try to rehabilitate her literary reputation, but I would point out that there are in any age always more than enough bad poets to go around and so one might suspect that the singling out of Kempner for particular abuse had something to do with the fact that she was a woman. Moreover, many of her poems are not about safely 'timeless' things like truth and beauty, but are concerned with more topical issues. Freud's defensiveness against women's 'topicality,' which we previously witnessed, again rises to the surface. Though crediting her with good intentions, he rails against 'the quite extraordinary clumsiness of their expression, which is linked with the tritest or most journalistic turns of phrase' (216). The parallelism between women and Jews that runs throughout the joke book again crops up as they are both associated with the corrupting power of journalism, which is now creeping into the previously sacrosanct realm of poetry. But this female Schmock has her sights set on more than just cultural capital:

'Wie glücklich bin ich,' ruft sie leise,
'Auch ich,' sagt lauter ihr Gemahl,
'Es macht mich deine Art und Weise
Sehr stolz auf meine gute Wahl.'

'How fortunate am I!' she softly cried.
'I too,' declared her husband's louder voice:
'Your many qualities fill me with pride
At having made so excellent a choice.'

This is just an excerpt from a longer poem, 'Der Kontrast.' The couple in question is getting ready to go to a ball. On the way they meet a beggar, but though the husband's pockets are full of money and his wife is laden with costly jewelry, he gives nothing. Male sexual egocentricity, which has turned the wife here into just a chance to engage in a little conspicuous consumption, thus plays out into economic stinginess when confronted by the poor beggar. Kempner is no revolutionary, but her work does show some sensitivity for the plight of women, the lower classes, and even of animals as another of her poems which Freud cites attests:

GEGEN DIE VIVISEKTION
Ein unbekanntes Band der Seelen kettet
Den Menschen an das arme Tier.
Das Tier hat einen Willen—ergo Seele—
Wenn auch 'ne kleinere als wir.

Between mankind and poor dumb beasts there stretches
A chain of souls impossible to see.
Animals have a will — ergo a soul too —
Even if a smaller one than we.

Her stylistic vulgarity is thus in sync with the overall challenge she poses to the patriarchal social order — the 'Herren der Schöpfung' (lords of creation) are reminded of their links to the 'lower' species. The comic effect of her poems could thus be seen as a product of the degrading effect it has on their objects, in both cases 'man.' Freud, however, prefers to redirect the comic against the poet herself and the leveling tendencies she represents. Her journalistic style links her both with the mass public sphere as well as a social agenda centering around issues that Freud seems hostile to.

Journalists make one other significant appearance early on in the book in Freud's discussion of condensation. 'Karl Kraus was responsible for another condensation with slight modification. He wrote of a certain yellow-press journalist that had travelled to one of the Balkan states by "Orienterpresszug." There is no doubt that this word combines two others: "Orientexpresszug" [Orient Express] and "Erpressung" [blackmail]' (27).

Karl Kraus was not only an important early critic of the effects of mass media; he was also one of the wittiest men who ever lived. This makes him an ideal case study in examining *Witz*'s place within the public sphere at the turn of the century. His work is therefore certainly deserving of lengthy analysis, even though Freud only mentions him twice. Yet the examples he chooses are both highly suggestive and illuminating. With regard to the one cited above, it raises the issue of blackmail, which was central to Kraus's critique of journalism. He devotes an entire essay to the subject, in which he half-jokingly raises the possibility of an etymological connection between *Erpressung* and *Presse* (the press; *Sittlichkeit* 58). Though probably not substantiated by *Grimm's Dictionary*, this link was borne out by the actual situation. It was common practice for smaller newspapers to raise money by blackmailing firms with the threat of publishing embarrassing articles about them if they did not pay up. Payment was usually made under the guise of *Pauschalien,* a lump sum given to the paper simply for the 'privilege' of advertising there (Pfabigan 65).

The type of blackmail that Kraus was most concerned to combat, however, was not so much commercial as sexual in nature. In his article 'Die Kinderfreunde' Kraus argues that the criminalization of deviant sexual behavior only serves to encourage blackmail through threats of denunciation. This tendency is fostered by a sensationalist press hungry for just such juicy scandals and more than ready to contribute to a mood of moral hysteria in order to sell papers. As an example of this, Kraus quotes Moritz Benedikt, the editor of the *Neue Freie Presse,* suggesting that homosexuals be castrated. After subjecting this idea to all the contempt it deserves, Kraus backs up his witty assault with a professional authority, invoking the name of 'Professor Sigmund Freud' to bolster his plea for the decriminalization of homosexuality (184).

Kraus's respect for Freud did not go unreciprocated. In fact, Michael Worbs describes Freud as 'the wooing partner' in this 'short-lived coalition' (151). Freud had written to Kraus in 1904 in praise of his account of the Hervay trial, another vice case in which a sensationalist press had played a less than constructive role. Freud would go on to make favorable mention of Kraus in the joke book and attempt to enlist his publicistic help in the Fließ-Weininger affair.[3] In 1906 he sent Kraus a letter with the following passage: 'I had naturally already read about the "Riehl" trial in the *Fackel.* Some parts are really "screamingly beautiful." People will once again praise your style and admire your wit, but they will not be ashamed of themselves, which is what *you* actually wanted to achieve. There are just too many of them and they feel too confident in their solidarity. We few should therefore stick together as well' (Worbs 158).

The Riehl case revolved around the exploitation of prostitutes by a bordello owner, who used blackmail to quash any resistance on their

3. This controversy revolved around Fließ's accusation that Weininger had plagiarized his theory concerning the basic bisexuality of human beings. Weininger apparently heard of these ideas through a patient of Freud's. Freud admitted using Fließ's ideas in his therapy, but his attempt to trivialize the matter, claiming that the idea of bisexuality had been around since Plato, failed to placate the enraged Fließ, who then broke with Freud.

part. Much greater issues are at stake, however, for the blackmailer is supported by a whole social system. 'The wheat of usurious blackmail grows when state and society exile sexual intercourse to the dark realm of disreputable concealment' (*Sittlichkeit* 234). Because prostitution was nominally illegal but hypocritically tolerated, the bordello owner, Riehl, working together with a corrupt and complicitous police force, could use the threat of denunciation to keep her restive 'work force' in line. The press managed to expose this one abuse, less, Kraus thinks, out of a sense of its role as social 'watchdog' than in the hopes of reaping profits from the extra newspaper sales generated by the whole affair. Whatever good might have come from the exposé is undercut because all is done in the name of the repressive morality that only serves to keep this rotten system as a whole running. It seems that Kraus stands alone in opposing his polemic *Witz* against these institutions (press, police, sexual mores) of 'state and society.'

In the above letter Freud shows his admiration for Kraus but doubts that he will meet with very much success. Though *Witz* may still have some entertainment value, Freud depicts it as having lost its normative effect in the mass public sphere. As we have seen, this realm was for him dominated by the 'comic of speech' of the journalists, whose 'joke-like productions' lacked the deeper seriousness of true *Witz*. Its moral force, the ability to provoke shame, has disappeared. Freud's pessimism may indeed have struck a responsive chord within Kraus himself. Kraus was constantly questioning the viability of his own publicistic enterprise and was moving away from the engaged muckraking journalism of the early *Fackel* to the elitist language mysticism that would characterize his work in the years preceding the outbreak of World War I.

A key text reflecting Kraus's development in this regard is his 1910 essay 'Heine und die Folgen' (Heine and the consequences). Here he tries to make Heine responsible for the 'impressionistic journalism' (*Untergang* 186) of the feuilleton. The rampant subjectivism of this sort of writing had in Kraus's view reduced language to a merely ornamental function, with any semblance of an objective discussion of the facts at issue falling by the wayside. This is allegedly due to the corrupting influence of Heine's *Witz*, which the feuilletonists took as their model. Kraus dismisses Heine's prose as a combination of '*Witz* without perception and point of view without *Witz*' (193). The apparent lapse into a hopelessly arbitrary subjectivity would indeed deprive *Witz* of any basis to go beyond amusement and actually move a larger public to action. As Freud indicated in his letter to Kraus, wit has lost its sting.

Kraus is good at diagnosing the crisis of *Witz* at the turn of the century, but it is certainly unfair of him to lay the blame solely on Heine's shoulders. What he overlooks is that the element of subjectivity had appeared in journalism long before Heine. With the rise of the moral weeklies in the eighteenth century, newspapers went beyond their previous role as being simple transmitters of information and attempted to edify and enlighten their public on an ethical level as well (Theurer 23–24). We have previously seen how *Witz*, in its ability to combine edification with entertainment, was a stylistic device well suited for these purposes. This process took on a political edge in the engaged political journalism between 1830 and 1848, out of which the turn-of-the-century feuilleton grew (Senoner 119). Heine's *Witz* did indeed play a seminal role here. But the glory days of '48 are long past, and for Kraus, Heine's wit is nothing more than 'an asthmatic hound' (*Untergang* 201). It has lost its political bite, as Kraus sardonically demonstrates by citing his poem 'Wartet nur! [Just wait!]':

> Weil ich so ganz vorzüglich blitze,
> Glaubt ihr, daß ich nicht donnern könnt'!
> Ihr irrt euch sehr, denn ich besitze
> Gleichfalls fürs donnern ein Talent.
>
> Es wird sich grausenhaft bewähren,
> Wenn einst erscheint der rechte Tag;
> Dann sollt ihr meine Stimme hören,
> Das Donnerwort, den Wetterschlag.
>
> Gar manche Eiche wird zersplittern
> An jenem Tag der wilde Sturm,
> Gar mancher Palast wird erzittern
> Und stürzen mancher Kirchenturm!

Because of my skill with lightning bolts,
You believe I cannot thunder!
You are much mistaken, for I possess
A talent for thundering as well.

This will prove itself most dreadfully,
When once the right day comes;
Then you shall hear my voice,
The word of thunder, change in weather.

Many an oak will be smashed
On the day of the wild storm,
Many a palace will tremble
And many a church steeple will fall!

Kraus's commentary: 'these are empty promises.' Palaces and churches remain standing, and so the *Blitz* of Heine's *Witz* remains empty braggadocio. Kraus dismisses Heine's wit because it has proven incapable of keeping its political promises, degenerating instead into harmless feuilletonism. The loss of its political brisance had cost *Witz* its critical position within the public sphere. But Kraus has another home in mind for it. 'All that is created remains as it was before being created. The artist brings it down from heaven as something complete. Eternity is without beginning. Lyric or a joke: the creation lies between the self-evident and the definitive' (202).

If *Witz* has lost its place on earth, then perhaps it can find refuge in heaven. This does not last long, however, for by the end of the essay this language mysticism has lost its pious tone and taken on an explicitly erotic character. Language becomes a sexual adventure, and Kraus has shown that he was also aware of the erotics of *Witz*. He criticizes the prudishness Heine shows in his attack on Platen's homosexuality and in an earlier essay had enlisted 'witty antitheses' in his defense of 'perversity' (*Sittlichkeit* 303). This may help explain why the alliance between Kraus and Freud was so short-lived. As Worbs remarks, Freud was highly suspicious of the anarchic sexuality which Kraus so passionately and wittily defended. Freud's own *Witztheorie,* on the other hand, was designed to keep these perverse drives under control.

Thus Kraus cannot be simply dismissed as reactionary in his attack on Heine and the liberal tradition he represents. He recognized the crisis it had reached, and his attempt to recover *Witz*'s edge by mobilizing it around issues of sexual freedom, to which Heine had proven hostile, was not without merit. Furthermore, we could certainly say that Kraus, as a bearer of the Enlightenment project of *Witz*, is not so far away from Heine as he might have thought. Despite repeated disillusionment, he continued his critical publicistic activity, thereby demonstrating that *Witz* could carve a place for itself within the mass public sphere. Kraus's greatest victory perhaps came in the 1920s, when his polemics against the newspaper magnate Imre Bekessy, who had built his empire on the basis of journalistic *Erpressung*, led to his being driven out of town.

Before we let ourselves get too enthusiastic over *Witz*'s potential within the mass public sphere, however, it would be well to remind ourselves of Freud's second allusion to Kraus: 'There is a witty and pugnacious journalist in Vienna, whose biting invective has repeatedly led to his being physically maltreated by the subjects of his attacks. On one occasion, when a fresh misdeed on the part of one of his habitual opponents was being discussed, somebody exclaimed: "If X hears of this, he'll get his ears boxed again"' (77–78).

The technique Freud wishes to illustrate with this joke is that of 'allusion by means of omission.' What is being left out in this case is the connection between the hearing of the misdeed and the slap in the face. The link, Freud tells us, is the probable publication by the writer of a satirical article, which would lead to his being physically assaulted. This gives us an idea of how dangerous the exercise of *Witz* within the mass public sphere can be and would support Freud's dour view of its prospects to effect real change.

This is fine as far as it goes, but Freud fails to discuss the second omission contained in the joke, that of Kraus's name. Kraus was no stranger to this sort of treatment, being the object of a campaign on the part of the major media of the day to ignore him out of existence. The tactic they employed was known as *totschweigen* (to kill with silence), with the idea being that, since no public figure can survive without publicity, Kraus must cease to exist as such if disregarded resolutely enough. This strategy failed to take into account Kraus's ability to maintain his public visibility through the founding of his own journal, *Die Fackel,* public readings which, though advertised little, were well attended, and participation in other cultural events. Moreover, as in the above joke, this strategy itself backfired to a certain extent, as omission only served to draw attention. The more people became aware of the campaign of silence against him, the more Kraus's reputation as a lonely fighter against the tyranny and corruption of the media increased. Still, *totschweigen* as a forerunner of attempts by some states to create 'nonpersons' is disturbing, particularly when it is backed up, as it is in the above joke, with the threat of violence.

The violent response to Kraus, both verbal and physical, was present almost from the very beginning of his independent publicistic efforts. In jokingly casting up accounts after the first quarter of the *Fackel,* he lists 236 anonymous letters of abuse, 83 anonymous threatening letters, and one physical assault (*Fackel* 9 [1899], 27). If Kraus cannot be ignored to death, then there are of course more direct means of attaining that end. Though there is nothing at all funny in these threats against Kraus's life, they do present us with a certain similarity with the attitude of the comic, which simply steamrolls over the subjectivity of its target. Freud has characterized the mass public sphere as being marked by the discourse of the comic, and now we begin to see to what extremes this can lead us. The X of the joke becomes a universal sign marking the possible fate of all 'witty and pugnacious journalists,' whose tendentious wit, however sharp it might be, still remains within the bounds of the social etiquette of the bourgeois public sphere upon which it depends for its very existence. But when the sublimated aggression it represents gives way to overt blows and death threats, then the potential for opening up a rational discourse which tendentious *Witz* also embodies falls by the wayside. Kraus himself expected no better and indeed came close to inviting such a response. In his article 'Recht und Pflicht, mich totzuschweigen' (The right and duty to ignore me), he declares that his critique of the mass media strikes to such a fundamental level that the only rational reply the press could possibly make would be to cease to exist. Kraus liked to set himself in life and death struggles with adversaries with whom no reconciliation is conceivable. Thus his brand of *Witz* lacks the corrective, redemptive powers of Shaftesbury and others who, while recognizing its critical powers, still held out the hope of ultimate consensus in rational agreement. The ideal of the all-encompassing Enlightenment public sphere had been developing cracks throughout the century and here breaks wide open as we find ourselves confronted with apparently implacable animosities. The transition from tendentious wit to comic abuse reflects this trend. Humorous aggression has become more partisan, less accountable to an ideal of rational universality, and more susceptible to lapse into overt violence. Not that this sort of phenomenon was unknown in the past. We saw how bourgeois *Witztheorie* itself took just such a hostile attitude toward excluded groups such as women and the lower classes. But now, at the turn of the century, the bourgeois idyll itself was quickly unraveling, collapsing under the weight of its own contradictions.

Kraus was a master at turning the contradictions of bourgeois hypocrisy into material for his witty polemics. This is nothing new, for we have seen *Witz* used in the past to critique its own class base, the bourgeoisie. What is remarkable is the degree to which *Witz* itself had been affected by the changes in the public sphere that we have been discussing. Edward Timms has dubbed Kraus the 'apocalyptic satirist' and has tried to show that, from about 1904 on, Kraus becomes less concerned with the concrete social situation of a given case instead permitting his satiric imagination to run away with him (47). An overly harsh sentence in a Vienna courtroom, for example, becomes the prelude to the Last Judgment. Kraus's tendency to absolutize, to attempt an existential refutation of his opponent, however witty, would seem more in line with the mood of the comic as described by Freud. It is certainly symptomatic of a public sphere where a genuine attempt at a rational exchange of ideas has ceased. This can easily lead to an apocalyptic mood where all efforts at communication and persuasion seem hopeless. One simply waits around for the inevitable end, passing the time with cynical observations that are not meant to serve as a warning but simply to show that one is above it all. Though only appearing twice in the book, Kraus provides us with a practical case study of the crisis of bourgeois *Witz* to which Freud had given theoretical expression. In tracing Kraus's career, we have moved from traditional, public-spirited *Witz* through its violent confrontation with the comic and on to Freud's last category, the resigned world of *Humor.*

The psychological model Freud offers in order to explain *Humor* is telling. In contrast to the intersubjective, social process of *Witz* or the subject-object struggle of the comic, *Humor* is centered purely within the psyche of the discrete individual. It is a solipsistic retreat from a world that has become unbearable. We have already made the acquaintance of *Humor* in our history of the development of *Witztheorie. Humor*'s first important theorist was Jean Paul, but it truly came into blossom only after the middle of the nineteenth century as a means of dealing with the disappointments suffered after the failed revolutions of 1848 (*Reallexikon* 1:732). The connection of *Humor* with thwarted revolutionary hopes is expressed in an example Freud takes from Victor Hugo's play *Hernani.* Hernani is both bandit and rebel against the king, though is himself of noble blood and, when finally captured, insists upon his feudal rights. 'A Grandee of Spain might cover his head in the presence of his royal master. Very well, then':

Nos têtes ont le droit
De tomber couvertes devant de toi. (230)

Our heads have the right
to fall before you covered.

Hugo wrote *Hernani* late in 1829, immediately following the banning of his play *Marion de Lorme* by the censors for its antiroyalist sentiments. With *Hernani* he still managed to critique the idea of hereditary monarchy and provoke a major literary scandal by breaking with the norms of classical French drama. All in all a fitting preface to the revolution of 1830, which not only toppled the French monarch Charles X, but also inspired German writers like Heine and Börne to take a more aggressive stance in their works. By taking us back to these events, Freud reminds us of the birth of *Junges Deutschland* and the resultant release of *Witz* from its Metternichean bondage. We should note as well that Hernani has an Austrian connection, for the emperor against which he rebels is Charles V, the most illustrious of the Habsburgs. Reference to this play could thus be expected to arouse any slumbering resentments against aristocratic privilege within the educated bourgeois public for which Freud was writing.[4]

But the heroic age of the bourgeoisie was really a thing of the past, and the invocation of these old dreams must have also served as a reminder of their actual frustration. Hernani could as well be taken as symbolizing the inability of the bourgeoisie (especially true in Austria) to shake off aristocratic rule once and for all and consolidate politically the predominance it enjoyed on the economic level. As a rebel, Hernani is a complete failure. In one scene he has Charles in his power, but cannot bring himself to commit regicide. Charles, on the other hand, has no scruples about wiping out Hernani's troop of bandits and later takes him prisoner without any great difficulty. Even the apparent defiance contained in Hernani's words cited above is merely a prelude to his complete collapse before imperial authority. After Hernani identifies himself as a nobleman, Charles pardons him and he gratefully swears undying fealty to his emperor.

This split in Hernani's character between bandit and nobleman is important for Freud. He begins this section with two examples of gallows humor, which he describes as the crudest form of *Humor.* 'A rogue who was being led out to execution on a Monday remarked: "Well, this week's beginning nicely"' (229). Another rogue, in a similar situation, asks for a scarf for fear of catching his death of cold, usually a praiseworthy precaution, but at this point rather superfluous. Freud sees 'something like magnanimity [*Seelengröße*]' in this attitude which permits the scoundrel to master his feelings of despair, but Freud's respect is 'inhibited by the circumstances of the humorous person.' Hernani, on the other hand, is able to overcome his roguish bandit persona by identifying with the nobility and is thus the object of Freud's unbounded admiration.

Humor would thus seem to rest on two moments: a rebellion against the social order followed by an identification with it. This latter element especially comes to the fore in Freud's 1928 essay on *Humor,* where he sites it psychologically within the superego, the internalized

4. Freud himself was certainly no stranger to such antipathies. Recall the 'Revolutionary Dream' in *The Interpretation of Dreams.*

voice of social discipline. To put this in historical terms, we might say that the bourgeoisie's inclination toward *Humor* stemmed both from its selling out to the aristocracy and the selling out of the proletariat, who were at one time its allies in the struggle to overthrow the old order. Fear of losing its own privileged position, however, induced the bourgeoisie to side with the aristocrats in quashing the demands for radical democracy being made by the lower classes, guaranteeing the failure of the revolutions of 1848. This is of course a highly schematized and oversimplified depiction of complex historical events, but still helps us understand just what is going on in Freud's theory of *Humor*. Whereas Hernani's grandiloquent resignation is expected to arouse our admiration, the gallows humor of the rogue merely saves us the need to feel sorry for him. Why should we, Freud asks, when he does not even feel sorry for himself? Indeed, according to Freud, in order to expend the psychic energy built up by this *erspartes Mitleid* (savings on pity), we would probably laugh as this humorous rogue is carted off to the gallows. Yesterday's revolutionary comrade-in-arms has become today's common criminal. *Humor* permits the bourgeoisie to effect this transition with at least a semblance of good conscience. They are able to maintain their progressive credentials by identifying with a romantic revolutionary like Hernani, who, at a safe literary and historical distance, poses no genuine threat to the status quo while at the same time cheerfully sending off real social outlaws to be hanged.

Freud next turns his attention to the New World and the works of Mark Twain. Here we find ourselves in a frontier society where aristocratic hierarchy would seem to have no place. Twain traces his family tree back to a member of Columbus's expedition, only to have this illustrious ancestor turn out to be just a poor stowaway, thereby ridiculing the idea of basing one's status on one's lineage. But the promise of a fresh start cannot long cheer the cynical mood of *Humor*, for America's darker side is also revealed in Twain's work.

> In his account of his brother's life, for instance, he tells us how he was at one time employed on a great road-making enterprise. The premature explosion of a mine blew him up into the air and he came down again far away from the place where he had been working. We are bound to have feelings of sympathy for the

victim of the accident and would like to ask whether he was injured by it. But when the story goes on to say that his brother had a half-day's wages deducted for being 'absent from his place of employment' we are entirely distracted from our pity and become almost as hard-hearted as the contractor and almost as indifferent to possible damage to the brother's health. (230)

In 1902 Freud drew a distinction between the Old World 'governed by authority' and the New World 'governed by the dollar' (Gay, *Freud* 562). *Humor* proves itself adaptable to both traditional and moneyed aristocracy. As with *Witz* and *Komik, Humor* operates on an economics of *Ersparnis*. What is being saved here is affective energy—in the cases we have been dealing with, pity. Whether the world be old or new, *Humor* saves us from having to show any sympathy for the lower classes and provides a bridge of identification with the upper classes, be they embodied in the merciful Holy Roman Emperor or a hard-hearted entrepreneur.

Twain's humor was not confined to the American frontier, however. He visited Vienna in the fateful year of 1897 and told of his experiences in the article 'Stirring Times in Austria.' This year saw not only the confirmation of the anti-Semite Lueger as mayor of Vienna but also the parliamentary storm aroused by the introduction of the Badeni ordinances. They would have made Czech the official language of Bohemia, a move that outraged the minority German-speaking elite of that province, who were determined to block the measure at all costs. Twain was in parliament to watch this battle, giving him firsthand experience of what Schorske has called 'politics in a new key.' *Key* is a deceptively musical term to describe the cacaphonies used by both sides to drown out the words of their opponents. According to Twain, all that could be heard above the din was the occasional catcall, showing how rational debate and exchange of ideas had been replaced by the one-way comic putdown. In the end, the military was called in to restore order, a victory of the army over the democratic public sphere that *Witz* had represented and which had been reduced to such a pathetic state.

Given this situation, succumbing to the prevailing mood of 'gay apocalypse' of which *Humor* was certainly a part was perhaps understandable. Freud himself is ambivalent here. On the one hand he obviously admires the ability of humorists to maintain their composure in the face of disaster. Psychologically, however, he relates it to the defense mechanisms, the psychic equivalent of the flight reflex designed to help the organism avoid pain. 'In fulfilling this task they serve mental events as an automatic regulation, which in the end, incidentally, turns out to be detrimental and has to be subjected to conscious thinking' (233). *Humor*, more sophisticated than the defensive processes of the neurotic, does not simply repress unpleasant events back into the unconscious but instead removes their affective charge. It enables us to emotionally deaden ourselves to an otherwise intolerable situation. In the case of 'treating' *Humor* then, it would seem that the problem is not so much in reasserting the primacy of the conscious thought of the ego but in somehow reinvigorating its emotional life. Yet I would also argue that there is indeed a degree of repression involved in *Humor*, that of its political dimension. The politics of *Humor*, as well as *Witz* and *Komik*, are certainly present for all to see in Freud's text, but it remains, on a conscious level at least, theoretically meaningless for him—a subtle form of repression similar to the bad faith of *Humor*, which sees yet refuses to see. Perhaps if we realize that what is at stake here is much more than mere quibbling over which jokes belong in which box, if we can break out of the theoretical straitjacket into which *Witz* had been placed at midcentury, a process aided and abetted by its transformation into *Humor*, then perhaps we can reengage our passions with the world around us. *Humor* relies on a feeling that the world is spinning out of control, beyond the power of anyone to set it right, and so one makes oneself as comfortable as one can in the 'Grand Hotel Abyss,' an attitude surely not unfamiliar to our own day and age. But before taking refuge in the nearest comedy club, where all the aggravations of modern life are resolved by one-liners and two-drink minimums, we should recall that the breakdown of *Witz* that Freud traces was by no means inevitable. The narrative flow of the book is complex, with numerous powerful countercurrents and unexplored side streams. *Witz*'s radically democratic and utopian agenda remains, I believe, a force to be reckoned with in the unconscious of the social psyche of modernity that Freud was instrumental in opening up to us.

EPILOGUE: THE POLYVALENCE OF WITZ

After making the long trek through two centuries of *Witztheorie* followed by a detailed analysis of a work of Freud's which proved to be remarkably dense and intricately plotted, the reader is certainly justified in wanting to pause and take stock of their own psychic economy, that is to say, to wonder to what purpose all this intellectual energy has been expended. The motly parade that I have assembled of famous, near-famous, and obscure authors, theorists, and politicians of the eighteenth and nineteenth centuries may have served an antiquarian interest, but its relevance to the late twentieth century is perhaps still unclear. True, I have made occasional gestures towards our own age during the course of this work, but now is the time for a more extensive discussion of this issue. What then is the place of *Witz* in the world today?

I have argued that Freud, despite his claims to a radical originality, stands at the end of a long chain of *Witztheorie*. Was he the end of the line? To be sure, theories of the joke continue to be produced, but their debt to the German tradition and to Freud in particular is usually not very great. The joke book itself remains one of Freud's lesser-known works, and he did not even take the trouble of making extensive revisions to it as he did with all his other major early works. The author himself would seem to be colluding in consigning his own book to oblivion. In the *Introductory Lectures on Psycho-analysis* he treats jokes as merely a diversion from his essential work on dreams (15:235). *Witztheorie* has traditionally suffered from nagging doubts as to its own triviality and Freud does nothing to dispel them. Is it then not frivolous of us to take up a line of inquiry which the master himself saw to be going nowhere?

Perhaps it is fitting that renewed interest in the joke book is in large part due to that great apostate from the psychoanalytic establishment, Jacques Lacan. Lacan has high (if ambiguous) praise for Freud's work on 'le mot d'Esprit'—'here all is substance, all is pearl' (33). His enthusiasm is understandable given the centrality of language to his theories. Jokes (as defined by Freud) are inherently linguistic phenomena and so might be likelier than the more visually oriented dream to provide the royal road to the unconscious. Still, even Lacan himself does not have all that much to say (at least not in the writings published so far) about this work he so much admires. The influence of *Witz* is probably more directly apparent in his style, which is laden with jokes and puns. Indeed, as Anthony Wilden points out, his reference to the joke book where 'all is pearl' plays on the colloquial meaning of the French *perle*—'goof, howler' (117).

As provocative as many of Lacan's witty formulations may be, they do raise certain methodological problems. Towards the end of chapter 3 I briefly mentioned Samuel Weber's argument for the significance of Freud's joke book. Fließ, Freud's 'first reader and critic,' had found the interpretations in the dream book a little too ingenious. Weber cites Freud defending himself against this charge: 'It is certainly true that the dreamer is too ingenious and witty [*zu witzig*], but this is neither my fault nor does it justify a reproach. All dreamers are just as insufferably witty, and they have to be, because they are under pressure, the direct way is barred to them. . . . The apparent wit of all unconscious processes is intimately connected with the theory of wit and of the comic' (Weber 84).

Freud thus finds himself compelled to put together a theory of *Witz* in order to protect his other theories about the workings of the unconscious from accusations that he is simply projecting his own intellectual acuity onto his patients and then generalizing about the nature of the mind. *Witztheorie* is not just designed to describe *Witz* but would also serve to put *Witz* in its place and keep its frivolity from undermining the much more serious processes of scientific thought. Weber remains skeptical of the success of Freud's project. He sees no reason why the freewheeling ingenuity of *Witz* which permeates dreams and jokes should stop there. Any theory that wishes to deal with *Witz* runs the danger of becoming 'contaminated by its "object"' (Weber 85). I would hope that the foregoing chapters have been enough to demonstrate that such was indeed the case with Freud. So it would therefore seem that the unabashed playfulness of Lacan and many of his fellow post-structuralist critics is a much more honest way of approaching the situation. Rather than attempting to straitjacket *Witz* in a narrowly rational theoretical discourse, they exploit the possibilities for a creative collaboration between the two.

While the appearance of the 'French Freud' may have had a very refreshing effect on the stale air of traditional psychoanalytic literary criticism (see Young 88), certain troublesome questions remain. The new Freud may be much more fun to work with and Lacan certainly avoids the stereotypical oversimplifications of vulgar Freudianism, yet one is often left to wonder whether radical posturing and willful obscurantism have taken the place of sound and incisive analysis. These sort of charges were, of course, leveled at Freud himself by many of his contemporaries. The Lacanians would seem less concerned with refuting such allegations as in taking them to a much deeper level. After having made an issue of the relationship between *Witz* and theory, Weber goes on to suggest that we may indeed have been 'fleeced' by Freud, whose theory cannot possibly live up to its billing as something scientific, rigorous and all-encompassing. A central theme in Lacan's work is the debunking of such illusory plenitudes of meaning; like Freud's nonsense jokes, the meaning is that there is no meaning. To prod the narcissistic ego out of its smug self-satisfaction is certainly a laudable goal, yet the constant repetition of this antipunchline, the constant frustration of the desire for meaning, can grow wearisome as well. Has the negativity of *Witz* reached a potency in this age of skepticism which dissolves all certainties and places all in flux? Perhaps, but recall that Schlegel, who ascribed a similar property to *Witz,* saw this as a precursor to a golden age, and it is this utopian moment in *Witz* which may yet return to make dupes of both Freud and Lacan.

Let us return to Weber now, who makes no secret of his debt to Lacan, though it is by no means an uncritical one. Weber radicalizes Freud's account of the psychogenesis of jokes. Remember that *Witz* arose out of childish play and is an attempt by the adult to recapture that happy state now made inaccessible by the censorship of reason.

The meaning of the joke serves to placate and distract this censorship and therefore, Weber argues, 'has for the *Witz* no intrinsic value; it is only instrumental, serving to eliminate temporarily the barriers to play' (93–94). As we have seen, the pleasure of play was located in the process of recognition, in the recovery of the familiar. This leads Weber to break down the apparent opposition between play and the discipline of meaning and depict both as serving 'the interests of the narcissistic ego bent upon reducing alterity to a variation of identity' (98). Indeed, the identity of the narcissistic ego is itself at stake in this flux of play and meaning. But the structure of jokes always demands the 'third person,' the listener who confronts the ego with 'that measure of alterity which it can never either fully appropriate or flatly reject' (108). The third person represents not only the social norms of the superego, which will sit in judgment on the teller's joke, but gives voice to the laughter of the id as well, which is also beyond conscious control and thus remains irredeemably other. Weber sees this situation epitomized in the nonsense joke, which plays with our desire for meaning but in the end frustrates our need for identity which intelligibility promises. Freud, 'who set out to unify and to totalize the membra disjecta of all previous joke theories' (116), is himself ensnared in this shaggy-dog story which he cannot bring to a satisfactory conclusion. He can never present to us the *Kern,* the essence of *Witz* that would explain it all, leaving us instead merely with handfuls of its 'fleece.'

Weber's problematization of the success of Freud's *Witztheorie* as a synthesis of his predecessors into a coherent whole certainly agrees with our own findings. Yet despite his skepticism, it is by no means clear that he himself has avoided being taken in by Freud. Freud's synthesis, I have argued, operates not simply on the abstract-theoretical level as he might have us believe, but also on the sociohistorical. It is this level of analysis which is essential to understanding much of the chicanery which goes on in the joke book, yet it is, for the most part, ignored by Weber. The terms which Weber uses to describe the ego's encounter with the other remain purely psychological and devoid of any social specificity. The third person, though supposedly representing the point of contact for the ego with the 'intersubjective order of society' (109), becomes the incarnation of the subject's superego, either as ego ideal or as derivative of the id. It is significant that Weber fails to offer any discussion of *Humor*, where the ego identifies with the superego, prostrating itself before this overwhelming otherness, but in the name of recovering its own narcissism. The humoristic ego is proof against Weber's subversion of meaning and the traditional notions of ego integrity bound up with this; indeed, it depends upon such dissolutions to justify its own passivity and resignation (all is meaningless, so why bother?). The humoristic turn, it will be recalled, came after the breakdown of *Witz*'s efforts to radically alter the structure of bourgeois society. Weber nominally sites the witty subject within society, but their relationship remains static. Society is just a placeholder for alterity, with no real possibility of modifying the iron triangle of id-ego-superego entering the picture. The sense of purpose and so of meaning which tendentious *Witz* had in its struggle with society is no longer present. If Weber feels that he has been fleeced by Freud, perhaps it is because he has gotten stuck in the same fatalistic trap.

Jeffrey Mehlman raises similar issues. Like Weber, he sees the joking ego as one 'which is alienated not secondarily, but in its essence' (460). To what degree this alienation opens the ego to something genuinely other remains, however, questionable. Mehlman bases his analysis of *Witz* on the tripartite model of joke dynamics Freud discovered in the *Zote*, but as in Weber, the 'third person' whom the joke addresses 'is less a term (a person) than a symbolic circuit, a structure of exchange which happens secondarily to find support or incarnation in an additional person' (449). The 'structure of exchange' is predicated upon the deflection of sexual energies at the root of the *Zote* 'from brute satisfaction to a "pleasure in signs"' (448). The third party becomes the Oedipal father who oversees this process, but contributes nothing essential to it, for, as Mehlman argues, sexuality is 'fundamentally a semiotic affair' (450). In making this assertion, Mehlman rejects Freud's own hypothesis that class pressures account for the movement from the unrestrained 'brute satisfaction' indulged in by the lower orders to the more subtle lewdness of polite society. Sexuality, like the ego, is alienated in its essence and both can offer merely an 'illusory plenitude' (454). 'To read Freud in the spirit we have suggested . . . no doubt entails a sacrifice. For it will be seen that the further we pursued our analysis of *Der Witz,* the more did the apparent object of Freud's analysis—jokes—disappear. Like the woman—the second person—in Freud's paradigm of the joke. I confess that this homology between Freud's model and our own undertaking strikes me as sufficient consolation for that loss' (460–61).

Jane Gallop has criticized Mehlman for so easily writing off women in the name of maintaining the integrity of Oedipal structures. That the jokes themselves fall by the wayside has even more far-reaching consequences, for as I have argued, these jokes themselves critique the logic of sacrifice, which both Freud and Mehlman subscribe to, and open up utopian possibilities that Mehlman would undoubtedly dismiss as a mirage of 'illusory plenitude.' The 'homology' which he offers as consolation is only attained in flattening out any points of opposition, anything that is truly other in this theoretical discourse which so prides itself on subverting such narcissism.

Jerry Aline Flieger makes a valiant attempt to break out of this post-structuralist vacuum. In her work on the relationship between Freud's joke book and the postmodern age, she argues that 'the use of psychoanalytic theory enables us to read 'text' as 'context,' an interaction or weaving of human subjects' (8). Yet for all her good intentions, her analysis is full of empty generalizations, which serve only to mask the repressive structures which it is supposed to criticize. She speaks, for example, of the 'human drama' being played out by Freud's 'cast of characters' that extends 'from Dora to Moses, from Oedipus to the Jewish marriage broker' (87). What holds this ahistorical jumble together is apparently 'the masterplot of human desire' (94), which she, like Mehlman, sees represented in the *Zote.* Her retelling of this 'Boy meets Girl' story is not without interest. Boy does not get Girl here, for the woman leaves the room when dirty jokes start to be told. Boy might get Boy, assuming the male listener laughs and and thereby establishes a homoerotic bond with the teller. But Flieger takes things a step further in asserting that Boy is Girl. Using Lacan's 'Seminar on the Purloined Letter,' which she takes as a theoretical model for farce, Flieger tries to show how people at their most active and aggressive (masculine) at the same time make themselves vulnerable and passive (feminine). The teller of the dirty joke is at the same time dependent upon the positive reaction of the listener for its validation. For Lacan, the phallus is not bound to one biological gender, but can be passed around, thus subverting these apparently immutable distinctions. Flieger goes on to write of the 'cultural variables' (118) which determine sexuality and open up the possibility that the 'wall' which separates male and female might someday be scaled, or at least graffitied with 'comic texts that play at "unworking" the phallocentric foundations of the Law' (119).

It should be pointed out that 'play at unworking' and 'playful unworking' are not necessarily the same. Despite the nod toward 'cultural variables,' there is no real analysis of the power structures which keep the phallus firmly in the possession of the males. The privileging of the sexual dynamics of the *Zote* as the model for all jokes further undercuts the possibilities of conducting such an analysis, since it leaves other important factors that go beyond issues of sexuality out of account. Maybe in our androgynous postmodern age we could actually start believing that on some level Boy is Girl. But how plausible is it to assert that Jew is Gentile, Black is White, or that Worker is CEO?

What seems to have been forgotten by all of these post-structuralist critics is that *Witz* was not just a matter of clever puns, startling paradoxes, and provocative nonsense. From the Enlightenment on it was seen as a tool for combining amusement with edification. The punch of tendentious jokes often contained a far-reaching yet immediate critique of repressive social structures. The post-structuralists represent the triumph of *Theorie* over *Witz*, encasing *Witz* in a theoretical jargon which both effectively isolates it from a broader public sphere and serves to mirror and perpetuate social relations of domination and repression within its discourse. The wall will only come tumbling down after it has been removed from its protective theoretical hypostatization.

The reading which I would oppose to the line offered by the critics discussed above follows Fredric Jameson's call for a rehistoricization of Freud. This must go beyond simply placing Freud within the context of turn-of-the-century Vienna or even of siting psychoanalysis within the history of the rise of the nuclear family. 'The conditions of the possibility of psychoanalysis become visible, one would imagine, only when you begin to appreciate the extent of psychic fragmentation since the beginnings of capitalism, with its systematic quantification and rationalization of experience, its instrumental reorganization of the subject just as much as of the outside world' (62).

The history of *Witz* in its development out of the medieval *Schwank* has given us a glimpse into the history of what Max Weber would refer to as the process of rationalization in Western culture from the Enlightenment up to Freud. *Witz* was both bearer and critic of this process of rationalization. Its use as an instrument of social discipline was balanced by the mediating role it often played in a society increasingly fragmented into autonomous, 'rationalized' systems. The combinatoric power of *Witz* enabled it to make surprising connections between these discrete life spheres, to make critical leaps that, with Freud, open up the space for a systemic critique when rationalization itself, as it is manifested in the psychology of *Ersparnis,* becomes the object of attack.

Yet the struggle around this systemic critique was not just over purely theoretical fine points, but was always being fought on very specific battlegrounds. Whatever *Witz* touched turned into contested terrain, including the very theory which constituted it. All the big issues were at stake here: class, race, gender, war and peace, utopia and apocalypse. *Witz* has not only played on both sides of every line, but has shown us how the lines of these apparently disparate battles in fact often interconnect. This is what I mean when I refer to the 'polyvalence' of *Witz.* Its Janus-faced character, its multiplicity of meaning, is not an ontological trait, not the product of some principle of ultimate undecidability, but the result of a multilayered political struggle in which it has been embedded from its very inception. A radically historical thinking of *Witz,* and thus of the bourgeois psyche, will therefore avoid any rhetoric which would reify *Witz*'s struggles into an apparently timeless human condition. The utopian vision in *Witz* may indeed prove inadequate to slake the unquenchable desire of postmodern consumerist society, but the progressive tradition it represents might still help guide us in creating a society where the needs of the millions who live in want are met.

One point must be granted to the post-structuralist critics I have surveyed, and that is that *Witz* does indeed represent a breaking point for the classical bourgeois ego. But this does not mean that the ego simply shatters into its Oedipal parts, thereby perpetuating the system which created it. In the first place, we must realize that the Oedipus complex is itself a historical construct, the repressive character of which *Witz* has called deeply into question. On my reading, *Witz* instead opens up the ego to a larger social psyche where various subjectivities, and not just Oedipal clones, both vie for a chance to be heard as well as interacting in an at times harmonious and mutually liberating fashion. The psychodynamics of this social psyche depend on the distribution of forces within a given historical constellation. Freud has certainly given us a fascinating map of his own times and perhaps has provided us with a benchmark by which we may evaluate our own. This book has yet to be written, but the institutionalization of *Witz* in postmodernity, be it in Lacanian theory or the yuppie comedy club, bodes ill for the realization of its critical and utopian potential.

Nonetheless, if there is one thing the history of *Witz* shows, it is the resourcefulness of this human faculty in the face of even the most adverse circumstances. We have seen it used to take on aristocrats, both hereditary and moneyed, anti-Semites, misogynists, and militarists. To be sure, *Witz* represents only a small point of resistance in the great psychosocial scheme of things, but one that is surely worthy of cultivation. Humor, from satiric polemic to comic put-down to absurdist put-on, has always been an important weapon in the arsenal of the Left, and not only in the German tradition with which I have been dealing. Our century has seen the appearance of dadaists, surrealists, situationists, and yippies as groups which used humor to further radical political and cultural agendas. This form of praxis therefore must have its theoretical counterpart if it is to be used intelligently and effectively. Theory alone will not make you the life of any party, social or political, but an awareness of the history of wit and the roles it has played in various social psyches would seem necessary if it is to work through its own conflicts and solve its own riddles. We have left *Witz* poised on a cusp between utopia and apocalypse; in the time since Freud's book I would say that this dilemma has only become more pressing. Let this study stand then as a contribution to the revival of a thoughtful Groucho Marxism and as a call to action. Tell a joke, change the world.

Bibliography

Alford, Steven E. *Irony and the Logic of the Romantic Imagination.* New York: Peter Lang, 1984.

Altenhofer, Norbert. *Harzreise in die Zeit: Zum Funktionszusammenhang von Traum, Witz und Zensur in Heines früher Prosa.* Düsseldorf: Schriften der Heinrich Heine Gesellschaft, 1972.

Arntzen, Helmut. *Karl Kraus und die Presse.* Munich: Wilhelm Fink Verlag, 1975.

Bauman, Zygmunt. 'Exit Visas and Entry Tickets: Paradoxes of Jewish Assimilation.' *Telos,* no.77 (Fall 1988): 45–77.

Bausinger, Hermann. 'Schwank und Witz.' *Studium Generale,* 11, no.11 (1958): 699–710.

Bebel, August. *Die Frau und der Sozialismus.* Stuttgart: Dietz Verlag, 1910.

Bergson, Henri. 'Laughter.' In *Comedy,* edited by Wylie Sypher. Garden City, N.Y.: Doubleday, 1956.

Birken, Lawrence. *Consuming Desire: Sexual Science and the Emergence of a Culture of Abundance, 1871–1914.* Ithaca, N.Y.: Cornell University Press, 1988.

Böckmann, Paul. *Formgeschichte der deutschen Dichtung.* Hamburg: Hoffmann und Campe Verlag, 1949.

Bodmer, Johann Jakob, and J. J. Breitinger. *Der Mahler der Sitten* (1746). In *Schriften zur Literatur.* Stuttgart: Reclam, 1980.

Börne, Ludwig. *Sämtliche Schriften.* 5 vols. Edited by Inge and Peter Rippmann. Düsseldorf: Metzler Verlag, 1964.

Bouhours, Dominique. *Entretiens d'Ariste et d'Eugène.* Paris: Éditions Bossard, 1920.

Büschenthal, L. M. *Sammlung witziger Einfälle von Juden, als Beyträge zur charakteristik der Jüdischen Nation.* Elberfeld: H. Büschler, 1812.

Cuddihy, John Murray. *The Ordeal of Civility: Freud, Marx, Levi-Strauss and the Jewish Struggle with Modernity.* New York: Basic Books, 1974.

Davidson, Arnold I. 'How to Do the History of Psychoanalysis: A Reading of Freud's *Three Essays on the Theory of Sexuality.*' *Critical Inquiry* 13 (Winter 1987): 252–77.

Drabek, Anna, ed. *Das österreichische Judentum: Voraussetzungen und Geschichte.* Vienna: Jugend und Volk, 1974.

Eagleton, Terry. *The Function of Criticism.* London: Verso, 1984.

Ehrenfels, Christian. 'Die sexuelle Reform.' *Politisch-Anthropologische Revue* 2 (1903–4).

——. 'Sexualethik.' In *Philosophische Schriften.* Vol.3. Edited by Reinhard Fabian. Munich: Philosophia Verlag, 1988.

Elbinger, Carl. *Witz und Satire Anno 1848.* Vienna: Wiener Verlag, 1948.

Fischer, Kuno. *Kleine Schriften.* Heidelberg: Carl Winter, 1896.

Flavell, M. Kay. 'Women and Individualism: A Re-examination of Schlegel's "Lucinde" and Gutzkow's "Wally die Zweiflerin."' *Modern Language Review* 70 (1975): 550–66.

Flieger, Jerry Aline. *The Purloined Punch Line: Freud's Comic Theory and the Postmodern Text.* Baltimore: Johns Hopkins University Press, 1991.

Flögel, Karl Friedrich. *Geschichte der komischen Litteratur.* Liegnitz and Leipzig: David Siegert, 1784.

Foucault, Michel. *The History of Sexuality, Volume 1: An Introduction.* Translated by Robert Hurley. New York: Random House, 1980.

Freud, Martin. 'Who was Freud?.' In *The Jews of Austria: Essays on their Life, History and Destruction.* Edited by Josef Fraenkel. London: Valentine, Mitchell and Co., 1967.

Freud, Sigmund. *The Standard Edition of the Complete Psychological Works of Sigmund Freud.* Trans. and ed. James Strachey. 24 vols. London: Hogarth Press and the Institute of Psychoanalysis, 1953–74.

——. *Briefe an Wilhelm Fließ, 1887–1904.* Frankfurt am Main: S. Fischer Verlag, 1986.

Freytag, Gustav. *Die Journalisten.* Stuttgart: Reclam, 1977.

Fuchs, Eduard. *Die Frau in der Karikatur.* Munich: Albert Langen Verlag, 1907.

——. *Die Juden in der Karikatur.* Munich: Albert Langen Verlag, 1921.

Gallop, Jane. 'Why does Freud Giggle When the Women Leave the Room?' In *Psychoanalysis and* ——. Edited by Richard Feldstein and Henry Sussman. New York: Routledge, 1989.

Gay, Peter. *The Bourgeois Experience.* Vol.1. *The Education of the Senses.* New York: Oxford University Press, 1984.

——. *Freud: A Life for Our Time.* New York: W. W. Norton, 1988.

Gerstenberg, Heinrich Wilhelm von. *Briefe über Merkwürdigkeiten der Literatur* in *Deutsche Litteraturdenkmale.* Vol.30. Edited by Berhard Seuffert. Stuttgart: G. J. Göschen, 1890.

Gilman, Sander. *Jewish Self-Hatred: Anti-Semitism and the Hidden Language of the Jews.* Baltimore: Johns Hopkins University Press, 1986.

Gottsched, Johann Christoph. *Ausgewählte Werke.* Vol.6, pt.1. Edited by Joachim Birke and Briggite Birke. Berlin: Walter de Gruyter, 1968–87.

Gray, Richard T. 'Free-Lancing: Heine's "Ideen. Das Buch Le Grand."' In *Heine-Jahrbuch.* 1988:32–66.

Grimm, Jacob, and Wilhelm Grimm. *Deutsches Wörterbuch.* Vol.14, pt.2. Leipzig: S. Hirzel, 1913.

Grunfeld, Frederic V. *Prophets without Honor: A Background to Freud, Kafka, Einstein and Their World.* New York: Holt, Rinehart and Winston, 1979.

Gutzkow, Karl. *Werke.* 7 vols. Hildesheim: George Olms Verlag, 1974.

Haberland, Paul. *The Development of Comic Theory in Germany During the Eighteenth Century.* Göppingen: Verlag Alfred Kümmerle, 1971.

Habermas, Jürgen. *Strukturwandel der Öffentlichkeit.* Darmstadt: Luchterhand, 1962.

Hecker, Ewald. *Die Physiologie und Psychologie des Lachens und des Komischen.* Berlin: Ferd. Dümmler, 1873.

Hegel, G. W. F. *Ästhetik.* Berlin: Aufbau Verlag, 1955.

Heine, Heinrich. *Sämtliche Werke.* 7 vols. Edited by Ernst Elster. Leipzig and Vienna: Bibliographisches Institut, 1890.

Hermand, Jost. *Der frühe Heine.* Munich: Winkler Verlag, 1976.

Hobsbawm, E. J. *The Age of Empire, 1875–1914.* London: Weidenfeld and Nicolson, 1987.

Hohendahl, Peter Uwe. *Literaturkritik und Öffentlichkeit.* Munich: Piper Verlag, 1974.

——. *Literarische Kultur im Zeitalter des Liberalismus, 1830–1870.* Munich: C. H. Beck, 1985.

——. 'Literary Criticism in the Epoch of Liberalism, 1820–70.' In *A History of German Literary Criticism.* Edited by Hohendahl. Lincoln: University of Nebraska Press, 1988.

Hömberg, Walter. 'Literarisch-publizistische Strategien der Jungdeutschen und Vormärz Literaten.' In *Deutsche Literatur: Eine Sozialgeschichte.* Vol.6. Edited by Horst Glaser. Reinbek: Rowohlt, 1980.

Huffzky, Karin. *Wer muß hier lachen? Das Frauenbild im Männerwitz. Eine Streitschrift.* Darmstadt: Sammlung Luchterhand, 1979.

Jameson, Fredric. *The Political Unconscious: Narrative as a Socially Symbolic Act.* Ithaca, N.Y.: Cornell University Press, 1981.

Jean Paul [Johann Paul Friedrich Richter, pseud.]. *Werke.* Vol.5. Edited by Norbert Miller. Munich: Hanser Verlag, 1963.

Jones, Ernest. *The Life and Work of Sigmund Freud.* Vol.1. *The Formative Years and the Great Discoveries.* New York: Basic Books, 1953.

Kaiser, Herbert. 'Karl Gutzkow: Wally, die Zweiflerin.' In *Romane und Erzählungen zwischen Romantik und Realismus: Neue Interpretationen.* Edited by Paul Michael Lützeler. Stuttgart: Reclam, 1983.

Kempner, Friederike. *Gedichte.* Leipzig: F. Lorber, 1873.

Kirchmann, J. H. *Ästhetik auf realistischer Grundlage.* Vol.2. Berlin: Julius Springer, 1868.

Kofman, Sarah. *The Enigma of Woman: Woman in Freud's Writings.* Ithaca, N.Y.: Cornell University Press, 1985.

Köster, Udo. *Literatur und Gesellschaft in Deutschland 1830–1848: Die Dichtung am Ende der Kunstepoche.* Stuttgart: W. Kohlhammer, 1984.

Kraepelin, Emil. 'Zur Psychologie des Komischen.' In *Philosophische Studien.* Edited by Wilhelm Wundt. Leipzig: Wilhelm Engelmann, 1885.

Kraus, Karl. *Schriften.* 12 vols. Edited by Christian Wagenknecht. Frankfurt am Main: Suhrkamp; Vol.1, *Sittlichkeit und Kriminalität.* 1987; Vol.2, *Untergang der Welt durch schwarze Magie.* 1989.

Lacan, Jacques. *Speech and Language in Psychoanalysis.* Baltimore: Johns Hopkins University Press, 1968.

Landmann, Salcia. *Der jüdische Witz: Soziologie und Sammlung.* Freiburg: Walter Verlag, 1960.

Larsen, Egon. *Wit as a Weapon.* London: Frederick Muller Ltd., 1980.

Lassalle, Ferdinand. *Gesammelte Reden und Schriften.* Vol.2. Edited by Eduard Bernstein. Berlin: Paul Cassirer, 1919.

Lavater, Johann Caspar. *Physiognomische Fragmente zur Beförderung der Menschenkenntnis und Menschenliebe.* In *Sturm und Drang: Dichtungen und theoretische Texte.* Vol.1. Munich: Winkler Verlag, 1971.

Lazarus, Moritz. *Das Leben der Seele*. Vol.1. 3d ed. Berlin: Dümmler, 1883.

Lepenies, Wolf. *Melancholie und Gesellschaft*. Frankfurt am Main: Suhrkamp, 1969.

Lessing, Gotthold Ephraim. *Werke*. Vols. 3 and 4. Darmstadt: Wissenschaftliche Buchgesellschaft, 1973.

Lipps, Theodor. *Komik und Humor. Eine Psychologisch-Ästhetische Untersuchung*. Hamburg: Leopold Voss, 1898.

Locke, John. *An Essay Concerning Human Understanding*. London: Oxford University Press, 1964.

Luise von Toscana. *Mein Lebensweg*. Berlin: Verlag Continent, 1911.

Macartney, C. A. *The Hapsburg Empire, 1790–1918*. London: Weidenfeld and Nicolson, 1968.

Marx, Karl, and Friedrich Engels. *Werke*. 43 vols. Berlin: Dietz Verlag, 1957–67.

Mattenklott, Gert. *Melancholie in der Dramatik des Sturm und Drang*. Stuttgart: J. B. Metzler, 1968.

Mayer, Hans. *Aussenseiter*. Frankfurt am Main: Suhrkamp, 1975.

McGrath, William. *Dionysian Art and Populist Politics in Austria*. New Haven, Conn.: Yale University Press, 1974.

———. *Freud's Discovery of Psychoanalysis: The Politics of Hysteria*. Ithaca, N.Y.: Cornell University Press, 1986.

Mehlman, Jeffrey. 'How to Read Freud on Jokes: The Critic as *Schadchen*.' *New Literary History* 6, no.2 (1975): 439–61.

Meier, Georg Friedrich. *Anfangsgründe aller schönen Wissenschaften*. Pt.2. Halle: Carl Hermann Hemmerde, 1755.

———. *Gedancken von Schertzen*. Halle: Carl Hermann Hemmerde, 1744.

Möser, Justus. *Harlekin*. Bad Homberg: Verlag Gehlen, 1968.

Müller, Volker Ulrich. *Narrenfreiheit und Selbstbehauptung: Spielräume des Humors im Werk Jean Pauls*. Stuttgart: J. B. Metzler, 1979.

Neumann, Norbert. *Vom Schwank zum Witz: Zum Wandel der Pointe seit dem 16. Jahrhundert*. Frankfurt am Main: Campus Verlag, 1986.

Oesterle, Ingrid and Günter. 'Der literarische Bürgerkrieg. Gutzkow, Heine, Börne wider Menzel. Polemik nach Kunstperiode und in der Restauration.' In *Demokratisch-revolutionäre Literatur in Deutschland: Vormärz*. Edited by Gert Mattenklott and Klaus Scherpe. Kronberg: Scriptor Verlag, 1974.

Oring, Elliot. *The Jokes of Sigmund Freud: A Study in Humor and Jewish Identity*. Philadelphia: University of Pennsylvania Press, 1984.

Oxaal, Ivar, et al. *Jews, Antisemitism and Culture in Vienna*. London: Routledge and Kegan Paul, 1987.

Pfabigan, Alfred. *Karl Kraus und der Sozialismus: Eine politische Biographie*. Vienna: Europa Verlag, 1976.

Platen, August Graf von. *Sämtliche Werke*. 12 vols. Hildesheim: Georg Olms Verlag, 1969.

Pulzer, Peter. *The Rise of Political Anti-Semitism in Germany and Austria*. New York: John Wiley and Sons, 1964.

Reik, Theodor. *Jewish Wit*. New York: Gamut Press, 1962.

Renner, Karl. 'Witz.' In *Reallexikon der deutschen Literaturgeschichte*. Vol.4. Edited by Klaus Kanzog and Achim Masser. Berlin: Walter de Gruyter, 1984.

Röhrich, Lutz. *Der Witz: Figuren, Formen, Funktionen*. Stuttgart: Metzler, 1977.

Roith, Estelle. *The Riddle of Freud: Jewish Influences on His Theory of Female Sexuality*. London: Tavistock Publications, 1987.

Rozenblit, Marsha. *The Jews of Vienna, 1867–1914: Assimilation and Identity*. Albany: State University of New York Press, 1983.

Ruge, Arnold. *Sämmtliche Werke*. Vol.3. Mannheim: Grohe Verlag, 1847.

——. *Neue Vorschule der Ästhetik*. Hildesheim: Georg Olms Verlag, 1975.

Schanze, Helmut. 'Friedrich Schlegels Theorie des Romans.' In *Deutsche Romantheorien*. Edited by Reinhold Grimm. Frankfurt am Main: Athenäum, 1968.

Schlegel, Friedrich. *Kritische-Friedrich-Schlegel-Ausgabe*. 35 vols. Munich: Ferdinand Schöningh Verlag, 1962.

——. *Literary Notebooks: 1789–1801*. Edited by Hans Eichner. London: Athlone Press, 1957.

Schnitzer, Manuel. *Rabbi Lach: Ein Kulturdokument in Anekdoten*. Hamburg: W. Gente, 1922.

Schnitzler, Arthur. *Jugend in Wien*. Frankfurt am Main: Fischer Verlag, 1981.

Schorske, Carl. *Fin-de-Siècle Vienna: Politics and Culture*. New York: Vintage Books, 1981.

Senoner, Erika. *Karl Kraus' Pressekritik in der 'Fackel' von 1899 bis 1905*. Ph.D. diss., University of Innsbruck, 1983.

Shaftesbury, Anthony Earl of. *Characteristics of Men, Manners, Opinions, Times, etc.* Vol.1. London: Grant Richards, 1900.

Simon, Richard Keller. *The Labyrinth of the Comic: Theory and Practice from Fielding to Freud.* Tallahassee: University Presses of Florida, 1985.

Spencer, Herbert. *Illustrations of Universal Progress.* New York: D. Appleton and Co., 1870.

Steinberg, Michael P. 'Jewish Identity and Intellectuality in Fin-de-Siècle Austria.' *New German Critique,* no.43 (Winter 1988): 3–33.

Stettenheim, Julius. *Wippchen's sämmtliche Berichte.* Vol.1. *Der orientalische Krieg.* Berlin: B. Brigl, 1880.

Sulloway, Frank. *Freud: Biologist of the Mind.* New York: Basic Books, 1983.

Theurer, Melitta. *Die Darstellung des Journalisten in Dramen von Hermann Bahr, Arthur Schnitzler und Karl Kraus.* Ph.D. diss., University of Vienna, 1983.

Thomasius, Christian. *Von Nachahmung der Franzosen.* Leipzig: Moritz George Weidemannen, 1687.

Timms, Edward. *Karl Kraus: Apocalyptic Satirist.* New Haven, Conn.: Yale University Press, 1986.

Twain, Mark. 'Stirring Times in Austria.' In *The Writings of Mark Twain.* Vol.22. New York: Harper, 1929.

Vischer, Friedrich Theodor. *Ästhetik.* Reutlingen: Carl Mäckens Verlag, 1846.

Waldberg, Max Freiherr von. 'Eine deutsch-franzözische Literaturfehde.' In *Beiträge zur neueren Literaturgeschichte.* Vol.16. Heidelberg: Carl Winters Universitäts Buchhandlung, 1930.

Weber, Samuel. *The Legend of Freud.* Minneapolis: University of Minnesota Press, 1982.

Weininger, Otto. *Geschlecht und Charakter.* Munich: Matthes und Seitz, 1980.

Weisse, C. H. *Kleine Schriften zur Ästhetik und Ästhetischen Kritik.* Hildesheim: Georg Olms Verlag, 1966.

Werner, Michael. *Genius und Geldsack: Zum Problem des Schriftstellerberufs bei Heinrich Heine.* Hamburg: Hoffmann und Campe, 1978.

Wernike, Christian. *Überschriften.* 1701.

Wienbarg, Ludolf. *Ästhetische Feldzüge.* Berlin: Aufbau Verlag, 1964.

Wistrich, Robert. *Socialism and the Jews: The Dilemmas of Assimilation in Germany and Austria-Hungary*. London: Associated University Presses, 1982.

Wolff, Christian. *Gesammelte Werke*. Vol.2. Hildesheim: Georg Olms Verlag, 1983.

Worbs, Michael. *Nervenkunst*. Frankfurt am Main: Europäische Verlagsanstalt, 1983.

Young, Robert. 'Psychoanalytic Criticism: Has It Got Beyond a Joke?' In *Paragraph* 4 (1984): 87–114.

Zweig, Stefan. *Die Welt von Gestern: Erinnerungen eines Europäers*. Frankfurt am Main: Fischer Taschenbuch Verlag, 1988.

INDEX

Other volumes in the series Modern German Culture & Literature include:

The Institutions of Art: Essays by Peter and Christa Bürger Translated by Loren A. Kruger

The Cinema's Third Machine: Writing on Film in Germany, 1906–1933 By Sabine Hake

A History of German Literary Criticism Edited by Peter Uwe Hohendahl

Bertolt Brecht and the Theory of Media By Roswitha Mueller

Art and Enlightenment: Aesthetic Theory after Adorno By David Roberts

Making Bodies, Making History: Feminism and German Identity By Leslie A. Adelson